12/6/95

For Preterm Health Services,
In memory of the victims
    of December 30, 1994,
and in honor of your brave
determination to continue
providing women with safe,
legal health care.

Miriam Claire

The Abortion Dilemma

Personal Views on a Public Issue

The Abortion Dilemma

Personal Views on a Public Issue

Miriam Claire

Foreword by

Marcy L. Bloom
Executive Director
Aradia Women's Health Center

 **INSIGHT BOOKS**

Plenum Press • New York and London

Library of Congress Cataloging-in-Publication Data

On file

The author gratefully acknowledges permission to quote from
the following sources:

The Ambivalence of Abortion by Linda Bird Francke. Copyright 1978 by Linda Bird
Francke. Reprinted by permission of Random House, Inc.

Recovering from Rape by Linda E. Ledray. Copyright 1986 by Linda E. Ledray.
Reprinted by permission of Henry Holt and Co., Inc.

Moscow Women: Thirteen Interviews by Carola Hansson and Karin Liden. Text
copyright 1983 by Random House, Inc. Reprinted by permission of Pantheon
Books, a division of Random House, Inc.

Broken Earth: The Rural Chinese by Steven W. Mosher. Copyright 1983 by The Free
Press. Reprinted with the permission of the Free Press, a division of Simon
& Schuster.

Abortion by Malcolm Potts, Peter Diggory, and John Peel. Copyright Cambridge
University Press 1977. Reprinted with the permission of the Cambridge
University Press.

Hills Like White Elephants excerpted with permission of Scribner, a division of
Simon & Schuster Inc., from *Men Without Women* by Ernest Hemingway.
Copyright 1927 Charles Scribner's Sons. Copyright renewed 1955 by Ernest
Hemingway. World Rights with Permission of Michael Katakis.

ISBN 0-306-45080-1

© 1995 Miriam Claire
Insight Books is a Division of Plenum Publishing Corporation
233 Spring Street, New York, N.Y. 10013-1578

An Insight Book

10 9 8 7 6 5 4 3 2 1

Printed in the United States of America

With love,
to my parents, in memory of their loved ones who were
murdered in the Nazi Holocaust
and to my wondrous son, Lucas, who is my heart

Foreword

*I'm going to get each and every one of you with a rifle, a scope,
and a silencer; so you'd better watch your backs all the time.
Killing babies is a mortal sin—and I'm going to kill you, too.*

Threats like these are terrifying and all too common at Aradia
Women's Health Center. Still, I am very fortunate. I feel empowered by my work because I am helping women in need of reproductive health care. Unlike my five colleagues in Brookline,
Massachusetts, and Pensacola, Florida, who were murdered for
providing quality health services for women, I am alive and well.
But I am also very frightened. Who will be next?

Tragically, violence against abortion providers is nothing new.
For more than 20 years, throughout the United States, the toll has
escalated. As of this writing, according to the National Abortion
Federation, there have been at least five murders, 41 bombings, 94
arsons, 68 attempted bombings or arsons, 547 clinic invasions, 587
acts of vandalism, 95 assaults, 226 death threats, two kidnappings,
34 burglaries, 210 incidents of stalking, 1833 acts of hate mail and
phone calls, and 312 bomb threats. These crimes amount to 4063
acts of violence and terrorism. How much more must abortion
providers endure? Where will women go for safe and compassionate health care if the terrorism continues to escalate? When
will the rhetoric about abortion end and the truth about women's
lives finally be told?

Abortion is not new to *any* society. It has been practiced since
the beginning of time, and has always been controversial. Women

from all economic classes, races, backgrounds, religions, and ages choose abortion for one fundamental reason—TO SURVIVE AND LIVE THE BEST LIVES THEY KNOW HOW. Women must be recognized as moral and ethical decision-makers, who deserve support and respect when faced with the dilemma of an unplanned pregnancy. Only by speaking out clearly and passionately against the terrorist campaign that continues to stigmatize abortion and marginalize abortion services can women choosing abortion and those of us who provide this care even begin to envision the day when we can feel safe again.

The Abortion Dilemma is an important component of realizing that day. In clear, concise language, Miriam Claire shares her respectful perspectives and honest insights about abortion and why women and men around the globe make this choice. She is not afraid to take on, analyze, and expose the inflammatory lies, rhetoric, and violent behavior of anti-choice militants. She implores all pro-choice advocates to get the message out that *abortion is not murder*—that abortion is indeed a moral choice. Claire skillfully discusses the illusive definition of a human being with its numerous scientific, moral, religious, and cultural nuances and viewpoints.

I became involved in the provision of abortion care because I saw, from an early age, how women's lives, including those in my family, were destroyed without access to safe abortion. Coming of age in New York City in the late 60's—before legalization—many of my high school girlfriends self-induced abortion with knitting needles or, if they were lucky, found a safe practitioner on the West Side of Manhattan or in Puerto Rico. Finding dead women in dumpsters was not uncommon in those years. Although this was the era of an exciting cultural and sexual revolution that afforded young women much freedom, it was also a painful and desperate time to be a *pregnant* young woman. It is even more terrifying that now, 30 years later, we are faced with the very real prospect of going back to the fear and terror of those times.

Close to 90% of the counties in the United States currently do not have an abortion provider. Even today, women must often travel great distances and risk violence from anti-choice fanatics to obtain their abortions. Abortion providers endure a great deal to help these women. The staff of Aradia Women's Health Center is sometimes scared but always steadfast. I'm proud of my work, and reading *The Abortion Dilemma* affirmed that pride and helped me let go of my fears, even if only for a short time. I know that every day abortion providers throughout the world are saving women's lives and helping women to regain their destinies. This compelling book will serve as an educational and counseling tool for providers, the media, the public, and those women who want to make an informed decision about the outcome of an unwanted pregnancy.

At the time of this writing, several anti-choice bills are pending in the legislature of Washington State. Once again, the most marginalized women in society—the young, the poor, and the geographically isolated—are in serious danger of losing their already fragile right to safe, legal abortion. I fear for their lives, as I do for my own. But I am very grateful to Miriam Claire that the *The Abortion Dilemma* is here to share her views about our work and why we do what we do.

Women all over the world will want to read this book. *The Abortion Dilemma* is a welcomed and invaluable resource that, with great empathy, explores why women make this complex choice. Its strength lies in its rational and compassionate ability to destigmatize abortion and logically silence anti-choice rhetoric. *The Abortion Dilemma* tells the truth about abortion and shares the realities of women's lives and choices.

Marcy L. Bloom
Aradia Women's Health Center
Seattle, Washington

Preface

The purpose of *The Abortion Dilemma* is to help you define how you feel about abortion and form an educated opinion.

If you are pregnant and considering an abortion, this book will help you make an informed choice. *Only you can decide* if abortion is the right choice for you.

For women who have had an abortion, reading *The Abortion Dilemma* will stimulate you and your partner to reflect upon the experience in a different light.

The Abortion Dilemma reveals how women and men around the world have responded to the reality of an abortion; how various religions and cultures view abortion; how abortion affects a woman's relationship with her partner; how abortion providers think and feel about performing abortions; how to sift through the maze of abortion propaganda and discern the facts; how medical abortion differs from surgical abortion; how preparing a living will can prevent anyone else ever making an abortion decision for you; about the implications for a woman of positive test results for both the HIV virus and pregnancy; about the special needs of rape victims who are impregnated by their attacker(s); about fetal abnormalities, prenatal diagnostic testing, and factors to consider before making a decision to continue a pregnancy when a fetal abnormality has been detected or is suspected; about adoption options; about the incongruous history of abortion legality and parental consent laws; and where to go for further education or practical help.

Abortion is an intensely personal public issue. It is important that abortion education be intimate, humane, and credibly scientific. Professionals in the various relevant scientific, medical, philosophical, legal, political, and religious fields tend to argue about abortion in academic language or inflated rhetoric that is ultimately too impersonal to have meaning for laypeople, especially those grappling with a real abortion dilemma. *The Abortion Dilemma* uses personal interviews with professionals and laypersons alike as an effective antidote to cold polemics.

I have asked questions that any person who thinks about abortion might ask, and have attempted to provide a variety of enlightening answers in language that can be understood by all. The texts of the majority of books available in stores and libraries on the moral issues surrounding abortion are convoluted and soporific. Professor Bernard Williams, then Provost of Kings College at Cambridge University in England when I interviewed him, presented me with a copy of one of his books on morality, which he felt might be relevant to my research on abortion. As he handed me the book he laughed and wished me luck reading it, saying that he considered it "virtually unreadable."

Professor Williams is indeed modest regarding his books on morality—his use of humor in writing about this very serious subject certainly helped me formulate my ideas for this book. In the Preface to his book *Morality: An Introduction to Ethics* he points out that most contemporary moral philosophy is "empty" and "has found an original way of being boring, which is by not discussing moral issues at all . . . the desire to reduce revealed moral commitment to a minimum and to use moral arguments in the role of being uncontentiously illustrative leaves an impression that all the important issues are off the page, somewhere, and that great caution and little imagination have been used in letting tiny corners of them appear."[1]

The pro-choice movement's arguments in favor of legal abortion leave me with the same feeling that Professor Williams describes so eloquently. Somehow, the key issue is not being addressed and is "off the page," because the question of whether abortion is murder is risky and unanswerable in an absolute sense.

In criticizing the present pro-choice response to the anti-abortion hysteria generated by Operation Rescue and other extreme abortion opponents, I do not intend to trivialize or diminish the remarkably successful efforts of millions of Americans involved in the process of legalizing abortion in the United States. But the intense preoccupation with individual and constitutional rights rather than addressing the concerns of abortion opponents is a mistake, because the general public and many people considering an abortion are confused and intimidated by the constant barrage of propaganda in the various media telling them that abortion is murder.

The estimated 50 to 60 million women worldwide who have abortions each year are not experts on abortion, morality, law, or politics. Neither are their partners, but somehow they have to make the choice. Those who do seek counsel from their religion, family, friends or doctor, often have to sort through a moral maze of contradictory and confusing views which in some cases are outright lies. Truth frequently becomes a victim of ignorance and fantasy.

Televangelism and slick marketing of simple answers to the complex issues surrounding abortion nurture ignorance, moral arrogance, and fanaticism. Reason, tolerance, and medical knowledge are my chosen weapons of defense against mindless dogma. Medical and moral education is the key to making an informed choice, not faith.

The Abortion Dilemma will help unravel the tangled yarn of anti-abortion rhetoric, which strangles the hearts of millions of caring people who are trapped in a moral web.

Acknowledgments

There have been so many people who have contributed to *The Abortion Dilemma* that it would take another book to fully acknowledge them as they deserve. Given the constraints of space and time, I hope that my grateful thanks to all who have helped over the years will be accepted without offense that you have not been named. You know who you are.

My warm thanks to all interviewees and the many people around the world who filled in questionnaires, wrote letters, phoned, read the various drafts of the manuscript, or simply confided thoughts in passing, for without you, this book would be a shallow diatribe. I have felt honored and encouraged by your trust and confidence that my research would be fruitful.

Staff at Marie Stopes International in England, Hospital Broussais in France, and the Planned Parenthood Federation of America have provided invaluable support, for which I offer thanks to all.

I am deeply indebted to my Editor at Insight Books, Frank K. Darmstadt, and his assistant, Jennifer Reynolds, for their sensitivity, constructive criticism and belief in the project. My thanks also to production editor, Daniel Kulkosky, publicist John Garger, and all the staff at Insight Books who have helped in ways big and small, but always friendly.

My warmest thanks to all who read and endorsed the book, especially Marcy Bloom, whose thoughtfulness and heartfelt Foreword offer sad insight into the reality of life for health care providers, who bravely continue providing women in the United

States with safe, quality health care despite ongoing violent harassment from antiabortion militants.

To Stan Irwin and the sponsors who brought me to America—thanks for so generously believing in me.

To my family and friends, thanks for patiently indulging me as I wrote the rewrite of the rewrite of the rewrite . . . the creative process is indeed evolutionary.

To all who "clipped" on my behalf, most of all my scissor-weary husband, thanks for being my eyes. A filing cabinet full of articles on abortion-related issues is bountiful proof of your diligence.

To my sweet and beautiful assistant Aketa, and my ever-gorgeous "bubble fairy niece" Michelle, thanks for keeping Lucas happily distracted so that I could write. Grandma Marie, thank you too!

To my parents, especially my mother—how can I ever thank you enough for all those years of loving support and encouragement? Thanks for being wonderful parents!

To my brother, David, thanks for the "marketing" feedback, helpful suggestions, publications, and faxes!

To my beloved "Redhead," thanks for taking care of us all and being a dream "sister." You've earned your "wings" Sandi . . .

To my poor "abortion maxed-out" husband, who yearns for the day when I will write a . . . well, on something other than abortion. You've earned your "Best Husband" Oscar and my loving thanks for all those little and big things you do to help.

To Walt Disney Productions, the late Jim Henson and the Muppets, Big Bird and Sesame Street, Lambchop and Shari Lewis, the late Gene Roddenberry, Steven Spielberg, George Lucas, Johnny Carson, Stan Irwin and my son, Lucas—thanks for making me laugh and keeping my imagination happy!

Contents

Prologue

The heart of the abortion dilemma is the need for a pregnant woman, and her partner or spouse, to make a choice between giving birth or not giving birth.

There are many complex personal, moral, religious, cultural, health, financial, and legal factors that may contribute in varying degrees to the sense of conflict that women and men all over the world feel when wrestling with the decision to have, or not have, an abortion.

Perhaps the most complex aspect of the dilemma of abortion is choice. When you choose to have an abortion, you are responsible for a decision to halt the development of a human life. That is the most significant difference between abortion and miscarriage. It is somehow easier to accept "fate" or "the will of nature" than it is to accept responsibility for our actions.

The following excerpts from interviews and discussions I had with women and men around the world, as well as from other specified sources, reflect the varied nature of the conflicts associated with a decision to have an abortion.

"If you don't want the baby and you don't want the abortion, what do you want?" asked my boyfriend. "That is my dilemma," I replied. "What I want is not to be pregnant. I don't mean that I want to have an abortion. I want simply never to have conceived so that I won't be faced with that decision."—A Greek Orthodox psychologist in England

My feeling was that I didn't want the child and I didn't want the abortion.—A Buddhist literary agent in the United States

I was scared and felt so very small and helpless. Here I was being led by the hand of my husband, who had made me pregnant, as if I was a small child. He was taking me to have an abortion. . . . I became suspicious of my husband's love for me. . . . I have never been able to talk to him about what I felt as a result of his decision. . . . The confrontation with the decision to have an abortion taught us a very valuable lesson: If we really didn't want a baby, then we had to take precautions to prevent it happening again.—A Muslim Israeli Arab educator/psychologist

The choice to have the abortion was made more difficult because I could not discuss the decision before nor confess it after to my Catholic priest in Hawaii. I was afraid of him, because he was against abortion and would probably have excommunicated me. His manner was harsh and cold. I had to bear the burden of my decision completely alone. Had I experienced such a dilemma in the Philippines, my priest there would have been sympathetic and helped me through the ordeal. He was more realistic in his approach to Catholicism, and seemed a kinder person. I feel that I could have confessed anything to him. I wanted to confess because I felt guilty about the abortion.—A Catholic Filipino woman

"Who would like to undergo an abortion?" queried Chen Shunkui, assistant Party Secretary of Sandhead Brigade during a family-planning meeting at an Equality Commune in China. This question was asked after the women in attendance, who had initially refused to have an abortion, were lectured on their duty to the commune and China. The need to control population growth for the good of the whole community was emphasized over and over again, in subtly varying ways. He reassured them that there was no longer a need to have many sons for security in old age as state welfare was provided for women who restricted the numbers of children to whom they gave birth. The question "was greeted with silence." One woman later cried out that she would "never abort." Eventually, 3 of the 24 women at the 4 day meeting agreed to abortions—to be performed the following day, 5 agreed to try to convince their families at home that they should abort, and 10 refused to abort. The remaining 6 women were fined for not attending the decisive meeting, and they would continue to be fined for each day they did not attend.— From Steven W. Mosher's *Broken Earth*[1]

I blocked out everything about the abortion—It was just another thing we had to do. We never talked about it then or now. The baby was just another victim of war . . . Three years after my abortion, it became legal in Hungary. Oh, the resentment . . . I consider myself a good Catholic, and like a good Catholic, I confessed my abortion to my priest. I was excommunicated. . . . "I felt worse about being excommunicated than I did about the abortion."—Mica Brody, a Hungarian Catholic who had an illegal abortion in the late 1940s just after Hungary was overrun by Russia. The punishment for abortion at that time was life imprisonment for the woman in Siberia and death or life imprisonment in Siberia for the physician. From Linda Bird Francke's *The Ambivalence of Abortion.*[2]

My friend was very supportive when I told him I was pregnant, but he left the decision about the fate of the pregnancy to me—I decided to have an abortion. . . . I felt I was carrying a girl fetus, so I named her "Lei," meaning spirit or gorgeousness in Japanese. I found a clinic near my apartment in Tokyo where I was lucky enough to have a young, sensitive doctor who listened to my thoughts with interest and concern. He said, "You seem to want to keep her spirit alive. Don't worry, you are not going to kill her. She will watch over you from her world and help you to be strong. Her spirit will be with you forever." . . . I almost fell in love with that doctor.—A Buddhist dancer in Japan

Here everyone is afraid of getting pregnant, terrified of having to have an abortion. It's difficult and painful; I should know, I had one at the hospital. Now they've started to give painkillers. But outside the cities they don't—only some kind of injection that doesn't work.—A Russian woman, as quoted in *Moscow Women* by Carola Hansson and Karin Liden[3]

Abortion is a common event indeed, and it is almost always devised and carried out without the husband's knowledge. The woman often manages to keep it secret, aided by the solidarity of the neighbourhood. The motives for aborting may be as various as family quarrelling, the failure to pay part of the dowry, or a serious offence. Also, a woman may be induced to abort by a desire for revenge against her husband.—A Basankusu woman in Africa, as quoted by A. Romaniuk, whose excerpt appears in *Women of Africa: Roots of Oppression* by Maria Rosa Cutrufelli[4]

If I'd had an abortion, I would not tell you—most Indian women, especially unmarried women, would not confess an abortion to you, for fear that someone in their family or community might find out. That would cause a social disgrace for an unmarried woman which might lead to the woman being outcast or murdered. Many unmarried women who've had abortions in India commit suicide, more because of the scandal and isolation associated with the pregnancy than because of the abortion itself. Abortion is legal in India, but there is still an enormous social stigma attached to pregnancy out of wedlock.—A female Indian Sikh

When my wife became pregnant in India in 1951, she had to have an abortion because we could not afford a child. I was responsible for educating and arranging marriages for my two brothers and four sisters, because my father had died and I was the oldest son. We were both students at the time of her first pregnancy. We felt that we could not risk the lives of seven people for one lifeless fetus. The conflict over the abortion for us did not stem from any moral concern for the fetus, but rather from fear for the health of my wife. Abortion was still illegal in India at that time—it was a very dangerous procedure.—A male Indian Sikh

I was married in the ghetto of Theresienstadt in Poland shortly after my arrival there in 1939, at the outbreak of World War II. Theresienstadt was a self-governed ghetto under the supervision of the infamous Nazi SS. All doctors and other professionals were Jewish. . . . One and a half years after my arrival, I became pregnant. Just before that time, abortion in Theresienstadt was forbidden by the German authorities, and if a doctor was discovered to have performed an abortion, he was jailed. I have no idea why the Germans suddenly forbade abortion. I went to several doctors first asking them and then begging for an abortion, but no one would help me because to do so would have put their own lives at risk.

On top of this pressure, my husband and I received a call to the "East." Such a call meant leaving Theresienstadt for an unknown destination. . . . I left Theresienstadt at the beginning of my third month of pregnancy. It was a terrible three-day journey. On the third night in the evening, we came to a halt and they opened the doors. There was terrible shouting and barking of dogs. Through the opening I could see only lights—I had no idea where we were. They shouted at us to get out of the wagons and to leave everything behind, so we sprang down surrounded by SS guards, dogs, and some people in striped uniforms that resembled pajamas. We had no idea what was going on. I asked one of these striped people to tell me where we were. He replied "Auschwitz," but he told me nothing of what that word meant.

Then we had to take showers and our arms were tattooed with our camp numbers. . . . There was a barrack in the camp that served as a hospital with Jewish doctors. I went to them and begged for an abortion, but no one was willing to risk death for performing an abortion. The Germans were not yet aware of my pregnancy, but the doctors could not have kept the abortion a secret as the Germans were constantly entering and leaving the hospital to check what was going on. I kept trying to get an abortion, but I did not succeed.

I worked in the camp, transferring stones from one heap to another. One day, we were told to get rid of our clothes and go to a "selection" where Dr. Mengele was standing with his hand straight up and his feet apart, signaling for people to go either to the left or the right. Can you imagine a woman, eight months pregnant, with a protruding belly, in that situation . . . what would you think? This is where instinct comes into action. I asked some of my young friends to stand in front of me in the hope that Mengele's eye would catch their bodies instead of mine. That was the only thing I could do. The girls arranged themselves in front of and behind me. We went, naked, before Mengele, and he waved me to the same side as the girls. On the other side were elderly women, ill people, and children. At that stage I didn't know exactly what the fate of the people who were waved to the other side would be, but I felt intuitively that they were in great danger. I wanted to live, and as there was a rumor that working hands were needed in Germany, I thought that we youngsters would be sent away. We were.

[Ruth was eventually sent back to Auschwitz with her friend, Bertha.] Bertha and I were a sensation when we arrived back in Auschwitz. We were the first two people ever to leave Auschwitz to travel to a destination in Germany and return alive. Everyone in Auschwitz was 100% sure that whoever left Auschwitz went to the gas chambers. Our return meant that there was hope for survival, even in Auschwitz.

We became so famous that Mengele heard about us and came to see us the next day. Mengele asked me to describe the situation that led to his passing me over during the selection—he couldn't believe that he had overlooked me. When I told him what had transpired, he replied with a sarcastic smile, "Oh, you give birth and then you will see." That was all he said.

During the remaining days of my pregnancy, Mengele came to visit me while making his daily "rounds" at the hospital to check on his experiments. Every day, this fascinating and good-looking young man would talk to me, almost as if he cared about my welfare. Then I began having labor pains. A Polish midwife helped me give birth as I lay on the ground on a blanket. There was no hot water, no antiseptic, no cotton wool, no nightgown, no diaper, no soap—nothing. She had a pair of scissors and after she cut the umbilical cord, she took the child and put it on a wooden cot where I lay with just one blanket. Despite the circumstances of the birth, I was elated when I was told that I had given birth to a baby girl . . . I think it was the biggest pleasure of my life, for she was my first child. There was indescribable pain and trauma associated with the birth, and yet the feeling of the baby coming out was incredibly beautiful.

The next morning, Mengele came and ordered that my breasts be bandaged. He forbade me to breast-feed my child. He didn't say it, but I knew that he wanted to use my baby for an experiment, to see how long a baby could survive without food. . . . I was forbidden to get out of bed. Every day, Mengele arrived to make his "notes," as if this process of starvation of an infant was a normal form of treatment. It was a crazy situation which made me feel as if I was going mad. After several days, I had no milk left in my breasts. My baby remained with me the whole time—I think Mengele wanted me to see her suffer. At first she screamed from hunger, but then her voice became gradually softer as she lost her strength. Her bones began to stick out and her belly became swollen. It was an unbearably frustrating situation. I was under guard the whole time, so there was little else I could do to help her. To compound the situation, the baby's diapers couldn't be washed, so the stench was terrible.

After 6 days, my baby was barely able to breathe . . . all I could hear was a faint whimper. Mengele observed that there was nothing more for him to note, and announced that I was to be prepared the next morning for him to come and fetch. I knew without doubt that this meant I was going to the gas chambers the next day. I started to scream and lost control. A woman doctor, who was also a prisoner, came and asked aggressively why I was crying. Her tone shocked me, as I hadn't realized that I was screaming. I was only just 21, and I desperately wanted to live.

Slowly, I managed to tell her my story, and that I was going to the gas chambers the next day. When she realized that I was one of the two who had left and returned to Auschwitz, she said that she must save my life. She left me then, and I lay crying, convinced that this was the last day of my life. After the lights had gone out as usual at 9 p.m. that evening, the woman doctor returned and told me that she had brought something which I was to give to my child. When I asked her what it was, she said that it was a syringe with morphine. She said that I had to kill my child. I didn't know how I could do it. So she started to talk to me in a hypnotic angel's voice, telling me that she had taken the Hippocratic oath to save human lives. Now she had to save my life, but my child could not continue living. She talked and talked until finally I was persuaded to do it. I gave the injection to my baby girl, who continued to cling to life for about an hour. Then she was gone, and part of me died with her.

Do I regret killing my baby? I've had horrible, recurring nightmares about it ever since. I can't say that I regret what I did, but the terrible moment of killing my child has returned to haunt me often, and I suffer indescribable pain. My husband has often had to awaken me at night to stop me screaming during these nightmares. Although my baby would have died in the gas chambers anyway, I was directly responsible for her death and will always have to bear the burden of that responsibility. I don't regret what I did, but I have had to live with it.—Ruth E., Israel

I have included Ruth E.'s story because it forces us to reflect on the tenuous nature of morality and ask ourselves whether we have the right to judge her actions in those extreme circumstances.

As it is common practice today for those who are against abortion to compare it with the mass extermination program that killed millions of people in concentrations camps in Nazi Europe, it is crucial that the reality of the difference between abortion and infanticide in that extreme situation versus "murder" be understood. Ruth E. killed her dying baby, but did she commit a "murder" in the same sense that the Nazis were murdering millions? If you believe that abortion is "murder," do you feel that abortion in a concentration camp such as Theresienstadt or Auschwitz would have been morally forgivable?

Most people feel that infanticide is wrong and yet, in Ruth's case, we are forced to adjust our concept of morality in order to understand and accept her behavior. Although we would like to live in a world governed by an absolute morality, unfortunately there is no such thing. Morality is not absolute; it is born of circumstance and survival needs. Killing is not always morally wrong.

When I presented the question of the morality of abortion and infanticide in a concentration camp to the ministers of religion and professionals interviewed in this book, the nearly unanimous response was that a woman in that situation could not be judged by anyone but herself and God. Most felt that there are circumstances in which killing is for the greater good. As the Nazis were known for savagely murdering babies in concentration camps by smashing them ferociously against walls and throwing them live into ovens, perhaps painless mercy killing in such a situation is forgivable?

The terrifying aspect of my abortion was fear that the Nazis would find out, because abortion was illegal in Germany at that time.—My widowed grandmother, who would probably not have been able to escape to Australia via England with her children, my mother and aunt, if she had gone ahead and had another child. Her fate, and that of her children, could well have been Auschwitz had she not had that abortion.

Your father and I married in August, 1944, a time when the impact of the news of the Holocaust via newsreels and the media brought home the horror in graphic detail. A short time later, we discovered that I was pregnant, but we both felt that it would be better not to bring a child into this nightmare world where genocide could be committed with such apparent ease. Abortion was illegal in Australia at that time, so once we had made the decision, a lot of "cloak and dagger" secrecy surrounded getting the name of a doctor who performed abortions, at a price. Your father was away in an Army camp in northern Victoria, so I had to try to communicate with him via a not very private telephone in the rooming house where I was living. Money had to be borrowed from Army friends. I was given an address by a doctor who had agreed to do the abortion, having accepted the reason I gave for wanting it. I was told where to go and to come alone. When I arrived, I was told to undress and put on a gown, and then I was blindfolded so that I couldn't identify the person who would carry out the procedure. I was terribly scared, mainly because of being blindfolded and all the secrecy needed to protect the doctor from being arrested. When I awoke, I got dressed and went home in a taxi, which we could not afford. My mother and sister knew what I was doing, so I went to their flat to recover. . . . When I became pregnant in early 1947, the very reason for which we had the abortion earlier became the dominant reason for not having one this time. Your father's whole family was murdered in the Holocaust—he was alone and wanted children.—My mother, who confided her experience of abortion after I began writing this book. Prior to that time, I knew she and my father were actively pro-choice, but they had never shared their personal experience. Neither ever regretted the abortion, but since my father suffered several strokes in 1986, he has become more expressive of sadness and openly mourns the murder of his family. He says that he sometimes wonders what the baby might have looked like.

My research has convinced me that there is no such thing as a universal or absolute morality that is applicable to all people, in all countries, of all religions, and at all times. Abortion produces intense emotional responses in people of all cultures, but for very different reasons. I hope that this book will contribute in some small way to fostering greater tolerance and respect for the opinions and feelings of others.

Introduction

On March 10, 1984, I had a surgical abortion at the Marie Stopes Clinic in London. I wanted to create something positive out of the trauma and negativity of the abortion, so I began researching and writing this book, hoping that it would one day help others through the experience of abortion. I never dreamed that I would still be working on the book 11 years later, or that I would have a second abortion in Los Angeles 5 days after a devastating earthquake, on January 22, 1994 (coincidentally, the 21st anniversary of Roe v. Wade, the landmark Supreme Court ruling that legalized abortion in the United States).

I was performing as a singer in "Evita" in London in 1984 when I discovered that I was pregnant. I shall always be grateful for the support that I received from the company at that time, including from those who strongly opposed abortion and yet were kind despite their beliefs. By coincidence, a colleague with whom I shared a dressing room discovered that she was pregnant at around the same time. She and her husband were thrilled with their news, but she became distressed at the thought that I was going to have an abortion. In total sincerity, she asked me if I would consider having the baby and letting her adopt it. I was utterly distressed at the thought of possibly giving up a child of mine for adoption. I thanked my colleague for her offer and tried to explain to her that just as her maternal instinct prompted her to make such an offer, my maternal instinct could never let me accept it. While I do believe that adopting out a child can be an expression of maternal protectiveness and caring, it was not my choice.

As I struggled through my own abortion trauma, I came to realize the complexity of the responses we all have to this very human dilemma. My experience was a struggle because I had not anticipated the terrible sense of emptiness that followed the abortion. It is probably difficult for those who are against abortion or who have not had one to understand that one can have an abortion without regret and yet still feel a deep sense of loss. The feelings seem contradictory—perhaps they are. If nothing else, I have learned that abortion produces many conflicting emotions that are not necessarily reconcilable or logical.

Making the choice to have an abortion can be difficult, and it is virtually impossible to know how you are going to react physically and emotionally after the abortion. All you can do is know your options, educate yourself about pregnancy and abortion, and learn from the experience.

Dr. Lawrence Scott is a warm, compassionate, caring, and sensitive physician (and attorney!) who has performed thousands of abortions in Los Angeles. I was lucky enough to be attended by him on January 22, 1994, when I underwent my second abortion. Dr. Scott has an extraordinary gift for explaining the facts of abortion in simple language and making women feel that everything will be alright. Patients breathe a sigh of relief after talking to him. I requested an interview with Dr. Scott after I had recovered from my abortion because I was so impressed by his humanity and intelligence. When I asked him how a woman can be sure that abortion is the right choice for her, he replied:

> Sometimes a woman is uncertain whether she is happy or unhappy about being pregnant. She didn't expect to be pregnant, but now that she is, in some way she may be delighted because she thought that she couldn't even get pregnant . . . Women often tell me that "It's nice to know that I can get pregnant even if it is an inconvenient time." There's a little test that I employ that sometimes helps patients in this situation. I ask the woman to "imagine that you have been sleeping and you wake up and find out that you aren't pregnant at all—it was just a dream. Really self-hypnotize yourself into

thinking that, and then when you finally snap out of it, decide whether or not you are happy or unhappy that you aren't pregnant." You'd be surprised how many ladies have called me back saying, "Dr. Scott, I laid back and thought about it, and God, I was kind of disappointed when I found out that I wasn't pregnant." Then I say that "maybe you had better reevaluate whether or not having a child is a priority now." Most women, however, call me up and say, "I was really relieved for a split second." Then I know that the woman really doesn't want to be pregnant now.[1]

If you are uncertain whether abortion is the right choice for you, try Dr. Scott's imagination test first. Writing answers to the following questions will further help you clarify how you feel and what is the best decision for you in your particular circumstances. If your partner and family are aware that you are pregnant and contemplating an abortion, share your thoughts, and this book, with them. Communicating about abortion is often very difficult, especially for couples, but it is important to make an attempt to understand each other's feelings and thoughts on the subject . . .

1. Why have you been considering the option of abortion?
2. Do you really want to have this baby?
3. How do you feel about aborting this pregnancy?
4. Can you afford a child financially?
5. Will having a child adversely affect your career/studies?
6. Could having a child negatively impact on your marriage/partner/parents/family or your other children?
7. Can you have a safe, legal abortion? If not, what scares you?
8. Is someone in your family hostile to you having an abortion?
9. Do you fear for your safety if you have an abortion?
10. Are you afraid of the abortion procedure?

11. Would you prefer to have a medical or a surgical abortion?

12. Could having a child threaten your physical health?

13. Do you feel that you can cope with the responsibilities of parenthood?

14. Are you willing/able to accept the changes in life-style that will inevitably follow having a baby?

15. Are you afraid to have a child because you don't know if you'll be a "good" parent and able to cope?

16. Have you discussed your pregnancy with the members of your family whom it may affect?

17. Does your husband/partner/family want you to have the baby?

18. Will your husband/partner/family stand by you and provide help if you decide to have the baby?

19. Could having a child now be dangerous for you or the baby in some way?

20. Are you afraid that a relative/partner/family member will become hostile and/or violent toward you or the baby if you choose to give birth?

21. Did you become pregnant as a result of being raped or incest?

22. If you answered yes to #21, are you concerned that your baby would become a victim too if you gave birth?

23. Have you tested positive for the AIDS virus?

24. If you have answered yes to #23, have you considered the possible consequences of giving birth in the event that you, your spouse, or your baby develop the disease?

25. Would having an abortion create a moral or religious conflict for you, your partner, or your family?

26. Do you believe that abortion is murder?

27. Could adoption be a suitable alternative to abortion for you?

28. Do you have medical insurance to cover the costs of pregnancy, birth, and any medical complications arising?

29. Do you need financial aid to pay for an abortion?
30. Is there a physician or abortion clinic close to your home? If not, is transportation a problem?
31. Do you need parental consent to have an abortion? (Minors)
32. Will your parents consent to an abortion? (Minors)
33. If your parents refuse to consent to the abortion, can you travel to a state where you will not need their permission or apply to a judge/court for permission? (Minors)
34. If your parents refuse to consent to an abortion, will you try to keep the baby or adopt it out? (Minors)

For millions of people around the world, abortion is a responsible decision that is made with a completely clear conscience, without any sense of regret. After reading this book, if you feel that abortion is morally wrong, seek an alternative such as open adoption or temporary foster care if you cannot keep the baby. If you cannot afford the medical costs of pregnancy and childbirth, there are charities that may assist you.

> In the few cells present at conception there is a potential human being—that is a certainty—but anything else is the subject for debate and ultimately resolution within each individual's conscience.—An American woman[2]

1

Women—How They Think and Feel about Abortion

A woman's feelings about abortion depend largely on her reason for choosing to end the pregnancy, the conditions during the procedure, and her response to the experience. There are many reasons for choosing to have an abortion. Perhaps underlying them all is a deeply maternal, instinctive feeling that the time is not right to give birth and that to do so would be detrimental to all concerned. If there is any doubt about the decision or any moral conflict, the emotional effect may be devastating. For some women, an abortion is one of the most profound events they will experience in life.

"My predominant feeling after the abortion was relief."[1] That reflection by English abortion counselor Andrea Butcher, during our interview in 1994, has been repeated to me over and over again by women around the world. It is the one response to abortion that is almost universal. Another English woman explained in a letter, "I felt mainly relieved at first—the guilt and the resentment of my boyfriend were buried by the initial sense of having solved the problem." Relief is the most common reaction after an abortion because fear of surgery and medical procedures, even when they are legal, is instinctive. Even women who have no emotional conflicts about abortion still express relief at the procedure being safely over, especially if it was illegal.

Mira Dana, a psychotherapist at the Women's Therapy Centre in London, has conducted postabortion counseling sessions for almost 20 years. In her view,

There are three general reactions women display after an abortion and on coming home from hospital. (1) Euphoria . . . an expression of the feeling of relief and freedom at having solved a problem, having got rid of a burden and having executed a decisive action. They will feel strong and powerful and in control of their lives. They will feel the need to laugh and have a good time . . . [and] keep excessively busy . . . feelings of loss, anger [and] guilt are of no relevance for them at this period . . . these emotions are bound to come later, sometimes even months or years later, sometimes in a disguised form, apparently with no connection to having had an abortion. . . . (2) Detachment— Some women will experience a sense of "shock" . . . numbness inside. They will go on doing ordinary activities they are used to doing, but with a sense of detachment, distance . . . unreality. This detachment is an attempt to avoid experiencing the painful feelings connected to the termination. . . . She may feel an inner emptiness . . . (3) Depression—Some women get into a state of depression which could be described as a general sense of hopelessness and diffused (unfocussed) feeling of blackness . . . feeling bad about yourself and your life and your environment, but without actually knowing what it is—a state of no specific emotion but this "darkness" . . . feelings of worthlessness . . . and that nothing is of much importance . . . [Other reactions may be] Fear of Sexuality . . . Many women need time after an abortion before they feel relaxed and able to have sexual relationships again because they fear another abortion. . . . Ambivalence—not only about having a baby. There are many issues in a woman's life about which she may be equally confused but which get "hooked" on the one issue of having a baby. . . . Envy—Often women feel envious of other women who have babies after the termination. . . . Some women will refrain from visiting their friends who have newborn babies as they feel it is too painful to be with them.[2]

Not all women feel loss, anger, guilt, and depression after an abortion, as Mira Dana suggests, but some do, and most women certainly experience at least one of those feelings.

Mira Dana has a deep perception and understanding of women's reactions to abortion and the problems created by having to keep the experience a secret. I believe she is absolutely wrong, however, in her belief that women don't get pregnant by accident, and that "getting pregnant and having an abortion is a statement. . . . Connected to its being a statement is the idea that an abortion is always an expression of a deep internal conflict."[3] That is simply not true for all women, though it may be for some, and in particular for the select group Mira Dana and other counselors see for postabortion therapy.

There is no 100% effective form of contraception other than abstention. For many women, unintended pregnancy results from a failure of contraception, including the pill. As Marie Stopes International abortion counselor Andrea Butcher noted in our phone interview, "I was using the cap and even took the morning-after pill, but I still became pregnant!"[1] Andrea Butcher's experience as an abortion counselor in London has led her to conclusions that directly contradict the thoughts of Mira Dana. It is important for women seeking counseling after an abortion to understand that therapists and counselors have different techniques and ideas on abortion. Selecting a therapist should be approached with the same care as choosing a physician, minister, or teacher.

Andrea Butcher spoke passionately during our interview about her anger at women's responses to abortion being misrepresented:

The idea that we all suffer to some degree when we decide to have an abortion makes me furious, because it's not true. Most women do not experience any guilt, remorse, or doubt. A number of women have said to me that they feel guilty about not feeling guilty after deciding to have an abortion . . . Only a minority of women feel unsure and ambivalent about whether or not they want to continue the pregnancy, and for them it can be a nightmare. I see very few people who actually have a moral qualm about abortion itself. For most women, abortion is *not* a decision that is looked back upon with regret and it is *not* generally viewed as something that

> will come back to haunt them later on—at least 90% of
> women feel no ambivalence about abortion. For most, it's a
> very straightforward, practical decision, based normally on
> economics. . . .[1]

During my research over 11 years, the most commonly cited reasons for an abortion were lack of sufficient income to provide for
a child and studies or a career that would be jeopardized by the
responsibilities of parenting. I have never met anyone who made
the decision to abort casually.

Some women confuse their emotional response to abortion
with their personal problems. An unhappy relationship with a
boyfriend, spouse, or parent is typically blamed on the abortion,
when in fact the problem in the relationship was present prior to
the unplanned pregnancy. Counselor Andrea Butcher observes
that

> When women take up the offer of postabortion counseling,
> they express feelings of confusion and sadness. Often, how-
> ever, I find that there are a whole lot of other problems in the
> woman's life and her reaction after the abortion is not sim-
> ply a result of the abortion. For example, the woman might
> be trapped in a very unsatisfactory relationship.[1]

A tragic example of just such an unsatisfactory relationship
influencing the decision to have an abortion was Maria Callas, the
great opera diva who was passionately in love with Aristotle
Onassis, the Greek shipping tycoon who wed the late Jacqueline
Kennedy Onassis.

According to the biography of Maria Callas by Arianna
Stassinopoulos,

> Ever since she had fully realized her dream of success and
> achievement, and even before she met Onassis, Maria had
> one overwhelming desire: to have a child. Now, at the age of
> forty-three, she found herself pregnant. It seemed a miracle.
> "I'm thirty-six," she had said, at the beginning of her rela-
> tionship with Onassis, "and I want to live—I want a child,

but I don't know if I'm capable of giving birth to another being." As the years went on Maria had tried to convince herself that perhaps she did not want a child all that much after all. It took the discovery that she was pregnant to make her see just how much she did want it, and just how much this had been a source of half-conscious but ever-present regret. All her instincts, everything in her that longed for life, wanted a child. Onassis did not. It was painful enough to have the man she adored reject, instead of celebrate, the child of their love, but he went further: he warned her that if she went ahead and kept the child it would be the end of their relationship. She was pitched into a torrent of doubt, fear, confusion. . . . Her abortion, at the moment when she longed for a new source of energy and meaning, was her life's greatest might-have-been. . . . Maria's longing to be needed by Aristo was further from fulfillment than ever.[4]

Giving birth is the ultimate human creation, and there is no artistic form that can fulfill that need or approach the greatness of nature. To have an abortion in an attempt to save a relationship when you really want to have the baby is a formula for self-destruction, and rarely will it save an ailing relationship.

Though it is fashionable to seek psychological explanations for human responses, the truth is that biochemical reactions in the body probably govern feelings far more than we presently accept. When a woman has an abortion, her hormones are thrown into chaos, causing a biological, hormonal, and psychological reversal. It is likely that feelings of sadness and loss after an abortion are as much induced by biochemical reactions within the woman's body as they are by emotional trauma or moral conflict. According to distinguished Canadian physician and high-profile abortion provider Dr. Henry Morgentaler, whom I was privileged to interview in 1986 and 1994,

The grief some women feel after having an abortion stems from a hormonal imbalance. . . . Being human also means having projections, images, and fantasies. Once you know that there is a potential human being inside you, you fantasize about having a child and the desire to have it. In your mind you skip the 9 months and it's there already. In a sense, you have the image of the child in your fantasy and that image is taken away. The potential has been taken away, at least for this particular pregnancy. It remains for future pregnancies. . . .[5]

The guilt some women feel after an abortion stems from blurred grief, disappointment, sometimes shame at not being able to carry the pregnancy to term, and, more rarely, because of the belief that they have killed a baby. What they have killed is a potential baby, a fantasy, an image of motherhood, and perhaps a dream to have a baby.

Grief and loss are the most confusing emotions associated with abortion. Somehow, because a woman chooses to have an abortion, it is not considered appropriate or socially acceptable for her to grieve publicly or, in many cases, privately. Psychotherapist Mira Dana ironically concurs:

Why would you feel sadness or loss about something you wanted to get rid of? On the surface it looks like a contradiction. . . . The fact that it was your decision which caused the loss does not allow space for mourning.[6]

Some women are surprised by the depth of their feelings of loss after an abortion, and they assume responsibility for this grief through a sense of guilt, because their choice to have an abortion brought about the loss. It is crucial for the mental well-being of women, and men, that they share their sense of loss with their partner, even if their partner doesn't entirely understand why they feel that way. Grieving secretly inhibits communication and can lead to the eventual breakdown of a relationship.

Women who miscarry spontaneously often feel this sense of loss and grief, but it is socially acceptable for them to mourn because they wanted to be pregnant. The most important way in which women, and men, need to be prepared for abortion is to understand what happens biologically, hormonally, and psychologically during pregnancy, and why the sudden halting of that process of growth is a shock to the woman and may be devastating in some cases. Women would then be in a better position to cope with their responses to abortion without feeling guilty and regretting the decision. It must be understood and accepted by all concerned with abortion that grief may be a part of the abortion experience, just as it is for women who miscarry naturally, even if the woman has no regrets or guilt about the decision to abort.

Many women fear that they will be unable to have children in the future after having an abortion. I interviewed several women who were unable to conceive after having an abortion and bitterly regretted the abortion. The abortion was never conclusively established as the cause of the inability to conceive, but the women nevertheless regretted having been given a chance to have a child that was forfeited by choice. The fear of future infertility is also common to women who miscarry spontaneously. The difference is, however, that women who choose to have an abortion feel that they have "tempted fate" by not accepting the gift of potential life. They fear that the "punishment" for this rejection of a potential child will be infertility in the future when a child is wanted.

In fact, it is possible that the opposite may be true, according to U.S. gynecologist and abortion provider Dr. Lawrence W. Scott, who observed during our interview that

> Women at the age of around 35 who have never been pregnant have a harder time getting pregnant than women who have been pregnant before and had an abortion. They are also more likely to deliver by cesarean section. . . . Patients often ask why this is so. I reply by offering an analogy. Suppose you bought a brand-new Rolls Royce on the 1st of January, 1990, and then let it sit in your garage for 5 years, and then on January 1st, 1995, you go out to drive your car. What do you think is going to happen? First of all, the battery juice is gone. Secondly, you've probably flattened your tires. But even after you have corrected these problems, you'll probably find microscopic dust in the motor, and after you start the motor, it will never run like the Rolls Royce of the

guy next door who bought a brand-new Rolls Royce and took it out just once a month and rode around the block. For some reason or another, our body suffers from so-called disuse atrophy. This notion applies to almost every part of our body. If you don't use the muscles in your leg, they waste away. If you get out on the beach and exercise them, they build up. To keep internal organs from scarring, they must be used. The female organs are expected teleologically to go through certain normal cyclic changes, certain hormonal changes, and if they don't, you pay a price for it later. Recent studies in this country and other countries have shown that women who are exposed to the hormones of pregnancy later in life have a lower incidence of heart attacks, strokes, and cancers in certain female structures. Getting pregnant now can be good family planning for the future, even if you have a termination. I am convinced of that . . . I have performed thousands and thousands of abortions and over 4000 vaginal end deliveries and hundreds of cesarean sections. I would have lost my license for making statements like this 10 years ago, but I have talked with other gynecologists and many of them feel pretty much the way that I feel. Contrary to how most people think, an aborted pregnancy can help preserve fertility and perhaps keep you from developing certain physical problems later in life.

Dr. Scott's profound observations probably hold the key to unlocking the mystery of the much publicized "studies" that suggest that having an abortion may increase a woman's chances of developing breast cancer.

It was reported in the *Journal of the National Cancer Institute* in November, 1994, that a study by Dr. Janet Daling and colleagues at the Fred Hutchinson Cancer Research Center in Seattle found that the risk of breast cancer in women who had undergone an induced abortion was 50% higher than in other women. The risk factor was highest in women under 18 who terminated their pregnancies after week 8 of gestation and in women over 30 years of age. Those so-called findings are in fact inconclusive and do not offer a plausible causal association between abortion and an increased risk factor for breast cancer. If indeed there is any possible connection between abortion and an increased risk factor for breast cancer, it is probably not the abortion that causes the increased risk, but rather disuse atrophy, as Dr. Scott described above, or possibly because of major changes in breast tissue during the early stages of pregnancy that might make it more vulnerable to cancer when breast development during pregnancy is not completed. The only way to establish any definite connection would be to conduct similar studies on women who have miscarried. It must be remembered that the number of women taking part in these studies is miniscule (just a few hundred) compared with the number of women having abortions, and the risk factor, even if it is eventually proven, would be so minute as not to be a relevant factor in an abortion decision.

When a woman becomes pregnant, regardless of any fears and doubts she may have about the pregnancy, the body "takes over" and seems to have a will of its own. Some women intensely dislike this feeling of being out of control of their body, whereas others have a heightened sense of being alive and are fascinated by these involuntary changes in their body, even if they are at times inconvenient. Some women feel that delaying the decision to have an abortion makes it more and more difficult to decide to have one, because the maternal desire for life becomes stronger as the pregnancy progresses.

Many women are afraid of the physical effects of surgical abortion, but some also express concerns about medical abortion. In Western countries where abortion is legal, there is of course much less need for fear of a surgical or medical abortion, but even so, most women are nervous before an abortion. Sadly, however, legality does not ensure safety in all countries where abortion is legal.

During a dramatic interview with me in Los Angeles, a woman from the Ukraine shared an ironic story of illegal abortion in a country where abortion is legal. She tearfully recalled the appalling conditions in hospitals that made her afraid to have another child and afraid to have an abortion:

> I had my first abortion in the Ukraine at the age of 24 because we already had one child and could not afford to have another one. I was not using contraception because there was nothing available in Odessa at that time. We were atheists, so there was no concern for the fetus as a human being with a soul, or any other kind of religious conflict. We were concerned about practical things—how to find food, shoes, and underwear, not to mention diapers. There were no Pampers in the Ukraine, or anywhere else in the [former] Soviet Union. There was no formula because there was no milk available, so I would have to stand in line to buy breast milk from another breast-feeding mother willing to go through the pain of manually pumping milk from her breast into a bottle. You can't be sure that you're going to have enough breast milk when you have a baby, so that was an important consideration. . . . To have a virtually "free" legal abortion in the Ukraine (it cost a few dollars nominal fee), you had to go to a hospital where students would perform the procedure, which jeopardized one's health. This involved waiting in lines which were so long that they would tell you to come back in one month's time, adding further risk to the abortion because it would be performed one month later rather than immediately. Only women who could not afford to have private abortions would have the operation in a hospital where they treat you like pigs. So I had an illegal "black market" abortion. It cost a fortune—the equivalent of $500 U.S. If caught, the doctor and I both risked going to jail. The abortion was performed in the home of the doctor, without anesthetic. I couldn't scream, because neighbors might hear, and that might have made the doctor nervous enough to make a mistake which could have killed me. The pain was unbearable, but I held the hand of the doctor's wife, who was with me throughout the procedure, and clenched my teeth in agony. It would have been too dangerous for my husband to

come with me, because the KGB watched Jewish doctors and Jewish people. A husband and wife walking into a Jewish doctor's home at night would have been suspicious if anyone had observed us. My husband waited outside. I never told him about the agony of the abortion.

Reliving the horror of her first abortion as she shared her story was terribly distressing for this woman, despite the passage of many years and her emigration to the United States. She emphasized repeatedly that the situation for women when they miss a period is tragic in the Ukraine and other former Soviet Union countries.

Legalizing abortion also does not guarantee that everything will go smoothly during the procedure, as the following interview with an Indian woman reveals.

At the age of 27, I had my first abortion in the city of Bombay, in India. At first I was in a dilemma because I wanted to go ahead and have the baby, but after talking to the doctor, she convinced me that it would be more practical to have a proper gap between children. She reminded me that I had to take care of the child I already had—that was my first obligation. The abortion was performed in a hospital. I was so nervous that I didn't become unconscious after they gave me the anesthetic. Three times, the doctor went away and came back, hoping that the anesthesia had worked, but it didn't, so they performed the abortion while I was conscious. I remember the scraping and scratching and then the machine they used to suck out the blood. I know how much time it takes and how painful the procedure is, because I felt it despite having had the anesthetic. I was sent home immediately after the abortion—I felt as if something had been cut inside my body. There was a lot of pain and bleeding after the abortion, and big clots of blood came out. I think I was about 2 1/2 months pregnant when I had the abortion. When I got home, I passed out for several hours—probably it was the anesthetic finally taking effect. After the abortion, for the first month I felt as if I had done something wrong. I kept thinking that I should have kept the child. I'm not a religious person, but being a mother already made me feel that I might have killed a child just like my daughter, whom I love very much. I felt guilty, but a year later, when I conceived again and gave birth to my son, I forgot about the trauma of the abortion. . . . My husband had no conflicts about the abortions (I had two in all) and he could not understand my feelings of remorse and guilt after the first abortion. Even though I had a legal abortion, I felt ashamed of the abortion because since I was married, I thought that there was no reason really why I couldn't have the child. Despite all the rational justifications for having the abortion, I still felt that I was doing something wrong.

An important lesson for all women, and men, is that when abortion is legal, you do not have to passively submit to a physician's will. Patients have choices, rights, and, contrary to popular belief, some measure of control over their medical treatment, if they choose to exercise it. If a general anesthesia has been administered and failed to take effect, you can speak up and ask the physician to wait before performing the abortion. If you are concerned about the quality of care, you can cancel permission to perform the surgery and go to another clinic.

By way of reassurance, U.S. physician Dr. Lawrence Scott compassionately observed during our interview that

The U.S. Centers for Disease Control and Prevention has shown that having a termination during the first three months of pregnancy is over 100 times safer than having a baby, and we know having a baby is a relatively safe thing these days. . . . There is absolutely no pain when an abortion is performed under general anesthesia. Before any surgery there is always anxiety, I don't care who it is. I've had surgery myself—four times—and even as a physician I am laying on the table and there's a little anxiety . . . it's normal. In 25 years of practice, I have always made it a point to make sure my patients were asleep before beginning the procedure. I have never once had a patient tell me that they felt anything, and I do not intend to change my technique in that regard. I always inform my patients that the procedure will only take a couple of minutes, that they will be asleep under the anesthetic probably no more than 8 minutes before they start to regain consciousness, and then 20 to 30 minutes after that the anesthetic will totally wear off and they will feel pretty much as they felt before. A small percentage of women have cramping and nausea after the procedure is over, but we have medicine to give them immediately for that situation should it arise. Suction aspiration is not only a safer procedure but it leaves the lining inside the uterus unscarred, unlike the old scraping techniques that sometimes caused perforation of the uterus. Women are greatly reassured when they learn that suction aspiration will most probably leave their ability to have children intact. Many women in the present day have as many as a dozen abortions and three or four children. I even had a patient who had 23 pregnancies—17 abortions and 6 kids.[7]

Unfortunately, not all physicians are as warmly communicative as Dr. Scott, but most will answer your questions if you summon the courage to ask. If a physician won't communicate, try to find another who will—it's your right to know what to expect before, during, and after an abortion.

As with any surgery, there are possible, rare complications during the abortion procedure itself, such as a seizure, heart attack, or allergic reaction to the anesthetic. It is important that you give your complete medical history to the physician prior to undergoing an abortion. Most clinics will provide a questionnaire to ascertain the relevant details of your medical history. If the clinic or physician does not request this information prior to an abortion, beware.

There are certain relatively common physical side effects of surgical abortion, most notably bleeding and cramping. Fever after an abortion is usually indicative of infection. Complications such as incomplete abortion (retained tissue), failure to terminate pregnancy (usually in pregnancies of under 6 weeks' duration), perforation of the uterus, and postabortal syndrome (severe cramping with little or no bleeding, usually caused by closing of the cervix, which prevents normal expulsion of blood after the abortion) are rare, but they do occur. Obviously, any complication after an abortion increases the physical and emotional distress a woman feels.

While it is normal not to bleed after an abortion, many women do bleed for a few days or spot for 2–3 weeks and more rarely up to 6 weeks, sometimes consistently and at times intermittently. This may be followed by a period of about 4–9 weeks in which the woman does not menstruate. Many women experience this period after the abortion when they do not menstruate normally as disorienting, and it has been described to me as a "no-man's-land" in which one is emotionally numb and "not really a woman" in the normal sense. The recommended abstention from sexual relations for 2 weeks after the abortion in order to prevent infection contributes further to this sense of floating in an emotional bubble.

While most women cope with the experience of abortion, some are so confused and traumatized that they need help. There are a variety of ways to get postabortion counseling: through your physician or via referral from the clinic where you underwent the abortion is the generally recommended approach; with a sympathetic minister of your religion or a charity; through some form of professional psychotherapy or with a psychologist or psychiatrist; talking with a close friend or relative; or via an organization, such as Planned Parenthood in the United States, that can refer you to an appropriate counseling service.

It is easy for vulnerable women to be led to believe that their personal problems are caused by abortion, when in fact they may stem from many other factors. The Christian organization Women Exploited By Abortion (WEBA) began in the United States in 1974. It has branches in a number of countries, including Australia, where I interviewed "Dawn," the national president. I have strong reservations about WEBA and other groups that offer counseling with a religious bias that is clearly anti-abortion on principle, but as

WEBA genuinely seeks to help women heal rather than recruit them for a political anti-abortion agenda, I am including their philosophy in this book because it may speak to some women. "Dawn" explained WEBA's aims when I interviewed her in Australia:

WEBA is not for women who don't have problems and are strong and able to cope. We use the term *exploited* not for all the people outside, but for ourselves, to help us overcome the guilt, because unless we work through the guilt we can't begin to work through the grief. . . . Abortion isn't a solution to the problem of an unwanted pregnancy—it's a failure to find a solution . . . WEBA's main aim is to help women who have had an abortion and feel later that they made the wrong decision come to terms with their abortion. The women associated with WEBA feel that they have been exploited by a society which failed to inform them of the side effects of abortion, and that abortion is in effect the taking of a human life. An important part of WEBA's formula for coming to terms with the grief associated with abortion is working through the following 11 points:

1. Recognition and acknowledgment of the human life of the embryo.
2. Name your unborn child to make his "human status" clear in your mind.
3. Accept grief and remorse as normal. You have a right to grieve.
4. Recognize your lack of knowledge, lack of maturity, and lack of understanding at the time you had an abortion.
5. Forgive yourself.
6. Forgive those connected in any way to your abortion.
7. Accept God's love and forgiveness.
8. Love your unborn child and let it love you.
9. Commit the unborn child to God (through prayer) or by a Mass (through the healing sacrament of the Eucharist).

10. Share your feelings with someone you trust.
11. Finally, understand that he or she did exist.

Women do need to be better informed about the possible side effects of abortion, both physical and psychological, before they undergo an abortion, but the problem with groups such as WEBA is that religious beliefs are etched into their teachings. Of the 11 points suggested by WEBA to help heal, numbers 3, 5, 6, and 10 are general in nature and could help just about anyone in a state of conflict about an abortion. But the remaining points are based on the religious presumption that an abortion is destroying a human being, and that may exacerbate a woman's feelings of guilt rather than alleviate them.

"Dawn" is a very bitter woman who blames her abortions for just about everything that went wrong in her life. Seeing oneself perpetually as an exploited victim is not conducive to healing a wounded soul, as the following interview with "Dawn" reveals.

I must say at the outset that I am totally opposed to abortion. . . . I nearly lost my life twice as a result of abortions. Once because of a hemorrhage and the second time as a result of anorexia. I was about 15 or 16 when I had my first abortion. . . . When I went to the doctor with my parents they asked me what I wanted to do. I said I would have the baby. They ignored my wishes and after discussing it with the doctor they brought me down to Melbourne to have an abortion. . . . I believe that abortion is murder. I would never have an abortion again, even if there were a danger that the baby might be born disabled. . . . The man I was pregnant to for the first two abortions didn't give me any support of any kind. He knew I was pregnant but he seemed to just disappear when it came to dealing with the pregnancies. But I went back to him, I guess because when you don't feel loved in your family situation you seek love elsewhere. As a 15-year-old, you do think that you are in love because of the feelings and sense of being loved which come with making love. And you also feel like you need to belong to someone. The sense of being alone and the need to be loved drove me back to him. Those feelings were intensified by the abortion and then a change of town and job which left me living physically alone. So I went back to him and became pregnant again. Then I had another abortion and moved to another state where I met a man whom I was going to marry. But I fell pregnant to him and when I confessed that I had an abortion he said that since I'd had one I could have another as he was paying off a car and it wasn't convenient for him to have a child at that point. I was very young and naive and not worldly in any sense. I wasn't even promiscuous. And yet I'd had three abortions before I even knew what was going on.

Dawn feels that she was exploited in every way, by her parents, boyfriends, and physicians. Surely a healthier approach to healing would be to take responsibility for her naive actions rather than angrily blaming society.

In some women, the fear of having a child and assuming the responsibilities that accompany parenting is so strong that the maternal instinct is fought throughout pregnancy and does not surface until childbirth. The following interview with an American woman living in New York City highlights these mixed feelings about motherhood:

I had been married for about four or five years when I became pregnant for a third time. (I'd had two prior abortions, one illegal and very painful, the other legal.) My first thought was that it was a blessing. My second thought was—what am I going to do? I don't want to have children and neither does my husband. I guess we were kind of self-absorbed. He felt that he couldn't be a good father and I felt that I would be totally inadequate as a mother. I used to walk down the street looking at other people's children; the more I looked at them the more nauseated I became. I attempted emotionally to have an abortion. That doesn't mean that I made an appointment anywhere. I did everything—I went to hypnotists, therapists, holy people . . . I called endless religious organizations. My feeling was that I didn't want the child and I didn't want the abortion. The process of the 9 months was quite extraordinary. The effort I put into trying to have an abortion on the one hand and yet on the other trying to love this unborn child I was carrying was remarkable. I was trying to muster up some love for this creature whom I saw as coming to destroy my life. I was 38, so I had amniocentesis, and I was still talking about having an abortion. Then I found out that it was a girl and immediately decided that I did not want a girl. During labor, I said to my husband that it was as if someone had given me some strange drug. The moment that little skinny, scrawny creature emerged I thought what a poor little thing she is—my fantasies and fears had envisioned this full-blown entity that was going to come and ruin my life. My husband held her in one hand and then put her on my breast. She immediately stopped crying and latched on. I felt "my creature"—she was mine. She instantly became everything. My husband felt the same way. I bless the day that my daughter was born. I have never for a single moment regretted her birth.

It is important to remember that despite all of the negativity associated with abortion, it can nevertheless be a positive, learning experience, particularly if it's safe and legal. An unplanned pregnancy is positive proof of fertility and womanliness. It can also make both the woman and her partner more conscious of contraception and responsible in their approach to using it. For women who feel out of control of their lives, taking control and making a decision about abortion can help clarify their goals and values.

Perhaps the most positive aspect of an unplanned pregnancy may be the pregnancy itself, for some women. Andrea Butcher sweetly reflected during our interview:

I must say that I did find being pregnant quite exciting, and it was nice to have friends with whom I could discuss that feeling who reassured me that it was okay to feel excited about being pregnant even though I was quite sure that I didn't want to go through with it. It's nice to have the space to feel that way.

It is, of course, paradoxical in the extreme to feel happy and unhappy that you're pregnant, both at the same time. But that's how some women feel, so we must just accept that not all human responses are logical.

There is only one reason I've ever heard for having an abortion: the desire to be a good mother ... women have abortions because they are aware of the overwhelming responsibility of motherhood.—Dr. Elizabeth Karlin, director of the Women's Medical Center of Madison, Wisconsin.[8]

Most women want to be good mothers and are a little anxious at some point during pregnancy about whether they're up to the job. It is a maternal instinct that prompts women to have an abortion, because they don't believe that they can provide emotional and physical sustenance for a child (or another child) at that time in their life.

2

Abortion Culture around the World

Abortion is not new. For thousands of years, women all over the world have gone to extraordinary lengths attempting to induce abortion. Linda Bird Francke noted in her book *The Ambivalence of Abortion* that as far back as 3000 B.C. in China,

> Women drank quicksilver fired in oil or swallowed fourteen live tadpoles three days after they had missed a menstrual period in the hope of bringing it on. Egyptian women in 1500 BC used various techniques for both contraception and abortion: an inserted plug made of crocodile dung and paste, a douche brewed from honey and salt. In more modern times, Russian women have attempted to abort themselves by squatting over pots of boiling onions, while members of certain Indian tribes climbed up and down coconut palms, striking their stomachs against the trunks.[1]

Today, many women still practice such folk remedies, particularly in preliterate communities, in countries where abortion is illegal, and when abortion is unsafe or shameful despite being legal. Abortion has been around for a long time and will continue to be, regardless of its legal status. It renders women equal in much the same way that we are all equal in the face of death. In a sense these folk remedies are timeless and acultural. Our modern attempts to bring on menstruation with deeply penetrative sexual intercourse or a bottle of gin and a hot tub are just as "primitive" as the methods practiced by preliterate tribes. When you're caught by an unwanted pregnancy, it doesn't matter how sophisticated your upbringing and education or what your religion is, you know you don't want to have a baby and you'll try almost any folk method to help mother nature abort the pregnancy.

It is worth recording more of these bizarre methods to gain a better perspective on just how widespread the desire for abortion is and has been since the connection between intercourse and childbearing was made thousands of years ago. According to Linda Gordon's book *Woman's Body, Woman's Right: A Social History of Birth Control in America*, a variety of extraordinary concoctions have been used in an attempt to abort, including "paste of mashed ants, foam from camel's mouths and tail hairs of the blacktail deer dissolved in bear fat."[2] One can't help but wonder who created these alarming brews—was it women trying to abort themselves, the local witchdoctor, a midwife, a medicine man, an anxious spouse, a physician, or perhaps a pharmacist? What is so remarkable is the resourcefulness of the inventors. Each seems to make use of whatever the local environment has to offer, even "turpentine, castor oil, quinine water . . . water in which a rusty nail has been soaked, hot herbs such as horseradish, ginger and mustard . . . ammonia and laundry bluing . . ."[1] Many of these potions worked not directly as abortifacients but rather by shocking the body through chemical injury to such an extent that it would spontaneously abort.

Self-inflicted wounds include douching with lye or inserting knitting needles or corrosive materials such as potassium permanganate, coat hangers, or chicken bones into the uterus. It should be remembered that even today, when abortion is illegal or unavailable, or when it's legal but secrecy is of paramount importance, these are the types of methods women use to try to rid themselves of unwanted pregnancies.

Emmenagogues—products that bring on menstruation—have been available under a number of guises for many years. Some emmenagogues are also abortifacients, that is, capable of aborting established pregnancies. There are records of solutions of gunpowder being drunk, and reports of death from ergot, lead, and other poisons recur in 19th century medical journals.[3] It was well known that these substances were sold under prescription as emmenagogues.

Among the herbal alternatives are savin oil of juniper, brown rice and figs, tansy, and pennyroyal, to name just a few. There has been very little scientific study of these herbal remedies, although savin oil is fairly widely recognized as an emmenagogue. It is also an additive of gin, which explains the old-fashioned remedy of gin and a hot tub. In England, the best known product of this type is Beecham's Pills. In 1897, around 6 million boxes of these pills were sold. Though they were reportedly used as a cure for other ailments as well, one cannot but wonder how many Beecham's Pills were consumed by women desperately seeking to terminate unwanted pregnancies.

In developing countries, many herbal remedies that supposedly act as abortifacients are available. For example:

> . . . in the Philippines an infusion of banana and kalachulchi leaves is drunk. Aqueous alcoholic infusions of barks rich in turpinols are also used. One of the most curious sites for the sale of abortifacients is in central Manila, next to the Quiapo. The Quiapo is the busiest and most loved church in Manila. Mass is celebrated in relays from 6.30am on Sundays and the church is crowded for many hours, with hundreds standing in the aisles. Immediately outside the church—in physical contact with its walls—are rows of booths. They sell three things: religious pictures (of a tinsel, folk art variety), candles (poorly cast in the shape of saints) and herbal remedies (of which those for late periods are the most important). A bottle of abortifacient medicine (always sold in the local San Miguel beer bottle) costs 1.50 pesos (25 cents). An average stall sells about 20 bottles on a Sunday to women going to or leaving mass. There are 40–50 stalls clinging to the walls of the Quiapo. The whole is a vivid demonstration that neither the congregation nor the priests perceive the intent to ter-

minate a very early pregnancy as a sin. Indeed, the Quiapo
on Sunday morning may well represent the busiest family
planning clinic in the Philippines.[4]

This ad hoc family planning service is culturally acceptable despite
its illegality, questionable efficacy, and conflict with the teachings
of the Catholic Church, the dominant religion of the Philippines.
Although family planning programs sponsored by foreign aid and
national investment are readily available, many women still prefer to use folk methods initially when confronted by an unplanned
pregnancy.

According to Susan Drummet, in an article that appeared in
the *Los Angeles Times* on January 24, 1995, in Mexico City, an elderly lady sells a herbal abortifacient for $30 per kilo at the Sonora
Market. To induce abortion, the 20 herbs must be soaked like tea
in a quart of water for five hours, after which a pregnant woman
drinks the whole quart all at once. Abortion is illegal in Mexico,
which is predominantly Roman Catholic, and yet there are an estimated 2 million abortions there every year. Approximately 5000
women die in Mexico annually as a result of illegal abortion.

In Africa, abortion has long been a popular form of "contraceptive" though that is slowly changing as various programs to
distribute "the pill" and other contraceptives free of charge have
been introduced. The methods used among traditional societies
have been favored for many generations, although it is impossible to ascertain exactly how long. "Decoctions from various plants
such as manioc, tobacco, yam, papaya, mango, frangipani—all of
which may be either taken by mouth or through the vagina"[5] are
most popular. In Zaire a strong variety of pepper known as pili-
pili is used. In large doses it is so strong that it can actually burn
the ovaries. "The Babindji of Kazumba take a potion made by cook-
ing babou roots . . . the Batshok know a substance they call mut-
shatsha which, in large doses, may be lethal."[5] Mechanical
abortifacients are less popular. These involve the insertion of sharp
sticks and stalks in the vaginal canal. It seems that for every tribe
there is a variation on a theme of herbal remedies combined with
mechanical devices. Most importantly, "by estimate, one third of

the blood bank store in Ghana goes to save women from the consequences of abortions, most of which are clandestine. Officially, abortion is a crime, and thus is concealed."[6] The lengths to which women around the world will go in order to abort an unwanted pregnancy, risking their lives in the process, are remarkable. The desire for privacy, an early termination, and control of the process of aborting seem to be major factors in the popularity of folk methods, especially in communities where safer, proven alternatives are available.

In Malaysia, despite the love of children and family life, women frequently seek abortions, largely in order to prevent too many pregnancies within a short period of time.

> Many resort to herbal potions, prepared by a local midwife or by other experienced elderly women, which are said to be often effective. Another popular method is drinking the juice of unripe pineapples or a strong ginger potion. If there is a delay in menstruation of one or two weeks and pregnancy is suspected, many Malay women assert that raw beaten chicken eggs washed down with a bottle of stout help to make the woman feel very hot and induce menstrual flow. A more costly and less frequent alternative is to drink a very large quantity of three star brandy.[7]

Another fairly effective method of both contraception and abortion is the displacement of the uterus by a skilled Malay midwife using external massage techniques.

Massage by traditional midwives is still a common practice in developing countries. Although it is a very painful process, millions of women submit to this torture rather than have unwanted children. It is an important method of fertility control and yet has never been scientifically studied.

Passing a foreign body through the cervical canal into the uterus has been used as a method of inducing abortion for thousands of years.

> In Hawaii, a special instrument made of wood, over 20cm long, slightly tapered and the same diameter as the average

index finger, has been described. The handle was carved with a grotesque head and the instrument, called a KAPO, regarded as an idol. The use of boiled twigs from thorn bushes remains common in India and in much of the developing world. One variant of the method involves the use of a straight twig or stick, usually about 20cm long. The woman is assisted by two friends and after placing stones on the ground and the twig upright above them, she is lowered so that the end of the twig enters the vagina when her friends, instead of supporting her, abruptly drop her upon the projecting stick, which with fortune will enter the cervical canal and uterus. However, needless to say, perforation of the uterus or vaginal vault is common and mortality and morbidity high. In some communities the need to prevent infection is crudely understood and procedures such as boiling or peeling the bark off a twig before use are routinely applied, whereas in other areas no sterile precautions of any kind are attempted.[8]

The tragic aspect of these folk methods of abortion is that they are not obsolete, even where abortion is legal. Each culture has its own variation on a theme of abortion folk tradition.

In Victorian England, steel instruments were often used—the ubiquitous crochet hook, umbrella ribs, hairpins, bicycle spokes, and, of course, knitting needles. Some of these instruments remain in vogue. Feathers are used in the Middle East and parts of Asia. In Western Australia in the years of the Depression, when farmers and their families were said to exist solely on wheat and rabbits, many women performed abortions using fencing wire. The aim of all such instrumental methods is either to rupture the membranes or so disturb the placental attachment that an abortion occurs.

Cervical dilatation is another method of abortion.

In China . . . dried asparagus lucides soaked in alcohol have been used as cervical dilators and this has also been a traditional method in Eastern Europe. In Japan, dried seaweed is used . . . slippery elm is another organic cervical dilator . . .

when tightly compressed dried organic material is introduced into the cervical canal and left in situ for many hours, it absorbs water from the cervical secretions, swells and dilates the cervix. Abortion usually follows after a day or so.[9]

Internationally, illegal abortionists have used a variety of methods ranging from safe to deadly. A common technique for providing a relatively safe illegal abortion in the United States prior to 1973 was to stimulate the onset of bleeding in the woman using either a saline injection into the amniotic fluid or instrumentation of the uterus and then admit her to a hospital on the pretext of a natural miscarriage for a safe dilation and curettage. It's a technique that's still used in countries where abortion is illegal or severely restricted. Both of these methods, however, could cause death if the woman were denied admission for treatment in a hospital, was unable to get to a hospital, or if she hemorrhaged severely prior to admission, and they rely on attending hospital staff turning a blind eye. Many of the horror stories of illegal abortion in the United States involved excruciatingly painful instrumentation of the uterus and use of rubber catheters that caused infection and hemorrhaging. The abortions were often performed by inexperienced physicians or lay people without any anesthetic or professional equipment. A current popular "folk" method in the United States for inducing a very early abortion up to about two weeks after a missed period is menstrual extraction. This involves insertion of a tube into the uterus and gentle suction of the endometrium (the lining of the uterus) out of the uterus. In addition to the risk of infection, the method does not always result in termination, as it is almost impossible to know if the embryo has been removed because it is so small at that stage in pregnancy.

The list of techniques used by illegal abortionists around the world is almost as extensive as that of folk methods.

Soft pliable objects that can be pushed through the cervical canal and will then lie within the uterine cavity irritate the uterus and cause abortion. They may also cause placental separation with fetal death prior to the actual onset of abortion. This method is particularly favored by experienced illegal abortionists. Both in the Western world and in the developing countries, the urinary catheter or other suitable small-bore rubber tubing is popular. In general, the abortionist inserts the catheter, leaving a short projecting end at the cervix, sends the woman home with instructions to remove it herself once the pains have become strong . . . it is usually understood that she may require physical assistance from trained personnel later.[10]

In Iran, the midwife or lay abortionist tapes the end of the catheter to the woman's thigh, and tells her to remove it after 24 hours and to go to the hospital when bleeding commences. Typically, the hospital is overworked, makes no effort to investigate the woman's history in depth, and proceeds with an immediate curettage.[11]

A popular Thai method of illegal abortion is infusion of liquids or use of rubber catheters.[11] The catheter is also popular in Latin America. One study in Paraguay revealed that 94 out of 249 illegal abortions used the catheter or "sonda."[12]

The following case study from England illustrates a scenario that could virtually be replicated in most countries where abortion is illegal.

A woman was admitted with uterine bleeding, a high temperature and septicaemia. Her condition became extremely serious and, being a Roman Catholic, she was given the last rites, still denying criminal interference. Shortly after she aborted and her condition improved. The expelled fetus was accompanied by a rubber catheter.[11]

Intrauterine injections using syringes containing a variety of fluids are used throughout the world to illegally induce abortion, "the commonest types being strong solutions of soapy water or Dettol solutions. In the Caribbean and some other areas, the preferred fluid was Coca-Cola, which in fact has quite good antiseptic properties."[11] Apart from infection, the main danger with this method is that the syringe can inject either fluid or air under pressure, and this air can then enter the placental sinuses, causing air emboli and possible death for the mother.

The list of variations on the theme of induced abortion is endless. At one stage in Great Britain, even toothpaste was used, inserted into the neck of the womb. Where abortion is illegal, or taboo despite being legal desperate women risk their lives. Sadly, the primitive and often dangerous methods noted above are *not* obsolete.

In countries where abortion is legal, dilatation and curettage (D&C), dilatation and evacuation (D&E), vacuum aspiration, RU 486, methotrexate, hypertonic saline, intraamniotic prostaglandin, and in very late pregnancies, hysterotomy (minicesarean), are the predominant methods. An early abortion (i.e., in the first 12 weeks of pregnancy) is universally recognized as being safer for women.

3

Is Abortion Murder, As Anti-Abortion Rhetoric Claims?

I have no idea at what point the fetus becomes a human being, whether it's always a human being, whether it has a soul or doesn't have a soul; one thing's for sure—IT'S ALIVE. An abortion is terminating something that's alive.— An American woman[1]

Abortion providers in the United States, along with their staff, patients, and volunteer escorts, are being terrorized by people who charge that they are "killing babies." Although there is opposition to abortion in other countries, protests rarely turn violent. Why are some Americans so passionate in their hatred of abortion and all associated with it that they are willing to murder? Is it because they are more moral than the rest of us? Are they alone privy to God's will? I doubt it.

Expert "marketing" of the notion that abortion is murder, via the pulpit and media, is responsible for the current hysterical antiabortion crusades in the United States. According to Frances Kissling, president of the Washington, D.C.-based organization Catholics For A Free Choice, "Catholic bishops were not particularly active on the abortion issue until it became legal in 1973. Then they immediately geared up for a campaign to recriminalize abortion."[2] Ms. Kissling went on to explain during our interview that

A group of Catholic women, largely feminists in New York City, got together after the bishops had started this campaign and said that there needed to be some organization that represented the views of the Catholic people. That's how Catholics For A Free Choice came into being—it was a reaction to the bishops' campaign to recriminalize abortion.[2]

That campaign was launched from the pulpit, via literature, and, most importantly, through repetitive advertising and exposure in the media. Christian-based religions and organizations were encouraged to unite in the name of "the cause."

In the aftermath of Catholic John C. Salvi III's horrendous Brookline, Massachusetts, murders of abortion clinic receptionists Shannon Lowney and Leanne Nichols on December 30, 1994, and the wounding of five others at the Planned Parenthood Clinic of Greater Boston and Preterm Health Services, it was reported in the *Los Angeles Times* on January 3, 1995, that Catholic Bishop Leo O'Neil and Cardinal Bernard Law, head of the archdiocese of Boston, were urging an end to abortion clinic protests. Bishop O'Neil cautioned that

> We all need a breathing period to walk away from this kind of tragedy and do some serious reflection about what is the best possible approach to getting across our message of the sanctity of human life.[3]

That is surely humble recognition that calling people to vehemently protest abortion and "protect babies from being killed" may be interpreted as a call to arms. The *Boston Sunday Globe* on January 1, 1995, reported on the front page that Cardinal Bernard Law made an urgent plea after the murders:

> The rhetoric needs to be cooled down. We need to keep our focus on the woman and the child and how best we can be of help to both. To have violence associated in any way with the pro-life movement is an utter anomaly.[4]

Some regular abortion protesters have heeded those admonitions, but others are resolute that they cannot sit back and "watch babies being killed." Eight dangerously misguided parishioners even demonstrated in support of John C. Salvi III outside the jail where he was detained after his arrest in Norfolk, Virginia. The holy war initiated by the Catholic Church in 1973 has clearly opened a Pandora's box that may be impossible to close.

After the murders, in the West Los Angeles newspaper *The Outlook*, it was reported on January 2, 1995, that Andrew Cabot, a regular abortion protester in New Hampshire, believed John Salvi to be a hero. "This is going to be, hopefully, the beginning of the war, and we'll win because we're right, and we'll once again have godly laws in our land,"[5] Cabot reportedly said. In the same article, Dr. Pablo Rodriguez, who is a Catholic and the medical director of Rhode Island's Planned Parenthood, said:

> The escalation of the rhetoric and the vilifying of the health-care workers by . . . leaders of these movements has served to inflame the passions of the fringe elements. . . . When you are being called a murderer and a baby killer from the pulpit, it's not too far for someone to take the law into their own hands if they are basically unstable to begin with.[5]

Dr. Rodriguez has received death threats and stopped attending his church for fear of being attacked. The Reverend Pat Mahoney, leader of the anti-abortion group Christian Defense League and former spokesman for Operation Rescue, said in the same article that he was rethinking his strategy on abortion protests, because "there may be a link between advocating the use of force and people acting it. It went from a more intellectual debate, and now it seems to be progressing into acting out that philosophy."[5] It is important to note that the causal relationship between rhetoric and violence is not just being recognized by pro-choice advocates. Even some staunch foes of abortion are reluctantly recognizing the link.

On January 4, 1995, Teri Reisser, the executive director of the Right to Life League of Southern California, was quoted in the *Los Angeles Times* as follows:

> An unborn child is a human being and in need of protection—we will never stop saying that. But that doesn't translate into us taking responsibility for some nut case who goes out and starts shooting people.[6]

Ms. Reisser grossly underestimates the power of rhetoric to arouse human passion. Hitler used it to inspire millions to murder and collaborate in heinous crimes. If the embryo or fetus is a human "baby," why wouldn't a decent person want to defend it? In the same article, Susan Carpenter-McMillan, founder of the Pro Family Media Coalition, lamented that

> We find ourselves being in the very awkward position of defending those we so deplore—the abortionists and any of their employees or providers. It's a real twist of fate. . . . But we are absolutely outraged.[6]

Why is it so surprising and horrifying to those people who daily exhort others to "protect innocent unborn babies" that people actually listen and do as they suggest? The entire so-called "prolife" movement must be held accountable for the current terrorist campaign against abortion clinics. To her credit, Susan Carpenter-McMillan's *Los Angeles Times* article on January 6, 1995, called for a new dimension to be added to the agenda of "sidewalk heroes" protesting abortion:

> ensuring the safety of those they condemn. This must include being aware of new faces among protesters, finding out where they come from and being on the lookout for those who describe murder as a solution. Then, at the first mention of violence, pro-lifers must immediately notify police and abortion clinic employees. Swift action could avert another murder.[7]

Ms. McMillan's practical suggestions are commendable.

In a *New York Times* article on December 31, 1994, it was reported that an FBI investigation "had turned up plenty of evidence of inflammatory rhetoric shared by the most militant abortion foes, but few signs of any anti-abortion network coordinating or financing attacks."[8] However, *Time* magazine, in its issue of January 9, 1995, reported that there is some evidence of the existence of a conspiracy, noting that a copy of the violently anti-abortion manifesto of a group called the "Army of God" was found among Paul Hill's belongings.[9] It is possible that the powerful rhetoric of the group's manual alone inspired Paul Hill's murderous behavior, along with his belief that killing abortion providers is justifiable homicide. Still, one can't help but wonder whether 30 signers (including Paul Hill) of a petition calling for the murder of abortion providers might not be orchestrating the violence. It was noted in an article in the West Los Angeles newspaper *The Outlook* on January 6, 1995, that John C. Salvi III drove over 500 miles, bypassing at least 180 abortion clinics, in order to attack two clinics in Brookline, Massachusetts, and then drove all the way to Norfolk, Virginia, where he was arrested shortly after firing at a building housing an abortion clinic. (There were no injuries in that shooting.) If he did bypass abortion clinics that were closer to his home, one can't help but wonder why he did so. Anti-abortion groups have described Salvi as a lone shark who was not affiliated with any of their groups, but police reportedly found a receipt from a Massachusetts-based anti-abortion group among Salvi's belongings, along with the name and telephone number of Virginia activist, Donald Spitz, who advocates killing abortion doctors. Salvi, who was a student with a low-paying job in a hair salon, was reportedly carrying $1000 in cash when he was arrested, and he had not picked up his last paycheck from work. Was he "paid" to attack the Planned Parenthood Clinic in Brookline because it was one of many clinics participating in the Population Council's trial of the French abortion pill RU 486? Why did Salvi select the other clinics that he attacked, when he had so many closer to his home to choose from? The truth will eventually emerge.

Marketing is the antiabortion conspirators' most deadly weapon. Human Life International distributes a variety of antiabortion pamphlets, as well as posters and plastic fetus dolls. A pamphlet that proclaims "Abortion is the Greatest War of All Time" is among the most widely distributed throughout the nationwide network of antiabortion publications. Father Matthew Habiger leads Human Life International's crusade against abortion. He calls clinics death camps and death mills and describes abortion as a holocaust. He is proud of his work and does not believe that the language of his publications is inflammatory. If that kind of inference is not inflammatory, I don't know what is!

Dissemination of information regarding the whereabouts of clinics and attending physicians is a common activity among even conservative anti-abortion groups and could be seen as conspiratorial because abortion protesters are implored to "defend innocent babies." Ask yourself what that expression really means. ALL exhortations to "protect innocent unborn babies" are inflammatory rhetoric and constitute a call to arms. Rhetoric can be a sinister force because it has the power to inspire violent behavior. In the March 27, 1995 issue of *Time* magazine, it was reported that "threads do link the most outspoken antiabortionists into a loose network."[10] The article noted that tactics are swapped and a manual with guidelines for clinic attacks is circulated. In January 1995, a group calling itself "American Coalition of Life Activists" released a "hit list" of 12 abortion doctors. *Life Advocate* is a magazine published by Andrew Burnett in Portland, Oregon. It is considered the "handbook of abortion militants."[10] If a hit list and handbook for militants doesn't spell conspiracy, what does?

It is essential that our concept of "free speech" be reexamined. Perhaps censorship is appropriate at times. The community as a whole has a right to say that it is unacceptable for talk shows to hold much-publicized debates on the ethics of killing abortion providers or for any kind of media to be used to promote or disseminate such ideas. Lawmakers should turn their attention to men like Reverend David Trosch of Alabama, who has been repeatedly reported in various media as saying unashamedly that he would congratulate John Salvi and shake his hand if he showed up on his doorstep. Perhaps that kind of verbal assault on decency should be grounds for arrest or, if not arrest, some other kind of punitive response, such as stripping of one's nationality and exile. Americans have a right to say that they don't want certain people in the country—that it's not okay to say anything you want if you are directly inciting people to harm others. Trosch regularly uses exploitive media to exhort people to do whatever they deem necessary "to protect unborn babies," even if that means harming those associated with abortion. It was noted in a whole-page advertisement in *The New York Times*, taken out by Planned Parenthood of New York City on January 5, 1995, that at one point Trosch even "tried to take out an ad urging that abortion providers be killed. The ad was rejected and Trosch censured, but the publicity that resulted from the incident has telegraphed this message nationwide."[11] It is absolutely essential that the power of rhetoric to inspire murder be recognized.

Attorney Morris Dees works at the Southern Poverty Law Center in Montgomery, Alabama. He has filed suit on behalf of the family of murdered physician, Dr. David Gunn. The suit holds John Burt and his anti-abortion group "Rescue America" liable for Dr. Gunn's murder, because, the suit claims, the gunman, Michael Griffin was influenced by the group's violent rhetoric. "We don't have to show that anyone pulled the trigger but that the shooting was encouraged to stop abortions."[10] That comment by Dees is strong evidence of the power of rhetoric, because he has won "two similar 'wrongful death' cases against the Ku Klux Klan in Alabama and a white supremacist group in Oregon."[10]

Historically, Christian-derived religious fundamentalism has dominated worship in the United States. In the days of the pioneers, it was acceptable to engage in shoot-outs over disputes and bear arms to defend life, limb, property, and beliefs. Although secular law based on the Constitution now rules the land, the tendency to solve disputes through violence is still woven threads through the fabric of life in the United States. No matter what the religion, an extreme fundamentalist approach requires a leap of faith that makes the intellectually and emotionally gullible susceptible to frenzy. The only way to stop that kind of extremism is by banning the rhetoric and educating the ignorant. Perhaps religion should be based less on faith and more on reason and knowledge. It might not provide as much comfort, but it would certainly breed less self-righteous arrogance. Blind faith and orthodox observance of religious ritual do not necessarily make people behave morally— history is a sad teacher of that lesson.

Constitutional rights were successfully invoked as the main basis for legalizing abortion on January 22, 1973, in the Supreme Court ruling on the case of Roe *v.* Wade. Since then, the pro-choice movement has focused its arguments in favor of legal abortion on a woman's right to privacy. Why should a woman have a right to privately murder, if abortion is indeed murder? It is essential to address the question "Is abortion murder?" if we are to succeed in formulating laws that satisfy the consciences of all Americans. As freedom to murder is not a constitutional right, it is no wonder that anti-abortion groups such as Operation Rescue, Lambs of Christ, Defensive Action, and Advocates for Life feel that they have the right to rise above the law in the name of a higher moral cause. They believe that abortion is murder and that the laws must be changed to prohibit abortion under any circumstances. It is nonsensical to respond to concern that abortion may be murder by saying that a woman has the right to privately decide about abortion. It is up to pro-choice advocates to get the message out that *abortion is not murder*.

Lest the reader fear that I condone the behavior of militant antiabortion groups, let me state quite clearly that I respect the right of people to believe that abortion is wrong, but I do not share that belief. Neither do I condone their fanatical disrespect for the present laws that grant women the right to safe, legal abortion in the United States. Most of all, I abhor their attacks at clinics, harassment of physicians, and total disregard for the feelings of the women seeking abortions at the clinics where they demonstrate and sometimes successfully stop abortions from taking place.

Murdering physicians and abortion clinic staff is truly perverse behavior for "pro-life" advocates. Punitive prison sentences and the death penalty will not deter future self-styled martyrs from engaging in what they believe is "justifiable homicide." Militant extremists are pseudo-heroes who feel that any form of combat is acceptable in defense of "innocent babies" being "murdered." The only defense reasonable people can muster against such fanaticism, other than improved security, is biological fact. We must arm ourselves with knowledge and use it to educate.

This chapter is dedicated to all abortion providers, abortion clinic staff, and volunteer escorts who risk their lives to provide women with the choice to have an abortion, and in memory of those who gave their lives or were injured for that cause. Five people have been murdered by anti-abortion zealots since 1993— Shannon Lowney, Leanne Nichols, Dr. David Gunn, Dr. John Bayard Britton, and James Herman Barrett. Dr. Gunn was shot by Michael Griffin in the Florida port town of Pensacola in March, 1993, because he performed abortions at the Pensacola Women's Medical Services clinic. Dr. Britton, who was wearing a bulletproof vest, and his escort, retired U.S. Air Force Lieutenant Colonel James Barrett, were murdered on July 29, 1994, by Paul Jennings Hill, a former Presbyterian pastor who was excommunicated for supporting Griffin's murder of Dr. Gunn. Hill blasted these men in the face with a 12-gauge shotgun as they drove up to The Ladies Center in Pensacola. Barrett's wife, June, was also shot. Paul Hill was sentenced to death, but the case was automatically appealed despite his request not to appeal, because he preferred to die a martyr to his cause. At the time this book goes to press, the appeal is pending. I pray that this chapter will help people who believe that abortion is "murder" to understand that performing an abortion is not the same as murdering a "baby."

Antiabortion protesters define murder in an absolute sense as morally wrongful killing, disregarding the legal meaning of the word. In all of the dictionary definitions of murder that I have read, the words *intentional* and *unlawful* appear in one form or another. In many definitions, including the one contained in the 1973 *Unabridged Random House Dictionary of the English Language*, murder is defined as the "*unlawful killing* of another *human being* with malice *aforethought*" or something similar. The word *unlawful* is very important, because it implies that killing IS lawful in some circumstances, but when it is unlawful, it becomes murder. Premeditation, unlawfulness, and a human being as victim are the three elements that define murder.

Premeditation definitely pertains to abortion because in one way or another the woman decides to have an abortion and takes steps to carry it out. That is by any definition intentional behavior.

Unlawfulness is a far more complex element, because laws change according to the views of a majority of people or as a result of a few imposing their will on a majority, regardless of whether there is evidence to substantiate them. At present, abortion is lawful in many countries, including the United States, and unlawful in others. There are states within the United States such as Utah, North Dakota, and Kansas, where it is extremely difficult to have an abortion despite Roe *v.* Wade, because of restrictive state laws and lack of providers.

The former USSR legalized abortion early in the 20th century. It was made illegal by Stalin in 1936, except for purely medical purposes, because he wanted to promote population growth. In 1955, Stalin's law was repealed, largely to protect women's health. It was felt that incentives to encourage motherhood were a more appropriate way of increasing the population than making abortion illegal and endangering women.

If we define abortion as murder according to its legality, the moral definition becomes absurd, because historically laws have been changed as a result of a whole series of factors and views unrelated to the fetus and morality. Lawfulness does not provide an acceptable, consistent standard by which to measure whether abortion is morally wrongful killing. Abortion can change its legal status from minute to minute, but murder cannot change its definition. If language is to have any meaning at all, the definition has to be precise and consistent.

The third element needed to define killing as "murder" is a human being, according to the majority of dictionary definitions. Almost all people who feel that abortion is murder believe that the fetus is a human being from the moment of conception, or from some time soon after conception, and that it has all of the feelings and rights of a born human being. It is a belief that has been the subject of debate among scholars, the clergy, and lay persons for centuries, because the definition of a human being is very elusive.

It is important to understand that the belief that the fetus is a human being from the moment of conception cannot be substantiated by any scientific or biological evidence. A belief by definition requires a leap of faith, precisely because there is no valid evidence to prove it. If enough people collectively believe, that doesn't convert the belief into a fact, although the communal feeling may become manifest in laws and religion. Just because more than 50% of the American people (according to various polls) believe that abortion is murder doesn't make it true. Many of those same people also believe that abortion is justified in some cases, especially rape and incest, and should be legally available. If abortion is murder, why should there be exceptions to a law against it?

The various religious views on abortion will not be discussed in this chapter, for they will not in any way help answer the question "Is abortion murder?" Religion is highly relevant to a personal quest for moral answers, but it cannot serve as a basis for laws in a pluralistic society. If we are to find a foundation on which to formulate laws that will satisfy the consciences of people of all religions, biological fact must be accepted as the only valid evidence to prove, or disprove, that the fetus is a thinking, feeling human being, because it presents some form of objective criteria.

Physicians and neuroscientists are the only professionals suitably qualified to provide biological evidence that will be useful in determining whether the fetus is a human being and hence whether abortion is murder. Of course the way physicians and scientists observe and interpret biological data is not universally consistent, but we must start somewhere, and they have the scientific knowledge that we need to build our legal foundation.

I was privileged to conduct the last extensive interview with the late Dr. Bertram Wainer, founder/director of one of the first abortion clinics in the world, the Fertility Control Clinic in Melbourne, Australia. Dr. Wainer made tremendous personal sacrifices, suffered financial ruin, and risked his life to help secure Australian women the right to have a safe abortion. All quotes attributed to Dr. Wainer in this book are excerpts from that interview.

When does human life become a human person? What value shall be accorded to the fetus? I think about it all the time. We all do at the Clinic. Yes, I'm concerned. . . . It would be a much more comfortable world if we didn't have to make decisions about abortions. At no time have I said that the fetus is zilch. . . .[12]

Dr. Wainer's recognition that the fetus is more than "zilch" encapsulates the essence of the problem in determining whether abortion is murder. Biologically, what is the fetus?

When I interviewed Dr. Henry Morgentaler, founder/director of the first abortion clinic in Canada, he reflected that

Unfortunately, most of the people who are against abortion do not seem able to make the distinction between potential life and a real live baby. When you go on the assumption that a fertilized egg is already a baby, which is completely crazy and nonscientific, then you have to be blinded by dogma not to understand that a microscopic cell is not a baby.[13]

The growth from a microscopic cell to a baby takes nine months. Even among physicians there are differences of opinion about when the multiplying cells have turned into a baby, which is one reason why most physicians prefer to perform abortions early in pregnancy, in the first 12 weeks.

Dr. Bernard Nathanson, formerly the head of the largest abortion clinic in the United States and founder of NARAL, an organization that helped bring about the legalization of abortion in the United States, is against abortion now

because the development of medical technology has given us a far greater insight into the life of the fetus which is a human being, biologically and scientifically. Abortion is the destruction of that life. I don't think that we can afford to engage ourselves in a program of killing of what the Nazi doctors used to call "lebens unwertes leben"—life unworthy of living. That was the motto of the Nazi extermination program. It is what we have been doing here in the United States.[14]

That argument is based on the belief that the fetus is a human being from the moment of conception.

Dr. Nathanson "cannot understand the difference" or distinction between a newly born baby and the newly created embryo and fetus. He attempts to demonstrate that the fetus is an aware human being capable of suffering in his film *The Silent Scream*, claiming that he is presenting abortion from the perspective of the fetus. (Why would anyone torture a "child," as he calls the fetus, for the purpose of making a film, if abortion is indeed causing suffering to the fetus?) He states in the film that the fetus has had brain waves for 6 weeks by the 12th week of gestation, which would mean that the brain waves developed at 6 weeks.

When I was shown this film by the president of Right To Life in Australia, Margaret Tighe, I felt uncomfortable with the propaganda tone of the film and the obviously greatly enlarged image of the fetus that was projected, but found that I did not have the scientific and biological knowledge to refute it. I determined that I would consult other equally distinguished physicians associated with abortion to glean their views of this film.

Dr. Wainer's views on abortion and the film *The Silent Scream* were strikingly in contrast to those of Dr. Nathanson. His view of the fetus was that "it is alive" and

> abortion is killing. Nobody can argue with that. When the fetus is inside the uterus it is alive and when the pregnancy is terminated it is dead—that by any definition is killing. The question is whether it is the killing of a human being. I think abortion is the destruction of something which is potentially irreplaceable, human and of great value, which is the tragedy of abortion. But it is not of greater value than the woman seeking the abortion. At the Fertility Control Clinic in Melbourne we've decided that the upper limit for termination of pregnancies is 16 weeks. Collectively, we felt that this was the limit within which we could perform abortions without constant moral conflict. The State limit by law in Victoria is 20 weeks. We feel that at 20 weeks if a woman went into labor the product of her birth would be put in a humidicrib

to give it the chance to survive. That would not happen at 16 weeks, which is why we feel more comfortable with that limit. Of course, as technology develops that cutoff point becomes more and more arbitrary, but we have made our choice according to our collective conscience.[12]

It is important that pro-choice advocates understand that terminating a pregnancy is killing something that's human and alive, but not yet "a baby."

Dr. Wainer considered the film *The Silent Scream* to be

an emotional film designed to exploit women's feelings. It's not an accurate picture of abortion. They have used technical gimmickry to produce its effects. It's now banned in Victorian schools because we were able to prove to the satisfaction of the Victorian government that they speeded up some of the sequences . . . it isn't the termination of an early [12 week] pregnancy as stated but of a more advanced pregnancy. An embryo isn't capable of responding the way it's suggested in the film. For an uninformed lay person, the film is fairly horrific. It was shown on National Television here in Australia in about early 1985 [shortly after it was released in January 1985]. We were interested to see what the effects would be in our clinic. Nobody canceled their appointment to see us as a result of the film, but many of our patients who had seen it were very distressed. The film used very slick, speeded up cinematography. The commentary was pompous and pretentious, and used loaded terminology such as calling the embryo "the child." I think it was a bad attempt to sway people to Dr. Nathanson's beliefs.[12]

Dr. Wainer's comments are profound, for they expose the illusory nature of Dr. Nathanson's film, which has been used extensively by anti-abortion groups to convince in excess of 150 million people worldwide that abortion is the "murder" of a thinking, feeling, aware human being capable of feeling pain and terror. The film has even had formal viewings at the White House.

U.S. molecular neurobiologist Patricia A. Jaworski produced a radio documentary entitled "Thinking About *The Silent Scream*" in 1985, in response to the release of Dr. Nathanson's influential and disturbing film. In her documentary she points out that movement is not an indicator of conscious awareness, feeling, or thought, noting that sperm and bacteria move, but are not capable of these responses. A female human egg and sperm are both alive, but that doesn't make them sacred or entitled to life. Ms. Jaworski's arguments are based on her knowledge of brain development and the premise that human life is a continuum. She accepts Dr. Nathanson's claim that a 12-week fetus is pictured in his film, unlike Dr. Wainer. Most importantly, she points out that the abortionist is in fact jabbing the back of the fetus and lifting it with an abortion instrument when Dr. Nathanson claims that the fetus is initiating movement and "rearing." A simple way to test her statement is to freeze frame at that point in the film and then move slowly, frame by frame. The still images reveal the truth. At one point in *The Silent Scream* Dr. Nathanson says that the fetus is "moving to the left side of the uterus, in an attempt, a pathetic attempt, to escape the inexorable instruments," and claims that the instrument is not touching the fetus. Ms. Jaworski shrewdly observes that technically he is correct, but in fact the membrane around the fetus is being touched, and that in turn touches the fetus. The power of an image and rhetoric are great, and when combined they can easily betray the truth.

Congressman Roy Rowland, M.D., was the Democratic Representative for mid/southern Georgia in the United States when I interviewed him in Washington, D.C., in 1986. He had received a copy of *The Silent Scream* in the mail, along with other films and data. Dr. Rowland felt that "the film was deceiving—it projected the fetus as being quite large when it was probably no bigger than the end of my thumb. I thought it was demagoguery."[15] As a physician, Dr. Rowland has the medical knowledge to refute propaganda like *The Silent Scream*, but one can't help but wonder how many politicians have been swayed against abortion by this film.

It is particularly disturbing when abortion is compared to Nazi Germany's murder of millions of people during World War II, but I recognize that to Dr. Nathanson and others who believe that abortion is the killing of a human being, there is no distinction. It is hard to refute this belief, but I feel the person most qualified to comment on that comparison is Dr. Henry Morgentaler, because he is a survivor of Auschwitz and Dachau concentration camps. In 1950, he emigrated to Canada where in 1967 he appeared before the Common's Health and Welfare Committee on behalf of several Humanist Associations to urge that Canada's restrictive abortion laws be repealed. The publicity that followed his address led to a deluge of requests from desperate women seeking safe abortions. After much agonizing, he decided to set up Montreal's first abortion clinic, thus bringing about a confrontation with Canadian law. In 1973, Dr. Morgentaler was tried on a charge of illegal abortion and was acquitted by a French-Canadian Catholic jury. This acquittal was reversed by the Quebec Court of Appeal in an unprecedented decision, the only one of its kind in the history of Canadian jurisprudence. It was later upheld by the Supreme Court. He was tried three times and acquitted in all. His case became a cause célèbre not only for women's groups and civil libertarians, but for many segments of the population. During this period, he spent 18 months in jail. Dr. Morgentaler won the Canadian Humanist Award in 1973 and shared the American Humanist-of-the-Year Award with Betty Friedan in 1975.

When I asked Dr. Morgentaler about *The Silent Scream*, he replied angrily:

> It's complete humbug—the same as Nazi propaganda. The Nazis portrayed the Jews as villains who were raping Germany and were responsible for the war—everything was blamed on the Jews. In this film the abortionist is the villain. I'm now the villain. So it's okay to attack me, to kill me, or do anything to me. It's the same kind of technique. Strangely, Dr. Nathanson sneers at the vile abortionist in his film and yet he continued to perform abortions after he wrote his books and

made the film. I really don't understand him. . . . The way that Dr. Nathanson describes the process of abortion in the film is horror propaganda. He talks of seeing a baby dismembered, its bones crushed, its chest crushed by the implacable instrument of the abortionist—it's all dishonest hype. He uses magnified images so that you have a foot-long fetus projected before you. . . . Everybody knows what a baby looks like. At 8 months you can say there's a baby, but just after conception there's just a few cells. To treat those few cells as if they were a baby doesn't make sense to me . . . to speak of unborn embryos is nonsensical. The fetus is human, but it is not a human being, a child, or a baby . . . it doesn't feel any pain because it doesn't have a brain that can feel anything until around 5 months. It has reflex actions which the brain doesn't interpret or feel as pain. There is a difficulty in saying up to what point of intrauterine pregnancy it is morally justifiable or responsible to terminate the life of this potential human being. When you're dogmatic, it's easy . . . you can say it's conception or x number of weeks, and that's the end of the discussion. But when you're not dogmatic, you have to take certain criteria into consideration . . . one of which is viability. The other major criterion is the beginning of brain waves. Both occur at around 5–6 months. Most abortions are performed before 12 weeks of pregnancy—about 95%. If abortion were even more freely available there would be fewer late abortions. The fetus has become viable earlier, sometimes as early as 22 weeks, so it would be better to ensure that as many abortions as possible occur during the first trimester (up to 12 weeks). . . . Up to what point is abortion justifiable? There are always difficult cases which require the weighing of one factor against another. The circumstances of the woman have to be considered. But I do think there should be an upper limit—I would personally place it at around 24 weeks, the age of viability. After that time, I think the woman should be offered the choice to give her baby up for adoption or to keep it, but abortion should no longer be an option . . . unless ultrasound or some other test shows that the woman is carrying a very severely crippled fetus that would be born a very crippled child.[13]

Most abortions are performed long before brain development would enable the embryo or fetus to feel any kind of pain or in any way be conscious of what was happening. Claims by anti-abortion protesters that abortions are routinely performed late in pregnancy are lies. It is extremely rare for abortions to be performed after 20 weeks.

Dr. Michael Bennett, chairman of the Neuroscience Department at Albert Einstein Medical School, observes that "you can't be a person without a brain, you can't be a dog without a brain, you can't be a cat without a brain, or a chicken without a brain."[16] Dr. Bennett is actively involved in research on the brain. The brain defines our identity. Theoretically, if a human being was born with the brain of a chicken, the person would behave like a chicken. Would we call it a human being, a chicken, or a chicken in a human body? The point is that the brain defines who we are and how we behave. Human brain development is the key to defining when a fetus becomes a human being.

According to Dr. Patricia Goldman-Rakic, professor of neuroscience at Yale Medical School,

> The premise of all of modern neurobiology is that the brain is the organ of . . . sensation, perception, and conscious experience . . . there is no thought without brain. . . . The brain is unique in that the cells undergo a process of migration. So when a cell is born, it's nowhere near having finished its developmental course. It now must move from its place of origin to a distant location and that can take, in some cases, weeks.[16]

Dr. Goldman-Rakic has been engaged in developmental neurobiology for over 20 years. Brain waves detected early in pregnancy signify the beginning stage of development of the brain, not an actively functioning brain.

The brain consists of approximately 100 billion cells, also known as nerve cells or neurons, which are connected in chain form so that information can pass between them. There are estimated to be 100 trillion connections between neurons in the human brain. During pregnancy, there are no neurons for the first 4 weeks. The neurons begin forming during the 5th week of pregnancy and continue developing until several months after birth; however, the peak period for their development is between 2 and 5 months of gestation.

The presence of developing neurons does not mean that the brain is functioning. Several other stages of development must take place first. The next stage is migration, which takes from 2 to 6 months. This is followed by the growth of dendrites, which are like branches of a tree growing out of the cell. Axons then develop from cells which control muscle movement. These may be several feet long, extending from the brain down the spinal cord.

The most important part of this development (which takes place over a period of months) is the formation of synaptic connections. Without them, neurons cannot pass information to other neurons. Synapses begin forming around the 28th week of pregnancy, fastest in the cerebral cortex, but most are formed during the first few years after birth. The speed at which this development takes place varies in different parts of the brain.

Although physicians and scientists differ slightly in their estimates of when brain activity reaches a point indicating that the fetus may be a conscious "person" capable of feeling pain, it is generally agreed that this occurs around the 28th week of pregnancy. Some (especially physicians who perform abortions) believe that pain may be felt by the fetus as early as the 5th month. Physicians researching the brain tend to time that stage later than physicians who perform abortions, the latter preferring to err on the side of caution. During the 8th month of pregnancy the fetus begins to show signs of sleeping and wakefulness.

Further insight is offered on the question of brain waves in a 6-week-old fetus by Dr. Dominick Purpura, a neurologist and neuroscientist, who was formerly the dean of Stanford University Medical School and is currently dean of the Albert Einstein Medical School, and Patricia Jaworski.

DR. PURPURA. Any electrical activity recorded from the brain is called a brain wave. One can record all kinds of oscillations back into the second or third week of embryonic life, but one can record all kinds of wild electrical oscillations from a couple of nerve cells sitting in culture too. That doesn't mean anything. It only means that all cells have electrical potentials. The human liver cell has electrical potentials in it. It can generate, if you will, certain types of quote "brain waves" but those cells are concerned with digestive enzymes. So the presence of electrical activity is common to virtually all cells . . . PATRICIA JAWORSKI. if you look at the fetus from the outside only, what Dr. Nathanson is saying [that the fetus is a fully formed and identifiable human being at 12 weeks] may appear correct. But if you look at what's going on inside, you realize that there are phenomenal changes occurring. The fetus is not fully formed at 12 weeks *in utero*, and in fact, is undergoing dramatic and revolutionary change at this time. The billions of neurons are still being created, they will be traveling for weeks to their destinations, and once there, they will be growing the trillions of dendrites and synapses they will need to function. As this is happening, the whole brain is being shaped. . . . DR PURPURA. Movements can occur at the very earliest stage; for example, reflexes of the spinal cord are demonstrable in the very earliest stages—the reflex movements that occur when even the mother feels life. You may have twitches and these twitches can cause the muscle to move in different ways—so movement itself, movement is the poorest judge, the poorest criterion for personhood.[16]

Ultrasound has contributed images of early fetal development and "movement" that further complicate our responses to abortion, because the images of reflex movements and responses to movement of the amniotic fluid make the embryo or fetus appear animated.

The human brain is the essence of a human being. If your heart stops beating, you are not considered dead until your brain waves have also stopped and you are pronounced "brain dead." It seems reasonable to apply that same approach to the fetus—it is not alive until its brain is capable of functioning. Prior to the development of synaptic connections in the brain at around 28 weeks of gestation, movements of the fetus are reflex actions that do not indicate pain or thought. Single cells also move, but that doesn't mean that they think and feel pain.

If we accept that the development of the brain distinguishes the fetus as a human being, then late abortions (in the third trimester) are problematic, because the fetus may well experience pain, and indeed, if born, could well survive. Fortunately, 95% of abortions are performed in the first trimester. Very late second trimester abortions are usually performed on a very sick or crippled fetus, or in order to save the mother's life. In the latter case, if possible, a cesarean section is performed and the fetus is given the chance to live. Contrary to misinformation disseminated via anti-abortion propaganda in the United States, abortions are not en masse being wittingly performed in the third trimester. Such cases are extremely rare.

The argument against calling late abortions murder rests more on the element of lawfulness than on whether the fetus is a human being, because in the third trimester the fetus could well be described as an unborn, developing, possibly viable human being. But if it is a very sick or severely crippled unborn human being, then painless mercy killing might be communally agreed to be acceptable, in much the same way that euthanasia is acceptable, to some. At that stage, the surgical procedure involved should probably not be called abortion, because it is more akin to surgery on a premature baby than abortion. If the community agrees that such circumstances would justify terminating the life of the unborn, possibly viable human being, then lawfulness would justify the killing and preclude it being called murder. If the community doesn't agree, then abortion in the third trimester could be defined as murder.

Without the three elements that define murder as murder,

killing is not murder, however much we hate it. Killing, though sad and undesirable, is not always morally wrong. If the mother's life is threatened in the third trimester, then a choice might have to be made between the mother's life and the unborn, possibly viable human being's life if a cesarean section is not possible (extremely rare). That would be a sad and tragic choice to have to make, but the arguments in favor of saving the mother's life are very potent, because she has a history of relationships and emotional ties which the unborn does not. She also has a better chance of survival than a premature baby.

A helpful definition of abortion appeared in the book *Abortion* by Potts, Diggory, and Peel. They define it as

> the loss of a pregnancy before the fetus or fetuses are potentially capable of life independent of the mother. In most mammals, this period extends roughly over the first two-thirds of the pregnancy.[17]

This definition is acceptable to me because it covers the first two trimesters prior to synaptic connections in the brain. The term *abortion* is inappropriate for third-trimester terminations because the procedure at that stage falls into the category of mercy killing and a different set of criteria apply.

A popular book among those against abortion is *The Abortion Holocaust: Today's Final Solution* by William Brennan.[18] Dr. Henry Morgentaler's response to this comparison of the Holocaust with abortion is that

> it is dishonest. There's simply no comparison between what took place in the concentration camps and what takes place during an abortion. Hopefully, reason will prevail. We have an era of unreason now with evangelists preaching simple things. But I suppose if you accept the premise that a fetus is a human being from the moment of conception, then I guess you would be justified in talking about the killing of innocent human beings and making comparisons with the Holocaust and murder. But if that premise is wrong, then everything else is wrong. I simply don't accept that premise.

It's based on a fallacy and an arbitrary dogma. A human body is made up of millions of cells, not just one or a few. The pictures presented in the book *The Abortion Holocaust* portray a 24-week-old fetus—not all, or even many, abortions are performed at that stage.[13]

To say that a human being exists from the moment of conception is absurd from a biological standpoint. It's simply not true. What does exist is the potential for a human being to develop during the next nine months.

While Dr. Morgentaler was in prison, a fellow prisoner asked him how he could justify killing babies. Dr. Morgentaler replied:

> They are not babies. If they were, I would not be performing abortions. . . . A woman who wants an abortion doesn't want to kill a baby. She doesn't want the product of conception to become a baby.[13]

No abortion providers anywhere in the world have told me that they would be willing to kill a baby. All have expressed one main reason for performing abortions: to protect women from being butchered and give them the option of a safe abortion.

When I asked Dr. Etienne-Emile Baulieu, the French physician who developed the abortion pill RU 486, what he would say to a woman who is concerned that abortion might be murder, he replied:

> If you believe that abortion is murder, don't have an abortion. People have the right to think what they want. Science is not going to tell anybody what is the beginning of a person. Science knows that there are sperm and ovum and both separately already contain unique gene activity. Then they merge and you have a fertilized ovum or embryo, which contains the merging of the two halves of the genes from the mother and father. This is a further step of complication which can be respected if you believe that it's animated and that the soul is entering at that time. I cannot pretend to know the answer to that question. Further on, you have implanta-

tion. In my opinion, there is no pregnancy before there is implantation. We diagnose pregnancy by the pregnancy test, which indicates that there is implantation. This occurs between 1 and 2 weeks after fertilization. Then you have development and about 4 weeks later there are the first signs of electric waves coming from the head. One could say that since death is attested by the lack of electric waves, why don't you say that life begins with the beginning of electric waves? *All* cells display electric waves provided that they are nutritionally good. But when does that life become a person? Nobody knows. I just feel that a person is somebody who is also recognized by others. Women say first, I have menses delay, second, I may be pregnant, and then they say I'm expecting a child. It's a progression. The limit between those stages is very subjective. Making a child is an affair of thinking, feeling, and love. Everybody has his or her own definition. It is up to each person to define whether there is, or is not, a person developing in the uterus. The definition of whether or not there is a person developing in the uterus may change for each pregnancy, depending on the circumstances of the people involved. Let people decide for themselves. Give them freedom and education about the biological continuum, but the decision regarding when the embryo becomes a respectable person is a private matter.[19]

Of the three elements necessary to define abortion as murder—premeditation, unlawfulness, and a human being—only premeditation can be reasonably and consistently described as an integral aspect of abortion. Unlawfulness tells us whether abortion is illegal, but not if it is morally wrongful killing, because history has shown that abortion has been made illegal for a variety of reasons that have no relationship to morality. Thinking, feeling, awareness, and an ability to experience pain are key elements of personhood, but the brain development of a fetus is not sufficient to respond in these ways until around 28 weeks of gestation. Abortion in the first and second trimesters cannot be defined as murder because the fetus is not a person in the sense that we understand personhood at that stage in pregnancy.

In the third trimester, lawfulness becomes the key element that would determine whether abortion is murder. If we decide that saving the mother's life or preventing a very crippled fetus from being born a severely crippled baby are insufficient reasons to terminate a pregnancy and we ban all late abortions, then abortion might well be considered murder in the third trimester, because there is a potentially viable human being *in utero*. If we decide that these circumstances would justify a late abortion, then termination in the third trimester would not be murder because it would be a lawful procedure, but it would be killing a possibly viable, developing human being, for which we must be willing to take responsibility. My feeling is that third-trimester terminations should be permitted to save the mother's life only if a vaginal delivery or cesarean section is not possible. If the fetus is fatally ill or severely crippled, then termination would be justified in my view, but I would call it euthanasia, not abortion. Those scenarios are extremely rare, but possible. Abortion should not be permitted in the third trimester for any other reason.

The product of conception is alive and undeniably made up of living cells, and after an abortion the form those cells take—an embryo or fetus—is dead. Any living thing will die when removed from its source of sustenance, and that by any definition is killing. Abortion kills the potential for a fetus to fully develop, but that is *not* murder, because it is not killing an actual human being.

4

Religious Perspectives on Abortion

Religious perspectives regarding abortion can be grouped as follows:

- Religions officially opposed to abortion: Assemblies of God, Buddhism, Roman Catholicism, Southern Baptist, Hinduism, Jehovah's Witness, Lutheran, Mormon, Greek Orthodox
- Religions with varying degrees of tolerance of abortion: Episcopal Church, Islam, Judaism, Presbyterian Church (USA), Salvation Army, Sikhism, United Methodist, Unitarian Universalist Association
- Religions that officially leave the decision up to the individual: Bahai, Quakers (American Friends Service Committee)

When I began researching this chapter, I was under the impression that most religions consider abortion murder, especially Catholicism. Gradually it emerged that this is simply not true: most religions that oppose abortion, including Catholicism, do not consider it murder, largely because the issue of personhood is insoluble. When does a human being become a human being and develop or acquire a soul? There is no definitive answer to this question.

The confusion on the issue of whether religions view abortion as murder arises because there are parishioners and ministers of virtually every faith who express the view that it *is* murder, even though there may be no theological basis within their religion.

I am always appalled by the moral arrogance of those who embrace the religious dogma of their religion and aggressively try to convert others, as if they were privy to an absolute truth. With a view to cautioning all readers against such moral arrogance, I would like to share the thoughts of Dr. Anthony Kenny, the Master of Balliol College at Oxford University in England. Dr. Kenny was the first person I interviewed when I began researching the morality of abortion. He was Father Anthony Kenny of the Archdiocese of Liverpool until he petitioned Pope Paul VI "to be allowed to return to the lay state" more than 30 years ago. Dr. Kenny is a renowned philosopher and authority on Aristotle, Aquinas, Descartes, and Wittgenstein.

I am indebted to Dr. Kenny, because he encouraged me to pursue the arduous task of writing this book, and offered the startling revelation that the Catholic Church did not always consider abortion a terrible sin. Dr. Kenny writes in his autobiography *A Path From Rome* that

In the 1970's many ex-priests received permission from Rome to marry or had their marriages recognized by the Curia. I have never wished to do so, for however much the pendulum of faith and disbelief may swing within my mind, I can never again imagine accepting the infallible authority of the Catholic Church and the full panoply of Catholic teaching. It is true that many of the things which I objected to in Catholic practice have altered since the Vatican Council, and it is true that many priests will now cheerfully deny in the pulpit doctrines which I could only doubt in solitary guilt. But I am old-fashioned enough to believe that if the Church has been wrong in the past on so many topics as forward-looking clergy believe, then her claims to impose belief and obedience on others are, in the form in which they have traditionally been made, mere impudence. This does not prevent me from placing great value on many things in the Catholic tradition, or from feeling nostalgia for membership of the Christian community. . . . I believe that the Church has been fundamentally right in opposing abortion no less firmly than I believe that it has been fundamentally wrong in opposing contraception. In so far as abortion is the termination of the life of an actual, identifiable, human individual it is wrong for the same kind of reasons as the killing of non-combatants in war is wrong. . . . [1]

I don't agree with Dr. Kenny's view of abortion, but he has my unreserved respect, because he does not need the crutch of moral infallibility to support his personal beliefs.

It is dangerous to accept the view of any person or authority on any subject as infallible, though it is certainly easier to abandon independent thought and accept simple, comforting answers to complex questions. One of the most disquieting aspects of life is not knowing, not having answers; perhaps that is why religion is so appealing—it seems to provide answers.

In the United States, where there are no centralized religious authorities, there are over 2000 religions derived from Christianity, but the only thing they seem to have in common is a belief in Jesus Christ. In other countries, there is less diversity within Christianity. The situation is so extreme in the United States that it is tantamount to religious anarchy: ten churches may share the same title—e.g., Baptist, Episcopal—but they may have ten entirely different viewpoints on any given issue. This makes it extraordinarily difficult to find a common belief regarding abortion, because it appears that all views are acceptable somewhere.

This chapter should be read with an open mind so as to allow each reader the chance to form an independent opinion on the morality of abortion. Perhaps there is something to be learned from all religions, and perhaps you should also beware of all religions, for they evolve from beliefs that cannot be substantiated by fact. Most religions require faith on the part of congregants, and belief that the tenets held are morally correct. However, a collectively shared belief is not necessarily true or morally right. If your congregation doesn't think as you do, "shop around" and find one that does. There you will get the support you need during your abortion dilemma.

It is important to remember that beliefs evolve. Fifty or one hundred years ago, each religion may have viewed abortion differently. The interviews in this chapter are presented with the understanding that they are not representative of all religions, or of the opinions of all congregations following each faith.

Consulting a cleric of your religion on the subject of abortion requires courage, because you won't know until you ask what the response will be, and it may well be negative. Most of us think we know what the general view of our religion is regarding abortion, but the truth is that the interpretation of the rules varies from cleric to cleric. This vulnerability to moral pressure and the individual whims of clergymen concerns me greatly, because it can further confuse women, and men, who are exhausted from the emotional distress caused by a confrontation with an unplanned pregnancy and abortion dilemma. Sometimes clerics will interpret religion in favor of the congregant, but at other times they use it to torment and intimidate.

The following thought-provoking interviews are intended to magnify the differences between the theoretical dogma preached from the pulpit and actual counseling that might occur between congregant and cleric. Almost all of the clergymen interviewed by me acknowledged there were circumstances that might lead to a moral compromise, such as rape, incest, or a medical threat to the mother's life. The prohibition against abortion is not absolute, even in the most dogmatically anti-abortion religions.

Father Michael Mannion is the director of the Newman Center and the Catholic campus minister for Glassboro State College in New Jersey. Father Mannion, an authority on abortion who teaches classes on the subject to other ministers, is a kind man whom I came to respect during our interview in 1986, primarily because he is caring and uncensorious.

The Catholic Church believes that abortion is morally wrong because it destroys innocent human life which is sacred from conception through birth and really through all stages of human existence. Human life contains the sacred, eternal soul which God gives us; the taking of that life at any stage of its existence is therefore morally wrong.

The Catholic Church does not view abortion as murder, because the word is counterproductive to dealing with the woman. A woman's whole biology, physiology, spirituality, and psychology leans towards the expression of the pregnancy in birth. When that is interrupted by miscarriage or intentional abortion, something in her hurts. It might be repressed or denied, but in a very true sense the woman is the second victim of the abortion . . . I am coming from a healing perspective. My experience as a counselor over the last 15 years has shown me that there is a basic "instinct of brokenness" which women feel after the experience of abortion.

Catholicism says that the lives of the mother and baby are equal. We believe that medicine should do everything it can to save both lives if the mother's life is threatened. I think that many girls who have an abortion are not guilty of serious subjective sin . . . there are times in life when people do things which are objectively wrong and yet subjectively, in the Lord's eyes, they may be innocent. The woman's hurt has to be faced before it can be healed.

If a woman is consciously and fully aware of the teaching of the church on abortion and chooses of her own free will to have an abortion, the church feels that she should be excommunicated. When a woman comes in for healing after she's had an abortion, the point to emphasize is not the excommunication but rather her coming to grips with the pain and brokenness of what's happened and finding a way back. The church that has said this is wrong is also saying there's a way back.

To any woman seeking to begin the healing process after an abortion, I would recommend the following: Take some time by yourself and find a spot where you can be alone, in silence. Close your eyes and imagine in the depth of your heart a God who still loves you and cares for you and wants to heal you in spite of the mistakes you've made and the problems you've encountered. Ask God to send into your life people who will reflect that vision of His love.[2]

The current (1869 conceived) official position of the Catholic Church is that abortion is prohibited under all circumstances, but that was not always its position. In 1588, Pope Sixtus V declared that abortion at any stage, for any reason, was murder. In 1591, Pope Gregory XIV reversed that opinion with the proviso that abortion was not permissible as a method of birth control or to cover up sexual sin. In 1869, Pope Pius IX decided that the fetus, although not ensouled, is directed to the forming of man, so therefore fetal ejection is "anticipated homicide." What is "anticipated homicide" supposed to mean—the killing of someone whose arrival or development is anticipated? In that case, there's no one there, and it's the killing of unensouled potential? It is extraordinary that such vague wording could be taken so seriously by so many for so long, but consoling that even within Catholicism Pope Pius IX's position has been vigorously debated.

Not all Catholics, including some nuns and priests, feel that abortion is a sin. Frances Kissling is the president of Catholics For A Free Choice, a Washington, D.C.-based organization that believes that Catholics should be encouraged to make their own choice on abortion based on "informed conscience." It is not an organization that advocates indiscriminate abortion on demand, but it does suggest that abortion is sometimes necessary and should be permitted within Catholicism. Ms. Kissling spoke with devoted eloquence and earned my greatest respect during our interview.

In the previous chapter, she explained how Catholics For A Free Choice was formed in 1973 in response to the bishops' multimillion dollar campaign to recriminalize abortion after Roe versus Wade legalized abortion in the United States.

If you look at public opinion polls in this country on the issue of abortion, you really find that there are probably only 15% of the Catholic people who agree with the bishops on the issue of abortion. The balance would agree with us, in varying degrees. Our support is, as with most social issues, bigger than the actual list that we work with.

Abortion is not subject to papal infallibility, which is something the average Catholic is unaware of; the institutional church is very reluctant to inform people of this fact. The Pope doesn't convince many people that abortion is wrong—that's the first thing you have to understand. We know that there is probably no place in the world where the Catholic people listen to the Pope on matters related to sexuality. Look at the situation in Italy: First abortion was made legal and then they had a referendum that took place in 1979 shortly after the Pope had been shot. He came out of his sickbed to campaign against that referendum and yet the Italian people voted two to one in favor of legal abortion.

I think that there is some overstatement of the extent to which Catholic women feel guilty about their abortions. Where is the evidence that Catholic women feel so guilty? Catholic women have as many abortions as do Protestant women in the same percentage as we exist in the population. We are 22% of the population in the U.S. and 22% of abortions in the U.S. are performed on Catholic women. No more, no less. We use contraception the same as everybody else does. These differences are artificially imposed upon us.

There is an official teaching of the church on the issue of abortion that says abortion is not permissible in any circumstances whatsoever, including to save the life of the woman. There are some rare circumstances where abortion is a secondary effect of another medical procedure in which it is permitted. It's always called direct versus indirect abortion. Basically, what they're saying is that if you have cancer of the uterus and you happen to be pregnant and it's necessary to remove your uterus because of the cancer and the ancillary effect of that is the death of the fetus, then that's permitted. But, if you have kidney failure, and your doctor says to you that carrying the pregnancy will put such a strain on your renal system that you will die and you should have an abortion if you wish to live, that abortion is not permissible. That is the position of the church.

The church does not say that abortion is murder. There was an interesting exchange that took place in the U.S. Congress in 1981 between then Cardinal Cook and Senator Leahy. Senator Leahy asked Cardinal Cook, "Does cannon law treat abortion as murder?" Cardinal Cook replied, "Well, ah, ah, ah, abortion is a grave moral evil and a heinous crime," but he went out of his way to avoid using the word *murder*. The historical basis for abortion to be seen as a heinous crime is sexuality, not murder.

Most people think that the church's objection to abortion is rooted in the Ten Commandments—Thou Shalt Not Kill—but the reality is that although in modern times there seems to be some implication that it comes from Thou Shalt Not Kill, it is not seen theologically as killing. Why? Because the Catholic Church has never had a position and does not have a position to this day on whether or not the fetus is a person. There have always been different opinions in the church on this issue. On the subject of when the fetus becomes a person, the church does not at this point in time have a position . . . theologians are still in disagreement. But they say that even though we don't know whether or not the fetus is a person, the fact that it has the potential for life is a sufficient reason not to destroy it. In Catholicism personhood is not a biological concept—it's a spiritual one . . . the moment we're looking for (which in itself is an arcane way of determining life) is the moment when God gives a soul to the fetus. God could do that at two months, five, six months—at any time during pregnancy. We'll never have a theological answer to this question. Which is why the church's teaching on abortion can never correctly become infallible. This one piece of information about personhood will never be available to us for as long as we live—it will always block the formation of an absolute position on the subject. It is a metaphysical reality, not a physical one.

There are seven sins for which excommunication is the automatic punishment. Five of them can only be committed by a priest. The two sins for which an ordinary person can be excommunicated are attempting to or successfully assassinating the Pope and procuring an abortion. If abortion is connected to murder, why is it the only kind of murder that is punished with excommunication? The church's answer to that question is that because it is so prevalent we have to make a rule because the norm of society is going away from protecting fetal life.

The church is not mad that abortions happen. It's mad that the law has said that women can make this choice and sanctioned the choice of abortion. If abortion were illegal and there were just as many abortions going on in this country as there are now, the church would not be doing one little thing to stop them. In every Latin American country that you can name, illegal abortion is rampant. Half the hospital beds in Columbia are filled with women who've just had illegal abortions. The church is doing nothing to try to stop those abortions. Neither do they preach about them. As long as it's illegal, even if the woman has an abortion, the order and law of the church is maintained.

Catholicism says that you have a right to your conscience and must be fully informed. But then when you say that you have fully informed your conscience and have read everything and know everything relevant they say no, no, what we meant is that you must inform your conscience in accordance with the teachings of the church. So they play these little games. The trouble is, the teaching on abortion is wrong. The Pope is wrong. This is a mistake, in the same way as it was a mistake in the 16th, 17th, and 18th century when the church said that slavery was okay. This is another mistake. The church, as with any other system, can always acknowledge its past errors, but never those which are going on in the present. Look at what happened with Galileo and the church—the whole thing was total nonsense.

We maintain a small list of people who can help Catholic women, including a priest to whom we send some women for counseling. I wouldn't send a person to just any therapist, and I don't believe that women should go to just any priest. . . . [She needs to go to] someone who will treat her with respect and dignity, who is going to give her honest information about what the church teaches, about the kinds of things I have mentioned in this interview, straightforward and honest medical information as opposed to lies, and who is ultimately going to allow her to make the decision for herself and stand by her whatever she decides. There are very few priests who come into that category. We find that campus and college pastors are more often sympathetic in the way which we think is desirable . . . many of them are women. The other thing that we're trying to do is to get people to the point where they understand that they can make their own decisions. People tend to seek authority and look upon the priest as being right by definition—if he says it's right then it is and if wrong then that is the case. We want to help Catholics get beyond that mentality. We also want them to know that there are other authority figures in the church, such as nuns, pastoral counselors who are nuns, psychotherapists, social workers, and other professionals who work in the various Catholic centers around the country. Contrary to popular opinion, there are many Catholic nuns who support our work, particularly in developing countries where those women in religious life are exposed to and work with ordinary people and see the kind of suffering that women go through as a result of machismo, poor health, and lack of nutrition. This makes them much more accepting of contraception and abortion than people believe. . . .[3]

There is no actual mention of abortion in the bible. As Ms. Kissling suggests, the desire to maintain authority and sexual taboos rather than a belief that abortion is murder are the strong factors behind the obsessive campaign of the Catholic Church against legal abortion. That desire to maintain authority and power was clearly demonstrated at the 1994 United Nations Conference on Population and Development in Cairo, Egypt. The aim of the conference was to set a 20-year plan for global population control that would be approved by consensus, not just a majority. The means by which population control would be exercised was the major subtext of the conference—empowering and educating women. The estimated world population in 1994 was 5.6 billion. The conference sought to get nations to agree to try to limit population growth during the next 20 years, so that the world's population would be 7.2 billion in 20 years.

Most countries, including those as diverse as conservative Pakistan and liberal Norway, initially supported compromise language that would have called for governments to confront the issue of the health risks of illegal abortion but not promote abortion as a family planning tool. Women were to be educated and empowered to make decisions regarding family planning. But the Holy See wouldn't accept the compromise language and set about using its vast political (and no doubt financial) influence on poor nations to convince them to change their vote, even allying itself with countries known to support terrorism, such as Iran and Libya. Pope John Paul II succeeded in disrupting much of the conference's noble agenda, all because he wanted to focus attention on the abortion issue and get his way. It is unbelievable that the world gave such credence to the wishes of the Vatican at the population conference. The Pope represents the Vatican, a state with a few thousand people most of whom are supposedly celibate men. The conference was arranged for states and countries, not religions. The Pope does *not* represent the millions of Catholics around the world—heads of state are elected to represent their wishes. And yet, the Pope wields enormous political power. It is dangerous for one man to wield so much power, especially when he believes that all methods of artificial contraception are deplorable and that abortion is inherently evil regardless of the intention or circumstances associated with the decision. Who is going to feed, clothe, house, educate, and employ all of these people he wants to bring into the world?

On July 8, 1990, *The Sunday Herald* in Melbourne, Australia, published an article by Margot O'Neill, who was reporting from Washington, D.C. The article was captioned "Church War On Abortion" and quoted former Roman Catholic priest Eugene Kennedy's cynical remarks when a public relations firm and pollster was hired by American bishops to sell the church's message: "You call in public relations operatives when the truth won't work. That's why PR . . . has become in business as in politics, the substitute for a genuine moral and ethical sense."[4] He went on to label the bishops' strategy "manipulative at best and numbingly amoral at worst." That strategy has created moral confusion and is inspiring men to murder. If you wish to read further and learn more about Catholicism from intellectually credible educators, call or write to Catholics For A Free Choice (see "Help" Directory).

By way of contrast, Rabbi Laura Geller, executive director of the American Jewish Congress (Pacific Southwest Region), wrote in a letter to the editor of the *Los Angeles Times* on October 27, 1991, that

Jewish tradition is unequivocal in its belief that abortion is not murder. All Jewish leaders and rabbis agree that there are certain circumstances where abortion is not only permitted, it is required! . . . The human dignity and health of the woman carrying the fetus are crucial dimensions of the sanctity of human life from the Jewish perspective.[5]

She wrote that letter in response to a pastoral letter written by Cardinal Roger Mahoney that was distributed to four million Catholics in the archdiocese of Los Angeles in October, 1991. In the letter, he implied that the Jewish belief in the sanctity of human life leads to the same conclusion about abortion that he holds— that abortion is "plainly . . . murder." As Rabbi Geller eloquently pointed out in her letter, "Nothing could be further from the truth." Reform, Conservative, and Reconstructionist Judaism take a more liberal view of abortion than Orthodox Judaism, but Rabbi Geller's general summary of the Jewish position is absolutely accurate.

Julia Neuberger was rabbi of the South London Liberal Synagogue in England when I interviewed her in 1985. She has led a highly distinguished career and is actively involved in many different areas of community service. She teaches Bible Studies at Leo Baeck College in London and occasionally lectures at Cambridge University and at schools and universities throughout England and abroad. My meeting with Rabbi Neuberger was fascinating, because she made me think about issues such as the morality of aborting a deformed fetus:

> There are a variety of Jewish attitudes to abortion. I think that most Rabbinic Authorities would come down against it, except to save the mother's life. The complication is to what extent they would come down against it and in what circumstances. It's not an absolute position, even in Orthodox Judaism, which is very hardline on many issues. Part of the reason is that in Judaism, Halachically (according to the Law) the fetus does not have a status as an individual until it is effectively half out of the mother . . . until it is emerging. So it is questionable whether the fetus has any right to protection according to Jewish Law.
>
> No Authority that I am aware of—Orthodox or Progressive—would allow an abortion because the child about to be born was going to be disabled or in some way incapacitated. Disability is not considered a reason for abortion . . . I am broadly sympathetic to the view that abortion to protect the fetus from future suffering should be permissible, but I think that if you ask disabled children whether they would rather not be alive, they would mostly say that they would rather be alive.
>
> Judaism doesn't talk in terms of when the soul enters the body. The whole question of the nature of the soul in Judaism is pretty complicated. A baby that dies within the

first 30 days of life after birth is not given a full funeral and is not regarded as a full human being. A stillborn child is not given a funeral at all. I have always found these practices extraordinary. My personal stand is that if the parents of a stillborn child want a proper funeral service for their baby, I will perform one even though it is not part of Jewish tradition. [After 30 days of life outside the womb, Jewish Law does consider the baby deserving of full burial rites.] If it brings some comfort to the grieving parents, then I consider that sufficient justification for breaking the tradition. The fact that a baby which dies before it is 30 days old is denied full funeral rights in Jewish Law is very interesting to me, because it suggests that you gradually become more alive as you get older.

I don't think that as a Jew one has the right to decide about whether a life should be born. Spontaneous abortion is nature taking its own course. It is the decision which makes abortion such a controversial issue. Judaism is a life-affirming religion which in my view precludes the right to make an arbitrary decision on the gift which has been conferred through pregnancy.

Although I am anti-abortion except where the mother's life is at stake, I must say that I find legalized abortion in England far more acceptable than the situation prior to 1967 when women were at the mercy of butchers or their own desperate attempts to abort themselves. Women have always had abortions and always will, regardless of whether abortion is legal or illegal. I believe that abortion should be legal in order to prevent the unnecessary deaths associated with illegal abortion.[6]

I don't agree with Rabbi Neuberger's belief that we don't have the right to decide about whether a life should be born. I think it is essential that giving birth results from a positive decision—every child born should be wanted. Her view is more in line with the Orthodox Jewish attitude to abortion, that it should be allowed only to save the mother's life and health. Most other Jewish movements are more tolerant of abortion and consider it a matter of individual conscience. All Jewish organizations support a woman's right to have a safe, legal abortion.

The Venerable Sangharakshita is the head of the Western Buddhist Order in England. He is a world-renowned teacher of Buddhism and has written many scholarly works on the subject, most notably *The Ten Pillars of Buddhism* published by Windhorse Publications in 1984 and *The Three Jewels: An Introduction to Buddhism*, which was first published in 1967 by Rider and Company.

To the best of my knowledge, no Buddhist group in the East or West has departed from the traditional Buddhist position, which is that abortion is the taking of human life and is tantamount to murder. The traditional Buddhist attitude is that the fetus is human from the moment of conception. The fetus is inextricably linked to the mother, in the sense that it is totally dependent on the mother, which therefore makes her responsible for its life.... The term *soul* isn't used in Buddhism for "theological" reasons.

If a woman comes to me for counseling regarding abortion, I initially explore whether her Buddhist faith conflicts with the decision to have an abortion in principle. Let me stress that I very rarely give anybody advice as such. Women do quite often come to me to discuss this particular issue. But here, as elsewhere, I try to help people to clarify their thinking and the issues at hand without actually giving them advice. I never tell anyone that they should do this or that. I try to get people to see the issue more clearly and to come to their own decision, accepting the risk that they may come to what I regard as an un-Buddhistic decision. However, we certainly would not cut off contact with a person for having an abortion. We don't believe in excommunication in principle. We feel that even if someone does break the Buddhist precepts in any respect or is guilty of unethical or illegal behavior, contact should not be broken, though neither should the action be condoned . . . breaking contact only makes the situation worse. We try instead to steer a middle path by making it clear that we disapprove of the action and yet leaving the door open to communication. . . . I can envisage a situation where the two alternatives, having a baby or having an abortion, may both be unethical from the Buddhist point of view, abortion being the lesser of two evils. That would not then make abortion ethical as such, but one would have to accept that having placed oneself in a position where a positive ethical choice is no longer possible, the least unethical choice is the most desirable.[7]

Buddhism is not an authoritarian, censorious religion. It aims to educate and set moral standards, but recognizes the autonomy of the individual in making decisions. Abortion is clearly viewed as murder, but Buddhism teaches that it is up to each individual to come to her own decision.

The following interview with a Hindu priest was conducted in London. The minister wished to remain anonymous because he felt that sharing his view that there is a point of compromise between Hindu dogma, which is against abortion under all circumstances, and reality, might not make him popular.

In the Puranas and the Code of Hindu Law, abortion is mentioned as one of the greatest sins. At any cost it should not be committed. If the mother's life is at risk, then the decision to abort would depend on whether the child in the womb of the mother is legitimate or illegitimate. If a legitimate child is needed as an heir, the family might well opt for the life of the child. Hindu society is very conscious of social prestige and honor. If the child is illegitimate, then it presents the family with a great dilemma. Although the religion forbids abortion, in practice for the sake of saving their social prestige and honor, families do go ahead and permit an abortion to take place. I think that there have been cases of "legal" Hindu abortions when the mother's life has been threatened, but the circumstances must have been very extreme.

Generally, it is believed that the soul enters in the seventh month of pregnancy, but some philosophers disagree with that because they believe that the soul enters at the moment of conception.

Rape is considered a sixth form of marriage in Hinduism—it is a "demonic" marriage. The man has forced himself on the woman so the child is considered illegitimate, but its life must still be protected. The chastity of the woman has been destroyed, but her child still has a right to life, providing that the mother's life is not threatened by the pregnancy. If the girl comes from a very high caste and there is family prestige to maintain, then obviously they wouldn't like to have the child. Then it would have to be adopted out.

Although abortion is legal in India, there is a high rate of illegal abortion, because Hinduism forbids abortion and, more importantly, because women need to be virgins when they marry. Shame and fear of being murdered by their family or husband for their indiscretion drive Indian women to risk illegal abortion. Secrecy is essential if they are to survive in their social milieu. The use of abortion for sex selection is also rampant in India. The majority of aborted fetuses are female, largely because families can't afford the expensive dowry required for girls when they marry. It is interesting to note that the pressure for a male heir in Indian society is so strong that even if the mother's life would be threatened by continuing the pregnancy, some families might risk her life if she were carrying a male fetus. No other culture places so much emphasis on the need for a male heir and use of abortion for sex selection.

Islam, like Judaism, mandates abortion to save the mother's life if it is threatened by pregnancy. The following interview with a Muslim educator was conducted in London, England. He chose to remain anonymous for fear of persecution by fundamentalist Muslims who might not agree with his view of Islam.

It is difficult to say that there is any one particular attitude to abortion in Islam, but perhaps the most common view is that abortion under certain circumstances is quite permissible. It is only in recent years that it has become safe to have an abortion. Previously there was a good chance that the woman would die, in which case the Muslim ruling would be against abortion because the mother's life was threatened. Now that a woman can have a safe, legal abortion, the general view seems to be that a "therapeutic" abortion is acceptable.

Islam believes that the fetus develops in approximately 40-day cycles. The soul is thought to enter after the third of these cycles, around the 120th day, though that of course is approximate. The mother's life always has priority. If a woman comes to me for counseling regarding an abortion decision, I would have to consider her particular circumstances. . . . The fundamental choice from an Islamic point of view rests on whether the woman can sustain the pregnancy without risk to herself. Aborting simply because you don't want a child would not be justified within Islam.

Aborting because you can't afford a child is also not deemed a good reason for an abortion in Islam. In reality, Muslim women do abort for a whole range of not very therapeutic reasons, including protecting the family honor. Sexual indiscretion for Muslim women can bring shame and dishonor to the family, and it is not uncommon for a brother, father, or husband to murder a woman who has been soiled by sexual intercourse outside marriage. Muslim women have been known to have their hymen sown up after an abortion, so that they will appear to be virgins when they marry.

If you have come to the conclusion that abortion is morally wrong, you will have formed an opinion deserving of respect, but no more respect than the opposite opinion, that abortion is not morally wrong. Perhaps you have concluded that abortion is permissible in some circumstances. Whatever your opinion, let it be one born from an "informed conscience" rather than from fear and confusion created by crusading bullies intimidating you with misinformation and lies.

5

Men—Their Feelings Should Also Be Considered

Ernest Hemingway's *Hills Like White Elephants* is a strangely haunting short story. The following extract epitomizes the tension and conflict that can fester between a man and woman confronted with the dilemma of an unplanned pregnancy and abortion.

"It's really an awfully simple operation, Jig," the man said. "It's not really an operation at all."

The girl looked at the ground the table legs rested on.

"I know you wouldn't mind it, Jig. It's really not anything. It's just to let the air in."

The girl did not say anything.

"I'll go with you and I'll stay with you all the time. They just let the air in and then it's all perfectly natural."

"Then what will we do afterward?"

"We'll be fine afterward. Just like we were before."

"What makes you think so?"

"That's the only thing that bothers us. It's the only thing that's made us unhappy."

The girl looked at the bead curtain, put her hand out and took hold of two of the strings of beads.

"And you think then we'll be all right and be happy?"

"I know we will. You don't have to be afraid. I've known lots of people that have done it."

"So have I," said the girl. "And afterward they were all so happy."

"Well," the man said, "if you don't want to you don't have to. I wouldn't have you do it if you didn't want to. But I know it's perfectly simple."

"And you really want to?"

"I think it's the best thing to do. But I don't want you to do it if you don't really want to."

"And if I do it you'll be happy and things will be like they were and you'll love me?"

"I love you now. You know I love you."

"I know. But if I do it, then it will be nice again if I say things are like white elephants, and you'll like it?"

"I'll love it. I love it now but I just can't think about it. You know how I get when I worry."

"If I do it you won't ever worry?"

"I won't worry about that because it's perfectly simple."

"Then I'll do it. Because I don't care about me."

"What do you mean?"

"I don't care about me."

"Well, I care about you."

"Oh, yes. But I don't care about me. And I'll do it and then everything will be fine."

"I don't want you to do it if you feel that way."[1]

Not once in this couple's conversation is the word *abortion* mentioned, and yet the fear and ambivalence about the pregnancy and abortion permeate the atmosphere and dialogue. She really wants to have the baby, she's afraid of the surgery, and she's doubting her partner's love for her. He doesn't want to have a baby, but neither does he want to hurt her, emotionally or physically. He's scared too, but tries to reassure her that everything will be alright. She wants him to change his mind about the operation and say that she doesn't have to go through with it. He doesn't want her to change her mind, but he also doesn't want to force her to do anything she doesn't want to do. She cares more about their relationship than she does about herself, which upsets him because he cares about her and doesn't want her not to care about herself. She just wants everything to go back to the way it was before she became pregnant, when things were alright. There has been tension between them ever since she told him she was pregnant.

An unplanned pregnancy forces a man to confront his feelings for his partner and whether he wants to commit to a long-term relationship with her and raising a child. It is one thing to enjoy a woman as a lover and quite another to have her become the mother of your child. Men don't like being cornered by pregnancy into commitment to a woman or child, and most of all, they don't like feeling guilty.

Many men do not communicate their feelings well, and during an abortion dilemma, if they have chosen to be supportive of the woman, they tend to ignore or suppress their own responses, largely because of anxiousness and concern for their partner. Some men have moral objections to abortion, but at the same time they don't want to be thrust into fatherhood, so they experience considerable conflict over the decision to abort. There have been several cases reported of men who offered to adopt the baby if the woman would carry the pregnancy to term, but in all cases the women would not consider having the baby and giving it away. Although a woman may not want to have a baby, it doesn't mean she would be willing to give a baby away, even to the father.

In this chapter, I have chosen to present mainly the responses of male artists, because they seem better able to express the intensity of conflicts and emotions associated with abortion for men. "The Illegal Operation" (pictured on the next page) is a work of art, created by Edward Kienholz, in response to "an incredible outburst of violent despair, depicting . . . the instant after a ferocious seizure of life."[2] It was created in 1962, before abortion became legal in the United States.

Writer Marc Marais longs for a child:

> My wife aborted my children without telling me during our marriage. It is absolutely unforgivable for a woman to make a unilateral decision to abort a pregnancy while married or in a committed relationship. If a woman is single or the preg-

Figure 1.   Edward Kienholz's"The Illegal Operation" 1962. 51 × 48 × 54 inches. From the collection of Monte and Betty Factor, Los Angeles.

nancy is life-threatening or the result of rape or incest, then she should have the right to make a unilateral decision regarding abortion . . .[3]

Marc Marais' frustration and anger at not being consulted regarding his wife's abortions have been echoed by many men during the course of my research.

Men have a legitimate grievance when they say that on the one hand they are being asked and forced legally to take responsibility for their children, and on the other they are being told that legally, they have no say in whether or not their wife or partner gives birth. It is unreasonable to expect a man to serve as a responsible provider and parent if he's not consulted on the issue of whether or not he wants to become a father. An American actor and musician recalled during our interview that he was

> furious and very hurt when I found out that my girlfriend had an abortion. She knew that I would have been happy to have a child with her and get married. I'm not against abortion, but I wanted to have children with her. I think she should have at least asked me how I felt since we were committed to each other—at least I thought we were.[4]

A man should not have the right to force a woman who doesn't want to continue a pregnancy to bear a child, but if he's in a committed relationship, he should at least be given the chance to express his feelings about the unexpected pregnancy and consulted about the decision to abort.

A painter, who chose to remain anonymous, wrote in response to my questions:

> The abortion experience made me feel love and great concern for my partner and her suffering . . . abortion was illegal in West Germany in 1972. It was not difficult to find a good doctor, just expensive. Although I was very much in love with her and would have been happy to have a child, I in no way resented her for wanting an abortion. I feel the decision should be a joint one, but the ultimate choice is the

woman's. . . . We took about two months to resume full sexual relations. Though my de facto wife did express a natural fear of becoming pregnant again, that fear did not as such affect our love or desire, only how we expressed it in lovemaking. Since we never found a satisfactory method of contraception we relied on the rhythm method—it was I who kept track of her cycle! In all our years together it only failed once. My wife accepted the abortion quietly—it's inevitability, the sadness, the physical confusion—but not without a little regret and fear. She would like to have children one day, as I would, though we are no longer together. I tried to give my wife every support possible, both physically and emotionally. The physical and psychological disappointment for a woman after an abortion is a concrete reality. Depression can also develop. A man can experience these feelings only second-hand, from outside. Although he cannot share the feelings, he can help with care, understanding, love and humor, until the natural cycle is re-established and the pain and disappointment fade.[5]

Such a caring attitude on the part of a woman's partner can go a long way to helping a woman through the trauma of an abortion.

Generally, men don't like to see a woman suffer, be it a girlfriend, mother, daughter, sister, wife, or simply a friend, and neither do they want to feel responsible in some way for that suffering. Guilt, frustration, and anger appear to be major contributing factors to the reluctance and sometimes inability of men to communicate their feelings on abortion. As one senior male entertainer remarked when I interviewed him, "At my age, I never have to go to a maternity ward and say I'm sorry." The same sentiment could be expressed regarding an abortion clinic.

"I have had four encounters with abortion over the years, at least where I was certain that I was the father." That remark by an Australian artist captures the essence of how many men think, especially when they're single and are first confronted by an unplanned pregnancy. "Am I really the father?" is a very typical thought, though it often goes unexpressed to the woman involved.

Another concern unmarried men sometimes express is whether the woman is being devious and trying somehow to trap the man into commitment or marriage. An American singer/songwriter recalls:

You just don't know with a woman whether she's telling the truth when she says she's pregnant. I find it hard to believe that our contraception failed. . . . The decision to accept paternity depends on how many other guys the girl is sleeping with. A man is in a very precarious position. With some women you can tell with a fair degree of certainty but with others you just don't know. . . . As far as I know, my girlfriend had an abortion. She had some other complications arising from a cyst on an ovary which was also removed during the same operation. If she hadn't had the problems with the cyst, she would have wanted to have the baby. My response to that was sheer panic. I wasn't in a position emotionally, financially, or physically to father a child. I knew that I didn't want to have a baby by her or anybody at that point. . . . I learned a lot from the confrontation with abortion. I learned that sex is not a toy to be played around with. Women's bodies shouldn't be taken for granted. Making love is a responsibility. I had no sense of grief or loss over the abortion—only a sense of relief. I was also very upset that it happened at all . . . that she became pregnant. I felt responsible and that I'd let myself down. . . . I think it's a woman's right to choose whether or not to have an abortion, but in my case I think it was right for her to consult me. I would have resented not being asked my opinion and feelings. I probably would have shot myself if my girlfriend had decided to have the baby. That failing, I would have done everything possible to be supportive, but I would not have lived with her just because she had decided to have the baby. Fortunately I was spared that choice. . . . My girlfriend was upset when I took her home after the abortion because I had made a prior arrangement to attend a concert which I was determined not to miss. She wanted me to stay with her to take care of her and give her the support she needed, but that night I simply said that the concert came first. She was very hurt. I guess it was childish of me, but she wasn't on her deathbed and I was not going to miss that concert for anything less than a matter of life and death. I think we both failed to protect ourselves properly . . . to take contraception more seriously. In the past I thought that it was a woman's responsibility to take precautions, but now I discuss it with a woman before making love and am well prepared for any spontaneous "emergencies" of passion—I have a drawer full of condoms. I don't want any more accidents. . . . When my girlfriend and I discussed her pregnancy I felt that she was being very sentimental and romantic. She wanted to have the child and didn't seem to think that a lack of money should prevent us. I was being very down-to-earth and practical. I wanted her to be "real" too, but I guess her thoughts were more governed by her maternal instinct. After the abortion she was very upset and emotional. We were able to discuss it, a little. The relationship lasted for about a year after the abortion . . . if anything, the abortion brought us closer. . . .[6]

This man was clearly terrified of the responsibility of becoming a father, particularly as he knew that he did not want to marry his partner. He could have been more supportive of his girlfriend after the procedure, but by his own admission, he acted insensitively and left her alone. A positive aspect of the experience was that he developed more respect for a woman's body and a greater sense of responsibility about contraception as a result of the confrontation with an unplanned pregnancy.

A poet living in Canada shrewdly observed that

an abortion puts a great strain on a relationship, largely by throwing into question its true nature and thereby administering the shock of disillusionment to one or both parties. . . . I have been involved in three abortion "situations." In the third one in particular, I was shocked by her failure to tell me of the situation at the time . . . but I was even more shocked by the great sense of relief I felt at having been saved from becoming the father of her child and thereby tied to her by a lasting bond. This appeared to me a revelation of my true feelings towards her, which were considerably less positive than I had supposed.[7]

Relief at not having to commit to a woman or child is a common response of single men after an abortion. It is easy to confuse sexual passion with love, and it is also possible to love without wanting to commit to a long-term relationship with that person. Men, and women, need to be more honest with themselves and their partners and not drift in relationships until a crisis like an unplanned pregnancy forces them to acknowledge how they feel.

Some men communicate thoughts and feelings well, but as a general rule, it is difficult for men to share their feelings with women when they are faced with an unplanned pregnancy and a decision regarding abortion. Single men in particular express great ambivalence about abortion, on the one hand being wary of accepting responsibility and on the other hand resenting not being given a choice about whether to have the abortion. Some men resent not being given the option to adopt their own baby if the woman chooses to have the baby and give it up for adoption. Although there are men who believe that abortion is morally wrong, the ambivalence most men express about abortion in general seems to stem more from doubt about whether or not to continue the pregnancy and make a commitment to the woman and child rather than about abortion itself.

It is up to women to open the door to communication with men on the subject of abortion, by asking them what they think and feel about the situation, and in turn honestly sharing their own thoughts and feelings. If women want men to be responsible fathers, then they must give men a chance to share the decision regarding the fate of an unplanned pregnancy.

6

Changing Dynamics between Couples Stemming from Abortion

One of the major problems women encounter when they have an abortion is lack of communication with their partner. This compounds their sense of anguish and frustration during the experience of having an abortion and makes them feel very lonely and insecure. An unplanned pregnancy often creates great tension between lovers and precipitates the disintegration or serious deterioration of their relationship. Sometimes men and women simply want different things out of a relationship and life, and an unplanned pregnancy suddenly sheds light on those differences. But lack of communication seriously compounds the problem. Less often, the couple is drawn closer by the experience. This chapter will open the door to communication between women and men who are locked in a prison of private anguish as the result of an unexpected pregnancy and abortion dilemma.

The most striking aspect of researching how couples feel about abortion was my difficulty in finding couples willing to talk about their experience together. Linda Bird Francke observed in her book *The Ambivalence of Abortion* that

> By the time a couple arrives at the clinic for an abortion appointment, their minds are for the most part made up, and rather than welcoming discussion of their motives, they clam up and refuse to open a painful subject. . . . How the people really feel rarely comes up, either in front of the counselor or

> with each other, before the abortion. And often . . . even after
> the abortion, couples, married or not, continue to keep their
> doubts or anxieties to themselves, each telling the other what
> he or she thinks the partner wants to hear.[1]

Women are generally more willing to talk about abortion than men. It is not difficult to find a man willing to share his feelings and thoughts on abortion if he is no longer involved with the woman he impregnated, but if he is still with his partner, he seems to feel threatened by the thought of sharing his experience in words, especially if his partner is present.

It appears that the main reason for this reluctance to talk on the part of men is the fact that abortion causes serious communication problems and emotional conflicts in their relationship with their partner. I also noticed during my research that women were fearful but curious to discuss their experience of abortion with their partner present, but were almost relieved when he refused or when they decided not to invite him to participate in the interview. It seems that both women and men were fearful of renewed conflict and tension over abortion, which might cause an emotional estrangement similar to what transpired at the time of the actual abortion.

One exception to that rule was an Israeli couple, whom I have named Nurit and Ari. I was originally scheduled to interview only Nurit, but when we began the interview and I asked if her husband would join us, he agreed quite willingly. They lovingly and very vocally disagreed with each other throughout the interview, but the level of trust and communication between them was striking. Their story is unique because she was a research student studying about the development of the embryo in medical school in Israel when she aborted a pregnancy in her fourth month of gestation. She discovered that she had been pregnant with twins when she expelled a second male fetus as she rose from a sofa. Uncertain about what to do with the fetus, she decided to take it to her lab where they preserved it in formaldehyde. Over 35 years later, Nurit still has the fetus preserved in a jar on her dresser.

I don't know exactly why I kept the fetus all these years. I never think of it as my offspring, but I didn't feel that it was right to just throw it away. I don't know why I brought it with me to America; I guess that I have some attachment to it. It never occurred to me to bury it, and I never felt the need to name the fetus. I have always referred to my son as my first born. The fetus wasn't born, so it didn't exist for me in that sense, and yet I keep it with me. I don't know why.

When her husband joined the interview, sparks flew as their misconceptions about each other's views on the abortion emerged. Ari recalled:

I didn't want my wife to have the first abortion, but when I realized her attitude, we decided that it would be best for us. I didn't want her to abort our child because having a child for me meant the survival of the Jewish people. I was born in Belgium and lost most of my family in the Holocaust. I felt that the abortion was killing a child, but that it was better to do it before we knew him . . . before he was born. My wife was more important to me than the fetus we lost. I didn't think my wife was right to preserve the fetus. To this day I think that she was wrong to do that. But it was part of her, and so it's her right to keep it, even if I disagree. This fetus represents death for me, but I am not afraid to face death. It also represents life, because you can see so clearly how life develops by looking at it. It represents my wife, because it was part of her.

In response to her husband's remark, Nurit reflected, "I believe that preserving the fetus was a celebration of life." After I interviewed Nurit and Ari, I became curious to hear how their children felt about the preserved fetus. Their son says that when he inherits the fetus, he will keep it as another form of memorabilia of his parents. He has no feelings toward the fetus, and does not believe that there was anything wrong with his mother preserving it, especially as she came from a medical background. Their daughter believes that it was morally wrong to preserve the fetus and that it should be buried.

There are distinct differences between the conflicts that an unmarried couple experience and those of a married couple, as well as some very obvious common factors. It is also interesting to note that the problems seem to be universal in many respects, crossing cultural, national, ethnic and religious boundaries. Obviously, each couple is different and will have a unique set of problems, thoughts, and feelings stemming from cultural and religious differences, but issues of commitment, responsibility, communication, contraception, caring, love, and understanding are human problems common to all couples grappling with abortion.

A surprise pregnancy out of wedlock is perhaps one of the strongest tests a couple will ever have to face, for it forces both the woman and the man to ask, "Do I love this person enough to have a child with him/her?" and "Can I make a commitment to live with my lover long enough to raise a child?" It forces both parties to make a decision about their relationship rather than letting it take its natural course, which might mean drifting for years without ever truly committing to each other. This upheaval often causes both to feel resentment and then the issue of who is to blame for the pregnancy begins to surface.

Pregnancy forces responsibility on lovers and tests their capacity for communication, understanding, caring, and love. Many relationships don't survive the test, and abortion becomes a source of great trauma and stress. Sadly, because of the lack of communication, couples who separate as a result of abortion often learn very little from the experience because they were unable to express their feelings to each other.

Married couples are usually committed to each other, if not to fidelity, so commitment is not the central issue. Economics, responsibility, and religion seem to play far more important roles in the conflict associated with abortion for married couples. "Do I want/do we want to have a child?" "Can we afford to have a baby at this time?" "Is abortion a morally acceptable choice if we decide not to have a baby at this time?" "Who is to blame for the pregnancy?" "Whose responsibility is it to take contraceptive precautions?" "Do we want another child?" These seem to be the driving questions behind the conflict for couples. Oddly enough, however, the problems of lack of communication, understanding, caring, and love seem common to both unwed and married couples, although the issues that trigger these problems may vary considerably.

Couples display a wide variety of complex reactions to abortion. To illustrate these reactions, I have selected two interviews I conducted, one with an unwed woman of Greek Orthodox heritage who was raised in England (where the interview took place) and whose partner was French. The second interview took place in Israel, with a married Arab Muslim woman who preferred that her husband not know what we were discussing during the interview, even though he was at home with their children at the time. Both of these couples survived the stress that abortion placed on their relationships, but the issues had not been resolved completely at the time of their interviews with me, despite the passage of months and years, respectively. These women expressed themselves very clearly, and it is my hope that reading their stories will serve as a catalyst to communication and understanding between couples. Even if the relationship eventually ends as a result of the issues raised, at least both parties will have learned something about each other and the meaning of responsibility in a sexual relationship.

(The names of the two couples have been changed to protect their identities, as they are well known in their respective countries.)

"Mariana" has chosen to remain anonymous because she fears hurting people close to her, especially her Greek father, who she feels does not fully accept that she is a grown woman involved in a sexual relationship out of wedlock. She also feels that he'd be hurt that she didn't share the abortion crisis with him and ask for his help. Mariana relates that if her mother had been alive, she would have confided in her. In yet another of life's paradoxes, she realizes that not telling her father is in some way illogical as her father is not naive—her own mother had an illegal abortion in Greece because she didn't want a fifth child. The abortion nearly killed her mother, but her father doesn't know that Mariana knows. Mariana's lover, Pierre, had originally been scheduled to participate in the interview with Mariana, but at the last minute he refused to come, apparently for fear of being confronted by unspoken demons of the past; Mariana believes that he was afraid of her feelings and his own feelings of guilt.

I became pregnant in the summer of 1983. I was absolutely thrilled when I discovered I was pregnant while Pierre, my lover, was away on holiday with his family. Part of my pleasure stemmed from the sheer joy of realizing that my body worked in the right way. . . . When Pierre returned from his vacation, he was at first thrilled to learn I was pregnant. He asked me to live with him, saying that he would leave his wife and children for me. I was ecstatic and we continued making love in a state of bliss as we contemplated the child we were going to have together.

A few days later, the reality of his commitment to me set in and he asked me to have an abortion. He'd had problems with his marriage for 5 years, but he had maintained it for the sake of his children. . . . Once he expressed his doubt about having the baby, I started to hate making love with Pierre. I still went through the motions, but I detested him for not wanting our child. I tried to understand how he felt, but I was torn between my love for him and my desire to have his baby. Suddenly the two were incompatible, and yet just a few days earlier we were fantasizing about a life of wonder together with our child. I became thoroughly confused emotionally and we had great difficulty communicating.

Abortion is a very personal and emotional issue for Pierre because his mother died after an illegal abortion in France when he was a child. He also felt guilty because he had just urged his wife to have an abortion not long before I became pregnant. When the reality of the situation set in, Pierre said that he hadn't changed his mind about leaving his wife and children, but my pregnancy was an extra complication which he didn't think he could bear. He felt that his wife would be terribly hurt if she knew that he was leaving her for a woman who was to bear his child after she had just had an abortion. He also felt that his children would feel rejected because he was not only leaving them but they would feel as if they were being replaced by a new baby if I had a child then. I think more than anything, he wanted me to have an abortion to make things as easy as possible for his children.

He said that he felt an abortion would be best for everybody concerned, but I pointed out that I was not sure that it was best for me. I wanted the child. I thought about it a great deal and told him that I was thinking of having the baby on my own, but I wasn't going to make a fuss or stir up any trouble for him. I told him that I would not make any demands of him, but he found the whole idea intolerable because he would be unable to ignore the fact that I was somewhere with his child. . . .

I found myself in a very precarious position. If I had the baby, I would have nowhere to live and no means of supporting myself and a child, but if I had an abortion, I could live with either my sister or Pierre. The whole situation made me very angry. I was very angry at the people close to me whom I felt had deserted me, but I was also angry at myself for being 32 years old and not responsible enough to be able to have my baby and support it myself.

I decided to have an abortion, but with a great fuss. I made the appointment and then I cancelled it. I then decided that I was ill and that I had an ectopic pregnancy. I had scans and was doing everything possible to convince myself that I wasn't pregnant, because what I wanted most was not to be pregnant. I don't mean that I wanted to have an abortion. I wanted simply never to have conceived so that I wouldn't be faced with that decision.

In the end, I made the appointment at the Marie Stopes Clinic (in London, England) and Pierre and I went together.

He was terribly sweet, but he was mortified by the whole situation because he knew that he was letting me down. I think he would be very hurt to actually hear me say the words "he let me down." It's one of the "unspokens" between us. If I could have persuaded him to come to this interview with you, and if he was honest, I think he would say, "I let her down." But he won't say it, and I won't say it, and as long as neither of us voices it, then it won't be "true" and he won't have to acknowledge that he hurt me.

A couple of days before the abortion we went out for lunch and I was going to tell him that I never wanted to see him again because I detested him. I was totally convinced that after the abortion I would not want to see him anymore. For some reason which is beyond rational explanation, I didn't actually tell him that I never wanted to see him again. I certainly felt that way.

When we went to the clinic, I was praying all the way there that he would say it was alright . . . that I didn't have to have the abortion and he would help me. Then I would get angry at myself for needing him. He looked terrible and was very upset. He was trying to be nice to me but my reaction was to tell him that I didn't want him to touch me, talk to me, or have any contact with me at all. I was quite cruel, because I felt angry and hurt.

I had so many mixed feelings as I lay on the operating table waiting for the anesthetist. I didn't want the abortion right up to the last minute before I lost consciousness. The strange thing is that after the abortion, I was elated. When the anesthetic wore off and I regained my senses, I wanted to have a party! The relief from 6 weeks of the worst pressure of my life was overwhelming. When Pierre came to see me in the evening, I was dancing with joy—he simply couldn't believe it. He'd thought I'd be awful towards him. That sense of elation lasted for several months.

A week after the abortion, Pierre asked, "Now you've had the abortion, where are we?" He was still with his wife and said that he felt we had made a mistake having the abortion as he still wanted to leave his wife to be with me. This made me incredibly angry—I couldn't believe that he could say such a thing after all I'd been through. I told him never to say such a thing to me again. All I wanted to hear from him was that we'd made the right decision. I couldn't cope with anything else.

A few weeks after the abortion, Pierre left his wife and we moved in together. For the first 6 months of living together, we were on a permanent high—it was one long honeymoon. That was about 2 years ago. We've rarely talked about the abortion since then except once, about 6 months after the abortion. I was still basking in the glow of romance and calmly asked him, without any hysteria or tears, how he felt about the abortion. He replied that at the time there was so much drama in his life with the breakup of his marriage and problems with his children that the abortion just became another thing for him to worry about. It was simply part of several larger problems all happening at the same time.

About a year after the abortion, I asked him again how he felt about the abortion. He seemed better able to see it as an isolated incident as he had emerged from the major problems which had plagued him earlier in the year. He said that he had found it a horrific time because I had hated him so much and he couldn't bear that or the thought of the alternative, having the baby. It had been so awful that he couldn't think of anything which he could say about it that would alter anything. That was the first time I realized that his silence at the time of the abortion was not a sign of indifference or him considering it unimportant. He just couldn't think of anything to say to help me, himself, or the situation.

Not long after we had discussed how he felt, I became pregnant again, or at least I thought I was pregnant. I did a home test which was positive. I was horrified, and so was Pierre. I told him that I didn't want to talk about it for a couple of days because I needed time to think. About 2–3 days later, he broached the subject, saying that he couldn't bear the thought of another baby at that time, and I agreed with him. The separation from his wife had been devastating for his children, his wife had turned nasty, and we were still getting to know each other as well as trying to provide a second home for his children. But worse than being unable to face having a baby at that time, I couldn't bear the thought of having to face another abortion. He asked whether the abortion had really been so awful. I replied that it was, and that I couldn't have another one. He told me I was being ridiculous, then asked, "If you don't want the baby and you don't want an abortion, what do you want?" "That is my dilemma," I replied.

Fortunately, 2 days later, my period arrived. It seems that I had spontaneously aborted as often happens in the early stages of pregnancy. After the natural miscarriage, Pierre and I did discuss our feelings a little. He couldn't understand why I was pleased to have come on naturally since I had said that I didn't want to have an abortion. True, but I had also said that I didn't want to have a baby either. Now I had what I wanted—I was not pregnant. He was terribly puzzled. I tried to explain to him that there was something about having an abortion which was very difficult to explain to anyone who hadn't had one. When talking to someone who has had one you don't need many words—you can just say you've had one and you feel lousy, and that communicates, because a woman who has been through the experience can agree that it's awful without needing an explanation of why it was so terrible. But if you're asked to describe the feeling to someone who hasn't had the experience, it's very hard to know what to say. I just couldn't make him understand that the natural miscarriage was not my responsibility, but my abortion was.

Pierre is normally very kind and comforting if I'm upset about something, but if he knows that I'm upset about the abortion, he can't comfort me, because he feels that it's his fault, and his guilt prevents him from being able to share his feelings or console me. I think he imagines that I feel a lot more resentment towards him about the abortion than I actually do. In a way, a lot of my anger at the time and even now is against myself rather than him, for not being independent in that time of crisis.

Each anniversary of the abortion since then I have been progressively more upset about the abortion. That's the strange contradiction which only those who've had an abortion can understand. Some women are not at all moved by the experience, but for those who are, the sense of loss increases with time rather than decreases. It has nothing to do with guilt, but rather with craving a child, and the anniversary reminds a woman of that emptiness which only a child can fill.

This year, at around the time of the second anniversary after the abortion, I became pregnant again. It's strange how mother nature works—it's almost as if the body has a will of its own and that some inner sense of time tells it to conceive around the same time each year. I had been advised to stop using "the pill" periodically, and as mentioned earlier, none of the other methods we tried were satisfactory. I was terribly depressed after the home test was positive. When Pierre wanted to know why, I said that it was because I didn't want a baby just then. His response was to say that it would be alright if we had a baby now, because he felt that we were ready to make the adjustment. He thought that it would be nice to have a child and said that he had become used to the idea. We had been through a period when he had questioned whether he wanted any more children, and I had to tell him that I respected his feelings, but I would ultimately have to leave him if he continued feeling that way, because I did want a child. I was not trying to blackmail him; I just wanted to make him see how much I wanted a child. When he expressed a positive response to this pregnancy, I realized that my initial unhappiness at discovering this pregnancy stemmed from a fear of hearing him again say that he didn't want our child. I desperately wanted to have a baby, but I wanted him to want to be a father too. Eventually, my period came, and I felt both relief and disappointment.

Not long ago, I suddenly found myself yearning to have a baby—somehow knowing that Pierre was willing to be a father to another child had triggered the release of all my maternal desire. I was finally free to have a child. Prior to that I kept feeling that one way or the other, pregnancy and a baby would create a terrible situation in which I would have to confront Pierre's not wanting a child with me, which would have made me feel rejected, or else I would have it against his will and have the horror of confronting his unhappiness. The worst scenario of all was the possibility of another abortion. Now I am free to follow my maternal instinct and have a baby, because I know he is willing to be a father to our child.[2]

When I sent Mariana a copy of the transcript of the interview, Pierre expressed a desire to read it. This surprised Mariana in view of his unwillingness to attend the interview. After reading the transcript, Pierre told Mariana that he'd had no idea that she had felt so strongly about the abortion at the time or since then, and he had not realized how desperately she wanted to have his child. He then suggested to her that they try to have a child immediately. Mariana was so overcome with joy at his response that she called me to share her news. She said that reading the transcript had removed that unspoken barrier between them and opened a whole new chapter in their relationship.

Although every relationship is unique, Mariana and Pierre's experience demonstrates many common misconceptions, practical problems, and communication difficulties that couples, unwed in particular, face when trying to cope with the dilemma of abortion. Most of all, their relationship mirrors the conflict of commitment and how great an impact that can have on the relationship and the decision to have an abortion. Sadly, abortion can be a very lonely experience for both a woman and a man, who at the time of crisis need each other more than ever. Communication is the only way for an estranged couple to find a way to comfort each other again.

Fatima is an Arab Muslim woman living in Israel. At the time of her interview, she was living with her late husband, Mostafa, who died suddenly of a heart attack about 10 months after we met in their home in Israel. Although he knew that I was interviewing his wife about abortion, Mostafa thought I was interviewing her as a professional educator. Fatima indicated to me that she was willing to share their personal experience as a couple, on the understanding that when he walked into the room, we were to change the focus back to general issues surrounding abortion. This was not because of any religious or social stigma attached to abortion in the Arab Muslim community in Israel, but because abortion and contraception had been the most divisive and destructive elements in their marriage and had almost caused them to separate. She felt that he would be deeply embarrassed to know that she had discussed their problems, as they had remained their secret. The same restriction applied to her children—when they entered the room, we were to switch the focus of the conversation.

Fatima and Mostafa's experience of abortion as a married couple highlights universal problems that married couples around the world face, most especially the battle over contraception. Their story is told from one side only, just as Mariana and Pierre's story is presented through her eyes only, but I feel that it is important for us to try to understand men who can't or won't express their feelings, as perhaps they may be feeling and thinking in a way that men who are willing to talk don't feel, or don't feel as intensely.

When we first got married we were both students. We thought that we would begin a family after about 4 years of marriage, once we both had our degrees. But we never actually took any precautions to prevent my becoming pregnant. We thought about contraception, but in practice we did nothing about it except trying to use the natural rhythm method, which didn't work. I think it was fear that prevented us from seriously thinking about contraception. We were newlyweds from very traditional families who warned us not to use any contraceptive "gimmicks" because they might ruin my chances of becoming pregnant. Traditionally, a woman was supposed to have her first baby in order to see if she was fertile and could actually have one. Although one tries to be logical in the face of such irrationality, there is a mystique about childbearing which makes one susceptible to that sort of pressure. I never thought of using the pill or any other methods seriously. We wanted children, just not then.

Three months after we were married, at the age of 20, I discovered that I was pregnant. All our calculations had been wrong. At first I didn't believe it; then I began to realize the seriousness of our situation. It was 1968 and abortion was still illegal in Israel at that time.

My husband had already received his grant to continue his studies for his Ph.D. in the United States. That was the dream of his life. We felt that to have children then would have made it impossible for him to continue with his studies. I was afraid to have the baby alone in the United States and to travel while I was pregnant. I didn't feel that it was right to have the baby in Israel and then travel to America, so I felt totally confused. My fear was greater than any natural maternal instinct, and I just couldn't see how I could cope, so we decided that I would have an abortion.

We hid my pregnancy from everyone because we knew that they would try to influence our decision and try to talk us out of it. But slowly I became aware that I wasn't 100% sure that I wanted this abortion despite all our discussions and agreement. I grew more courageous as my pregnancy progressed. I guess I was becoming adjusted to the idea of becoming a mother. I felt hurt when my husband agreed that I should have the abortion, but I didn't show my hurt to him at that time. I hoped that he would start feeling "fatherly" and that he would change his mind—he was 26 years old. My primary reason for wanting the abortion was because we were going into an unknown situation and we both wanted to finish our studies, but as the pregnancy progressed, my maternal instinct sprang to life and I didn't really want to go through with the abortion.

It was my husband who made the appointment with the doctor at a private hospital. I went along with him all the time thinking that I was just going along with his wishes—he was leading me, but I wasn't really going by choice. The whole idea became vague to me . . . I wasn't going, not really. I felt scared, very small, and so helpless. Here I was, being led by the hand of my husband, who had made me pregnant, as if I was a child. He was taking me to have an abortion.

All these small pictures were hurting me, but I didn't fully realize how much. I was afraid that I might die as a result of the abortion, or that if I didn't die, that I would be unable to have children in the future. I wasn't afraid of God or anything abstract—the fears were practically based.

The doctor was a very old Jewish lady. She was very smart, and I think she sensed my fear. She said that she didn't feel that I was ready for an abortion; that it was a decision that had to come from within. So she gave me 3 weeks in which to go away and think about it. She asked whether we were sure that for a degree we would want to give up our baby. We had 3 weeks in which to discuss it, and if we still wanted to have an abortion there would be time enough to have one safely. I thanked God when the doctor said that we should go away and think about it. Now we could reexamine our decision.

After that, I became suspicious of my husband's love for me, because he didn't change his mind about the abortion. I have never been able to talk to him about what I felt as a result of his decision. The longer I was pregnant, the more I wanted the baby. I no longer cared about degrees or anything else—I just wanted my baby. I was supposed to be logical and reasonable and not present any obstacles to my husband's development, but as time went by, the conflict of interest became greater and greater.

When we went back to the doctor, the first thing she said was that we had come late. I felt as if she was treating me as a mother—that she understood my feelings. My husband was scared too; she could see that. He felt that it was his responsibility though he never said so. He was not at ease with himself and was obviously disturbed. It was as if we were both waiting for someone to tell us to stop being so stupid. Everyone has their troubles, I thought, but that is no reason not to have a baby. The doctor examined me and said that the baby was now too big and she would not perform the abortion because it would be too dangerous. Once my husband heard that it was dangerous he immediately said no, we wouldn't have one if that was the case.

We went home without saying a word to each other. Then the next day we raced with joy to his family to tell them I was pregnant. Things improved from the moment it was decided that I couldn't have the abortion. My husband had proved his love for me because he was not willing to sacrifice my health for a late abortion. He wasn't willing to submit me to that danger despite knowing that the grant money probably wouldn't be enough to cover us with a child. I have never regretted being unable to have the abortion. Having my baby boy was simply wonderful.

The confrontation with the decision to have an abortion taught us a very valuable lesson—that if we really didn't want a baby, then we had to take precautions to prevent it happening again. So we decided that I would use an IUD, which worked successfully for 4 years, at which point it was removed because we had decided that we wanted a second child.

We returned to live in Israel, where we had our second child, a daughter this time. Afterwards, my fear of the IUD surfaced. To be honest, it hurt. I hate taking drugs of any kind, even aspirin, so the pill was not an alternative. I had been in a little pain for about 6 months when I originally had the IUD inserted. The memory of that pain suddenly returned after the birth of my second child, and I didn't want to go through it again.

There started to be a tension between my husband and I, because he wanted to have sex and I didn't—I was afraid of becoming pregnant again. I knew that I wasn't ready for another baby and that I must find an alternative method of contraception. I believed that it was my husband's turn to take responsibility for preventing any further unwanted pregnancies. Our sex life was very badly affected and a distance developed between us. We thought that if we went to the United States for his sabbatical it might help us to rebuild our relationship. We spent a disastrous year there: I had two abortions, both under a local anesthetic. He occasionally agreed to use condoms, but occasional isn't enough. I remained adamant that he should take the precautions.

The first abortion made me terribly angry and very worried. I didn't want to have the abortion. My daughter was now 3 years old and I felt ready for another child. He was absolutely certain that he didn't want another child. He had two; that was all he wanted. Our relationship was bad. I didn't want sex; he wanted it. He thought that I didn't love him anymore, which led to a loss of trust in me . . . I became angry and said that if he didn't want this baby, then I didn't want any baby from him. But I swore that he was never going to have sex with me again unless he did something about contraception. I told him that I wanted another baby. He didn't, so it was up to him to do something about it, or else stay away from me. I couldn't have any more abortions.

But the rubbers didn't work satisfactorily; when a man is about to have an orgasm he doesn't think about anything else in the world except coming. So it wasn't a reliable method. I didn't like them either—it's such an artificial method of contraception.

I played courageous and went and had the abortion. I was trying to save my pride and had the abortion in a very angry state. I didn't have time to dig too deeply into my feelings. Later on I felt that I had been stupid. It was my right to have the baby. It was more part of me than of him. If he can make a decision that he doesn't want a child, then I can make a decision that I *do* want it. This only struck me after the abortion. You learn; after each experience in life you learn.

Why did I have the second abortion? More clashes. We still hadn't found a satisfactory method of contraception. I started playing games with myself to convince myself that I didn't really want another baby after all those years. Now, 8 months after the first abortion in the U.S. I was to have another. My husband did try to be kind, but it didn't help. He wanted to be close to me but I was deeply scarred from the first abortion and all the conflict over contraception. I think that he did feel guilty but I believe that he was also in pain himself. Now if the situation were to be mentioned, he would say that it was my decision. He would deny responsibility for the decisions to have the abortions. He might say it was our decision, but more mine—it's as if he would try to block it from his mind. We have never really talked about it, but I think that's what he'd say.

After two abortions I was even more resolute in my stand on abortion and contraception. I was physically weakened by the abortions and became anemic, but I was much stronger mentally. Now I had the courage to fight for what I believed. I think my husband sensed that and he suggested that I might have an operation—that I should have my tubes tied. He thought that would be the best solution. *For him!!* "Why me?" I asked. "Because you don't want children and look what's happening to your health," was his answer. I said that I knew all that, but that we were back to square one—I still felt that it was his responsibility to take the precautions. I told him to think about it. He did. He decided to have a vasectomy. I agreed. It was his decision—he didn't want to have any more children, so it was his decision to make. I still had a question mark as to whether I wanted a third child. I told him that if this situation continued we might well separate and I might decide to have another baby. So I left the choice to him. I told him that he had to prove that it wasn't me that he didn't want to have another child with but that for all the mental and other reasons, he simply didn't want any more children. He asked if I really looked at it like that—he really hadn't understood how strongly I felt on the subject. I said yes. I think that he was a little shocked when I agreed to him having the operation, but he went through with it.

After that our marriage became very much stronger. I went with him to the hospital when he had the vasectomy. He seemed surprised that I agreed to his having it because it was irreversible—my operation wouldn't have been. But I told him that it was he who didn't want to have more children, so it was he who had to take action. Somehow having the vasectomy proved to me that he loved me. He really didn't want to have any more children. We had fears that we might want children in the future and be unable to have them together, but he made his decision and I have felt very much more secure in our relationship as a result.

As Muslims we had no particular religious conflicts regarding the abortions. I was educated religiously that up until 120 days the fetus has no soul—that you are not dealing with a human being up to that point, but rather with what is going to become a human being. My conflict about having the abortions stemmed from my feminine, maternal instinct, not from my religion. I felt grief and loss, not guilt.

The conflict over contraception is universal. Many women shy away from sexual relations after an abortion, not because they love or desire their partner less, but because of fear of becoming pregnant again. Insensitivity by a man to this fear on a woman's part can trigger great anger and hostility in the woman and often signals the breakdown of the relationship. Fatima's remarkably candid interview highlights the tremendous misinterpretations we can make in analyzing the behavior of others, especially those we hold most dear. It is truly a mistake to think you "know" someone. Women frequently tell me that they want their partner to intuitively understand how they feel about pregnancy, abortion, sex, and contraception, without them ever having to voice a thought. That is an unrealistic expectation of men. Women have to articulate how they feel and what they want from their partner, and in turn listen to his needs with understanding. Perhaps the saddest part of loving is that we can't always give loved ones what they need, even if we understand the need and would like to fulfill it. But if we don't even have the chance to understand, then there's no hope at all of fulfillment. Women and men need to try to communicate better on so many subjects, but especially about contraception. Avoiding unplanned pregnancies is a joint responsibility.

7

Doctors and Nurses—Living in the Twilight Zone between Science and Feelings

"Why are doctors who perform abortions in America willing to risk their lives to do abortions?" asked Londoner "Mary" during our phone interview about her experience with RU 486. "To help women," I replied. Throughout my interviews, that has been the universal response of doctors who perform abortions. They care.

Dr. David Grimes, professor and vice chair of the Department of OBGYN, University of California, San Francisco, noted matter-of-factly during our interviews that

> My feelings as a doctor should never interfere with what I do for my patients. There are many aspects of medicine that may not be particularly fun or enjoyable or pleasant, but I have an ethical obligation to do what's best for my patients and not take my own personal convenience into consideration.[1]

Like many abortion providers in the United States, Dr. Grimes has bravely continued serving his patients despite threats against his life.

Dr. Henry Morgentaler, family physician, Morgentaler Clinic in Toronto, Canada, confided:

> To me, there is no conflict or contradiction in a doctor delivering babies as well as performing abortions. In each case, he's helping a patient. That is what you have acquired your

knowledge for and that is what it is your moral obligation to do. . . . I have never had any regrets about performing abortions.[2]

Almost all of the abortion providers interviewed by me cited witnessing the agony suffered by women as a result of botched illegal abortions as a prime motivating factor for their performing abortions. Some acknowledged experiencing personal conflicts about performing abortions, especially in the second trimester, while others, like Dr. Morgentaler, felt no conflicts because they were saving women from being butchered to death.

Suitably qualified doctors who refuse to perform abortions usually object on moral or religious grounds, but more and more are shying away, particularly in the United States, because it is simply too dangerous to perform abortions. The reasons why some doctors who do perform abortions feel conflicts are complex, as revealed in the following interview with Professor J. G. Schenker, Chairman of the Department of Obstetrics and Gynecology at Hadassah University Hospital in Jerusalem, Israel.

> I try to do as few abortions as possible. My interest in gynecology is particularly focused on reproduction. Most of my research and that of my clinic is focused on how to solve the problems of infertile women. On the one hand, we spend so many hours trying to help couples create life and on the other we help women destroy it in five minutes. For me, this creates a definite conflict. But there are two circumstances in which I am always prepared to carry out an abortion in spite of that conflict. One is when the pregnancy endangers the health, both physical and mental, of the woman. The second is when the fetus is malformed. In those two circumstances, it is easy for me to perform an abortion. What is difficult is when a woman comes who is ambivalent in her attitude to her love of her boyfriend and hence her pregnancy. It is very hard to accept any kind of casual attitude to abortion when you spend so much of your time trying to help couples achieve pregnancy.[3]

Professor Schenker's feelings have been echoed particularly by nurses during my research. Watching infertile couples go through the often exasperating process of trying to conceive can be heartbreaking for doctors and nurses. A display of insensitivity or ambivalence on the part of a woman having an abortion can trigger resentment and even hostile behavior toward her. At the time of my first abortion in London in 1984, a friend was desperately trying to get pregnant using every known method of fertility treatment. I couldn't bring myself to tell her that I'd had an abortion, because I thought she might be offended that I was destroying a conception that she was desperately trying to create.

Some women have expressed horror at having an abortion in a ward where women are having babies, recovering from a miscarriage, or undergoing fertility treatment, because they sense resentment from the other women and nurses. An Irish nurse living in London explains how that resentment can be triggered and fester.

Before I first assisted a doctor during an abortion, in 1977, I believed that abortion should never be permitted under any circumstances. It totally went against my very strict Roman Catholic upbringing. But then I realized that there were some circumstances in which abortion seemed justified. Mostly, I assist with abortions performed at between 6 and 12 weeks of pregnancy—I would not assist at 16 weeks. I remember one girl in particular who came in for an abortion. She was about 24, and she'd had five abortions. Quite honestly, when she spoke to me, I couldn't even answer because I was so mad at her. She wasn't sorry or sad. She was to blame, and I just couldn't stand it. I refused to assist on her abortion. I resented her for her lack of feeling about the situation and the fact that she was more than likely going to go out and do exactly the same thing again. All the nurses, even the most hardened ones, resented that girl. Many nurses resent girls coming back for a second time. Sometimes I do, but if she's young I can forgive her a second mistake, and of course, it depends on the circumstances. I try not to judge the girl, but it is difficult not to. For instance, if a girl has been raped, then I feel a lot of sympathy for her. We had one case of a woman who had her tubes tied and still became pregnant, so there was a lot of sympathy for her. It is also acceptable to me if a woman has an abortion for health reasons. . . . It is always kinder to get rid of the pregnancy if it is not wanted. . . . When I handle a fetus, I switch off. . . . We had two women who came and had abortions, then were sewn up afterwards. They were Arab women. To me, that was disgusting and hypocritical. They were both unmarried and came as private patients. They knew they were under threat of death if it was discovered that they were not virgins, so why did they have sex in the first place? To be sewn up afterwards just seems terribly hypocritical to me. I resented the fact that they knew what they were doing when it came to having an abortion, but they didn't seem to know about contraception or abstinence. I don't know why I felt this way, but it was my reaction. . . . Sometimes I feel so hostile to women having abortions. There they lie in hospital beds beside women who are trying desperately to have children, or who are about to have a baby, and they are being blasé about their abortions. That sort of casualness makes me feel nothing but contempt for women.[4]

This nurse certainly is judgmental, even though she tries to be fair. She clearly resents women who seem to her to be casual about abortion and contraception, possibly because she cannot conceive and blames this on an abortion she had after being raped as a young woman.

I began asking doctors and nurses how they felt about abortion after a number of women seeking abortions in London reported encountering hostility from physicians and nurses. I was curious to understand what might cause people in the medical profession to behave in a manner that a patient experienced as hostile. Andrea Butcher, an abortion counselor at the Marie Stopes Clinic in London, has verified that the attitude of the Irish nurse quoted above was not an isolated one.

When I worked for the family planning association a year before my own abortion, part of my job was running courses on abortion awareness for National Health Service nurses who worked on abortion wards. I dealt with both student nurses and experienced staff. There was this predominant idea amongst some nurses that women who had more than one abortion should be punished, which is why it was decided that they needed training in abortion awareness! If someone came in for a second abortion, the nurse would give her a prostaglandin so that the woman "wouldn't do it again." The nurses felt that it was up to them to "teach the woman a lesson." That was a common practice. They would hold women back from having the abortion until they were 12 weeks pregnant and then give them a prostaglandin. This occurred up until as late as 1984. Their attitude was that the women had been told about contraception, they'd had an abortion, so they should know better than to get pregnant again by mistake. There was this feeling that there was something wrong with a woman who got pregnant twice or more by mistake. I would ask them, "Where is this safe, reliable method of contraception with no side effects?"[5]

Underlying a desire to punish a woman for having an abortion is the feeling that she is to blame for the pregnancy and decision to abort, which is very unfair to women. Don't men have a responsibility to take contraceptive precautions too? I myself was warned by a friend in England not to have an abortion on the National Health System, because that would mean a delay in the abortion and having it in a public hospital where she said I would encounter hostility. For some reason, the attitude of nursing staff to a woman having an abortion is generally better in private clinics specializing in abortion than in public hospitals, though the reasons for this vary depending on the culture. Perhaps the most obvious reason is that a nurse working in a private clinic has chosen to work with abortion patients as a vocation, but a nurse in a public hospital may have less choice about her assignments and, if she feels ambivalent, less opportunity to act on her feelings.

It is important to understand that the majority of medical professionals providing abortion services to women do not feel that way—most are caring and sympathetic in attitude. But, some women still do encounter hostility at times, especially among dogmatically religious medical personnel, when abortion is illegal or only recently legalized, and when contraception is available. A startling example of this was reported in the *Los Angeles Times* on April 5, 1992. Canada's Northwest Territories Status of Women Council reported that 85 women had suffered agonizing pain during abortions that were performed without anesthetics at Stanton Yellowknife Hospital. One of the women, who were mostly of Indian and Inuit (Eskimo) ethnicity, reported that as the doctor completed the abortion, he said, "This really hurt, didn't it? But let that be a lesson before you get yourself in this situation again."[6] Another victim who had become pregnant after being raped reported that the abortion had been far worse than the rape. She stated that she had been pinned down during the abortion and had experienced excruciating pain. The victim was given no counseling and no sympathy. One woman who was scheduled to undergo both an abortion and a tubal ligation reported that just before the abortion, she was advised by the doctor that, "The anesthesiologist does not believe in abortions; we will administer the anesthetic following the abortion, for the tubal ligation."[6] It is hard to control one's anger at people who inflict that kind of suffering on others because of a personal belief. Medical personnel who feel strongly against abortion should not be in any way involved with the procedure, and they certainly should not be in a position to administer so-called treatment to vulnerable women.

Great opposition to abortion even when it is legal can put medical personnel under pressure, and in turn cause them to seem distant at times when perhaps they really do care, but are preoccupied with their own problems. In Eastern European countries, most contraceptive methods are unpopular or unavailable, so many women have more than 20 abortions. The coolness of medical personnel to women's suffering in countries such as Russia stems more from insensitivity to their pain rather than from hostility to the women for returning over and over again for abortions.

Dr. Bernard Nathanson now regrets having performed abortions.

> I ran the largest abortion clinic in the world for 2 years. I had no conflicts whatsoever at the time I was doing the abortions. I changed my mind because the new scientific data which we were getting from advanced technology persuaded me that we could not indiscriminately continue to slaughter what was demonstrably a human being.[7]

If the fetus in its early stages of development was so "demonstrably a human being" as Dr. Nathanson asserts, there would be no debate over abortion.

Congressman Roy Rowland, M.D. was the Democratic Representative for mid/southern Georgia in the United States when I interviewed him in 1986. I was curious to know how a physician who was also a politician would view abortion. He had been active as a politician for about 10 years at the time of our interview.

> The two abortions which I performed while working as a doctor were done during the first trimester of the pregnancy. In both situations, after consultation with my colleagues, the family, and the patient, I felt that the mother very definitely was in danger . . . so I felt there was a good reason for each abortion and did not experience any personal conflict in performing them. My position is that there are instances in which abortion is possibly justified, such as in cases of rape, incest, or when the health of the mother is in danger. . . . The decision to have an abortion rests between the woman who is pregnant, her physician, and God. It's a personal decision. . . . Abortion should not under any circumstances be used as a method of contraception. I find that most people in my constituency generally feel the same way. . . . Abortion should be legal but I don't think that there should be abor-

tion on demand; once a fetus is at the point where it can live independently of the mother, there should be no question of performing an abortion. But earlier is a gray area . . . It distresses me that the Court became involved in this issue; I don't think that the Court should have become involved, and Congress shouldn't become involved either—it is not a politician's business to decide whether a woman should have an abortion . . .[8]

Ideally, politicians and judges shouldn't be involved in the debate on abortion, at least not as professionals. Abortion should not be illegal or legal. It is a medical procedure that should be monitored for safety by the medical profession.

During our interview, Dr. Bertram Wainer indicated that if women were ever treated badly again in Australia and denied the right to have a safe abortion, then his passion for the cause of legalizing abortion would once again become aroused. That passion was originally born of a combination of compassion for women and anger at those who would harm women by forcing them to have dangerous, illegal abortions.

My whole professional training was to prolong life, to nurture and protect it. Abortion is clearly at odds with that ethos. . . . I have never refused to perform an abortion because of any personal conflict. I have postponed abortions because I felt the women needed more time to think about them. I remember one woman said to me that if I didn't perform the operation she would go home and do it herself (she was a Catholic nurse) and that if it went wrong then I would be to blame. I had point-blank refused to perform the operation. Confronted with that sort of emotional blackmail I immediately said yes. All my patients receive a consumer evaluation form to send back two weeks after the abortion. It asks various questions such as "Do you regret the decision?" and other questions of that nature. The Catholic nurse wrote that she was a bloody murderer and that I was one too. She wrote in red ink and said that God would punish us both.

I remember talking to one couple for many hours. They had no good reasons for having an abortion. They were married, financially secure, professionally settled, and wanted eventually to have a family. Their only reason for wanting an abortion was fear of becoming parents. They wanted an abortion the same day that they came to the Clinic. I felt very strongly that it was not the right decision, so I made them come back another day to give them time to think about the decision. In the end they decided to have their baby and were thrilled with it. . . . I never refuse to perform an abortion, but I do procrastinate in order to give the woman time to think very carefully about what she wants so that when the time comes she knows exactly, and will hopefully not regret the decision.

I have never felt hostile to a woman seeking an abortion. I think that if a woman comes for her 100th abortion it would probably be an injustice to foist her as a mother upon a child. (I did have a Yugoslavian woman come to me who had had 24 abortions, mainly in Yugoslavia where abortion is considered a method of contraception. She didn't know any other way. We taught her about alternative methods of contraception. I never felt any hostility towards her for having so many abortions.) People make the allegation that women who have unwanted pregnancies are "stupid" or irresponsible. Were that to be the case it is the last reason to be punitive and to force maternity on such persons.

I sometimes get upset by the aggression which I am confronted with in a woman . . . a general hostility which some women feel towards men. A woman finds herself pregnant, the man accuses her of tricking him, or implies that he can't be sure it's his, or he simply doesn't want to know and so he's off and she's on her own. She comes to our Clinic and is confronted by another man. She hasn't had sex with him but she is on her guard all the same—men aren't to be trusted in her view. She is so angry. You can feel it, like a wave of fury beating against you, merely because you're a male. I do understand why they get angry, and I don't judge, but sometimes I feel crotchety when they take their bitterness with life and bitchiness out on me. Doctors get ulcers because they know that they can't take their frustrations in life out on their patients! Sometimes I wish that more patients did likewise!

No man knows what it's like to be pregnant or to have an abortion. We are dealing with people who are equal but different. How can I judge the women coming to me? Judges and politicians may think they can, but I don't think that judgment is mine to make. I'm sure that there have been doctors involved in performing abortions who have hated women. From my own historical research I have learned of a lot of exploitation of women both physically and financially. There was a lot of unnecessary brutality in the early days. If you felt at all sadistic towards women, that was an area where you had them totally in your power.[9]

The later the abortion, the stronger the conflict a physician may feel. Dr. Lawrence Scott explains:

I don't like to perform abortions after 16–17 weeks. It's an emotional thing with me, not medical. I don't like to see fetal parts. When I start to see little hands come out, it bothers me, even though I know the fetus is not completely developed and cannot feel any pain. It just bothers me. In the early 70s, when I first started doing abortions, we didn't have ultrasound. I was doing an abortion on a woman whom I thought was 16 weeks pregnant, but during the procedure, I discovered that she was in fact 22–23 weeks pregnant. That shocked me. I have confined my abortion activity to the first trimester for a long time now as a result. I totally adore and love children, so when I see these little body parts, I start seeing kids, and it bothers me. And you know the probability is that if the pregnancy is left alone, you are talking about a person in a matter of 2 or 3 or 4 months.[10]

Dr. Scott's feelings about performing abortions in the second trimester have been echoed by many of the doctors I interviewed. They all feel more comfortable from a medical and ethical point of view if the abortion is done in the first trimester. The doctors also stressed that it is far safer for a woman to have an abortion in the first 12 weeks of pregnancy.

It appears that a combination of compassion for women and anger at militant anti-abortion fanatics motivates those brave American doctors who are now risking their lives in order to perform abortions, particularly in extremely anti-abortion states such as North Dakota. Dr. Susan Wicklund has been forced to hire security guards to protect her from members of the Lambs of Christ, an extreme anti-abortion group that regularly and systematically harasses her in an attempt to dissuade her from flying into North Dakota from Minnesota in order to perform abortions. No local doctor is willing to risk his life or the safety of his family in order to perform abortions there. Dr. Wicklund expressed enormous anger, as well as great courage, during a 1992 interview broadcast on "60 Minutes" — anger that she had to risk her life in order to provide a service to women that she believes they have a right to receive since abortion *is* legal in the United States. Fifty doctors refused to appear on that "60 Minutes" episode for fear of reprisal by antiabortion groups. It was estimated in that same program that only about 50% of doctors who formerly performed abortions in the United States are still performing them. It is believed that most stopped out of fear for their lives and the safety of their families.

Dr. Warren Hearn is one of three doctors in the United States who is still willing to perform late abortions. He works behind four layers of bulletproof glass in his office in Boulder, Colorado. His life has been threatened, his car has been tampered with, and demonstrators have tried to run him over. In 1988, five shots were fired at him. Like Dr. Wicklund, he refuses to be bullied into not performing abortions, and he is outraged that militant psychological terrorists are successfully intimidating doctors. He too is both angry and compassionate, and he is incredibly brave.

Northern Nevada's only abortion clinic for 200,000 square miles is run by Dr. Damon Stutes. The clinic is a high-tech fortress that was built after Dr. Stutes' former clinic in downtown Reno was firebombed four times. Dr. Stutes recalled his response to those firebombings in an article by Margot Hornblower that appeared in *Time* magazine on January 9, 1995. "I was mad as hell—and afraid."[11] Despite his fear he has continued performing abortions for the same reason that he began performing them: to protect women from being killed by illegal abortions. He has never forgotten the two 12-year-old girls in his hometown of Lansing, Michigan, who died after illegal abortions. "With me, it is primal. . . . Abortion is a lifesaving operation." Dr. Stutes and his wife Lynne, who helps run the clinic, fortunately managed to save enough money to build the fortress, but sadly, most abortion providers aren't in a position to invest that kind of money in security systems. Many are presently involved in campaigns to raise money for increased security, which is now considered an operational cost.

Physicians are dedicated to the preservation of life. Abortion presents an inherent conflict because it involves stopping a life from developing. Most physicians who perform abortions resolve this conflict by focusing on their role as healer and provider of a medical service that benefits the physical and mental health of women and saves them from the perils of a "back alley" abortion. For some physicians this is not enough justification for an abortion, and eventually they are forced by their conscience to stop performing abortions, or else to participate only in very selective cases. The later the abortion, the stronger the conflict and moral doubt become.

If you are contemplating an abortion, try to understand that physicians and nurses are human beings, not gods, and that as a patient, you should seek out a physician with a positive attitude about performing abortions. The best way to do that is to contact a major organization such as Planned Parenthood in the United States for a referral to a clinic or physician (see "Help" Directory).

I hope that those American doctors presently being terrorized by religious fanatics derive some solace from the knowledge that they are working to save lives, a very important and noble cause. At a time when abortion clinics and their staff in the United States are being subjected to bombings, arson, assault and battery, death threats, stalking, burglary, vandalism, and murder, it is especially important that the courageous doctors who perform abortions and their support staff receive our heartfelt thanks.

8

RU 486 and Methotrexate—Abortifacients that Offer an Alternative to Surgical Abortion

RU 486 (mifepristone) and methotrexate are abortifacients that offer a safe alternative to surgical abortion in early pregnancy. (An abortifacient is a drug, or device, that causes abortion.) Although each drug can be used alone, they are more effective when used in conjunction with a prostaglandin.

The main advantages of medical abortion are that it can be performed very early in the pregnancy when it has a higher success rate than surgical abortion; it is not invasive; it requires no anesthesia; there is no risk of perforation of the uterus or injury to the cervix; recovery is faster; the side effects are usually milder; it seems more like a "natural" miscarriage than an abortion; it gives women the feeling that they have more control over their body and awareness during the procedure. RU 486 can also be used as an emergency contraceptive or morning-after pill.

Some women prefer surgical abortion because they will be less conscious of the abortion and the passing of blood, tissue, and the embryo or fetus; the procedure is over in about 10–15 minutes; there are fewer office visits required.

RU 486 was developed in 1980 by French physician Dr. Etienne-Emile Baulieu and fellow researchers. Since the first trials in 1981, more than 130,000 women in France have medically terminated pregnancies using RU 486 alone or in combination with a synthetic vaginal or oral prostaglandin. In 1992, France switched to the oral prostaglandin Cytotec (misoprostol), because it has fewer side effects in their experience than vaginal prostaglandin, and is easier to administer. RU 486 has been legalized in England, Sweden, and China, and there have been extensive trials around the world, including in the United States, with a view to legalizing it in other countries.

Methotrexate was first used as an abortifacient in 1952.[1] It has been used in Brazil and many developing countries as an abortifacient, but under uncontrolled conditions. In the United States and other countries, it is used fairly widely as a medical treatment for unruptured tubal pregnancies. It is also used in the treatment of malignant tumors of the placenta and other malignancies, as well as some leukemias, rheumatoid arthritis, and psoriasis. Trials of methotrexate as an abortifacient for normal pregnancies have been conducted in British Columbia, New York (University of Rochester), Pittsburgh, San Francisco, and Kansas City. Others are underway as this book goes to press.

There is one very important difference between RU 486 and methotrexate for American women. Methotrexate is legally available in the United States, while RU 486 has not been approved by the FDA, and may well never be approved because of political opposition. Of course there will be just as much political opposition to methotrexate as there is to RU 486 once it becomes widely known that methotrexate is available and being used as an abortifacient, but little can be done to stop methotrexate's use because of its prior approval by the FDA. (Once a drug is approved, it can be used for any medical purpose by a physician.)

RU 486 (mifepristone) is an antiprogestin that blocks the action of the natural hormone progesterone, which prepares the lining of the uterus for a fertilized egg. Pregnancy cannot occur or be maintained without progesterone, because the lining of the uterus softens and breaks down, thus bringing on menstruation. Taken alone, it is about 80% effective in terminating pregnancy within a few days of administration. RU 486 is effective as an abortifacient only in the early stages of pregnancy because the ovaries produce progesterone at that stage. By 9–10 weeks of gestation, the placenta produces progesterone in greater amounts, resulting in the RU 486 antiprogestins being "outnumbered" by the natural hormone. RU 486 is taken orally in tablet form.

Methotrexate is an antimetabolite that inhibits dihydrofolic acid reductase, thus interfering with DNA synthesis, repair, and cellular replication. Pregnancy is terminated because fetal cell growth is impaired. Taken alone, methotrexate is effective as an abortifacient, but it works slowly, which could be considered a disadvantage. (It could take up to 3 or 4 weeks after the administration of methotrexate for bleeding to begin.) The success rate using a combination of methotrexate and vaginal misoprostol appears to be about 95%, the same as for RU 486 combined with oral misoprostol. This combination also works considerably faster than methotrexate alone. The success rate using methotrexate and misoprostol may in fact be even higher: if the women were left alone to abort without medical intervention by concerned physicians during trials, they would probably all eventually abort. Methotrexate used alone to treat early ectopic (tubal) pregnancies has been shown to be 94% effective. It is administered by injection and is considered safe and effective as an abortifacient up to 56 days after the last menstrual period began.

Prostaglandins cause contractions of the uterus, and are naturally released from the lining of the womb during menstruation. Misoprostol (Cytotec is the trade name) is presently the most favored synthetic oral prostaglandin being used in combination with RU 486, largely because it has fewer side effects. It is usually taken 36–48 hours after RU 486, or administered vaginally 3–5 days after methotrexate. Some countries still use a vaginal prostaglandin with RU 486 (gemeprost is favored) or administer it by injection. When used with RU 486, misoprostol increases the success rate of termination from around 80% to 95%, if used within 49 days after the last menstrual period began. The success rate of RU 486 with misoprostol decreases between 49 and 63 days after the last menstrual period. (About 1% of failures represent continuing pregnancies, and the other 4% are incomplete abortions that have failed to lead to expulsion of the embryo.)

It is recommended that a surgical abortion be performed if medical abortion using RU 486 or methotrexate is incomplete or the pregnancy is not interrupted. There have been cases of pregnancy continued to term after a failed abortion using RU 486 combined with a prostaglandin. The women changed their minds when they discovered that they were still pregnant and refused to have the recommended surgical abortion. All but one delivered normal babies. The exception was a woman who underwent a sonogram in the second trimester that revealed fetal abnormalities. She then had a surgical abortion. It is not known whether RU 486 or the prostaglandin caused the fetal abnormalities, because congenital abnormalities occur "naturally" in 6% of newborns (1% are very serious and 2–4% are considered serious to minor; the other 1% are very minor defects.)

As methotrexate is known to cause severe fetal abnormalities, it is essential that a surgical abortion be performed if methotrexate fails to completely terminate the pregnancy. The drug's manufacturer (Lederle) recommends that pregnancy be avoided for at least one ovulatory cycle after taking methotrexate. The drug has been used effectively for years in the treatment of gestational trophoblastic neoplasia, but no problems with future fertility or congenital abnormalities in subsequent pregnancies were detected, according to an article by Dr. Mitchell D. Creinin that appeared in the October 19, 1994, edition of the *Journal of the American Medical Association*.[2]

Mifepristone is a widely tolerated drug but it is contraindicated for women who are suspected of having an ectopic pregnancy or adrenal deficiency. Dr. Etienne-Emile Baulieu cautions:

About 5 in 1000 pregnancies (0.5%) are ectopic. The rate of ectopic pregnancies is increasing because of sexually transmitted diseases. If ectopic pregnancy is not detected, the woman goes through a disaster, regardless of whether or not she uses RU 486, because it will rupture with heavy internal hemorrhaging. The contraindication to use of RU 486 for ectopic pregnancies is not because of RU 486 itself, but because of the danger of ectopic pregnancy. This is why I insist that a woman should be medically examined if she wants an abortion of any kind, surgical or medical. Ectopic pregnancy presents a great risk. Prostaglandins have some contraindications in their own right, but millions of people already take misoprostol for duodenal ulcers and it is well tolerated. Prior spontaneous miscarriage is not a contraindication for use of RU 486.[3]

In the United States, it is hoped that widely available early medical abortion will diffuse opposition to abortion because any general practitioner could prescribe and administer the drugs, making it virtually impossible for protesters to detect where or when women are having abortions. Although that may be true, some pro-choice general practitioners have told me that while they welcome the possibility of widely available medical abortion, they would refer a woman to a gynecologist for treatment rather than risk error resulting from their inexperience in gynecology. Small-town GPs might be more willing to take that risk, however, as they tend to have more experience with pregnancy and associated complications than "big-city" physicians who refer pregnant patients to gynecologists.

In England, the following contraindications are listed in a 1994 publication by the Birth Control Trust as applying to mifepristone (RU 486) and prostaglandin combined, although they probably in reality apply to prostaglandin rather than RU 486: pregnancy of 64 days or greater; chronic adrenal failure; long-term corticosteroid therapy; rheumatic fever; known allergy to mifepristone; hemorrhagic disorders; treatment with anticoagulants; smokers over 35 years of age. The same publication also notes that caution should be used in treating patients with asthma, chronic obstructive airway disease, cardiovascular risk factors, renal or hepatic failure, prosthetic heart valves, and pregnancies of 56–63 days amenorrhea.[4] Other articles suggest that it is important for diabetics to inform the doctor of their condition before taking RU 486. The side effects of RU 486 range from none to light uterine bleeding as well as symptoms similar to those of normal pregnancy: nausea, headache, weakness, and fatigue. (It is impossible to distinguish if these symptoms are caused by the pregnancy or RU 486.)

According to the manufacturer, methotrexate is contraindicated for women who are nursing or who have a history of hepatitis, chronic liver disease, ongoing kidney disease, alcoholism, immunodeficiency syndromes, bone marrow hypoplasia, leukopenia, thrombocytopenia, or significant anemia. In addition, Dr. Mitchell Creinin noted in an article in the December, 1993, edition of *Contraception* that women who have taken prenatal vitamins or medications containing folate, who have a history of inflammatory bowel disease, or a known intolerance of methotrexate have been excluded from studies of methotrexate.[5] The side effects of methotrexate taken in the small dosage required to abort a pregnancy appear to be negligible based on studies to date, but according to the manufacturer, they may range from none to nausea, fatigue, dizziness, chills and fever, leukopenia, decreased resistance to infection, malaise, and ulcerative stomatitis. No drug-related symptoms were reported in the medical literature when methotrexate was used to treat ectopic pregnancies. Some women have complained of headache, dizziness, nausea, vomiting, and difficulty sleeping after taking methotrexate to abort a pregnancy, but as these can also be symptoms of "morning sickness", it has not been definitively proven that methotrexate caused the symptoms.

The side effects of prostaglandins can include nausea, vomiting, diarrhea, hot flushes, hypotension, cramps and abdominal pain on the level of a very heavy period, uterine bleeding similar to a heavy period that lasts for about 1 week, or bleeding and spotting that are not heavy but last for 1–3 weeks. Prostaglandins with or without RU 486 and methotrexate are contraindicated for women with a history of asthma and chronic pulmonary disease, or who are over 35 and smoke heavily, because prostaglandins can cause cardiovascular problems.

For the record, according to Dr. Etienne-Emile Baulieu, "There has never been a cardiovascular reaction to RU 486. The reactions recorded have been to the prostaglandin Sulprostone."[3] (There was one abortion-related death after an injection of Sulprostone in a 31-year-old woman who was a heavy smoker in her 13th pregnancy. She suffered cardiac arrest and died several hours later. Two other women who were heavy smokers over 35 also had cardiovascular problems after an injection of Sulprostone, but recovered completely. Sulprostone is no longer recommended for use with RU 486, even though the risk factor is considered very low, 1 in 20,000.)

When new forms of medical treatment are discovered, there is often controversy. Never has that been truer than in the cases of RU 486 and methotrexate. It is easy to get caught up in controversy and debate over the ethics of abortion, forgetting that real people are faced with making decisions about abortion that are intensely personal and divorced from academic debate.

"I was terrified of a surgical abortion ... [and] terrified of keeping the kid," said a Los Angeles woman, one of nearly 400 women who participated in the initial trials of RU 486 at Los Angeles' County–USC Medical Center's Women's Hospital between 1984 and 1990. She was the mother of 11-month-old twins and didn't feel able to cope with another child at that time. Fear of infection during a surgical abortion was a strong factor in her choice of medical abortion. She was 5 weeks pregnant when

> I ... took three little [RU 486] pills ... on Tuesday. On Thursday, I started bleeding, little spots. Friday morning, I went back for the shot of prostaglandin, which helps to expel the fetal matter. They make you wait half an hour after the shot before you can leave. And they tell you to get someone to drive you home. My husband drove me ... After I got home, I started cramping. It was really minor cramping. And to my amazement, it only lasted two hours. That day, I aborted. The matter came out on two sanitary napkins. You couldn't really tell if it was fetal tissue. It just looked like a heavy menstrual period. I bled for a total of 10 days. I had so little pain—only two hours of pain in the whole thing, but I was also dizzy for several days.

I felt my head was encased in cotton balls and I was very sleepy. . . . Physically, taking the pills was a dream. But emotionally, I was very angry . . . I had weeping fits. Sometimes I'd just look at my kids. My husband was depressed about it too. He loves kids. His way of dealing with it was not talking about it. But he supported my decision 100%. . . .[6]

Many women have a misconception that using "a pill" to abort is easier than having a surgical abortion. Emotionally, medical abortion can be just as distressing as surgical abortion. Physically, it seems to be easier for some women, especially if the pregnancy is aborted very early.

"Mary" had a medical abortion with RU 486 in London.

My first abortion, at age 19, was surgical. I chose RU 486 for my second abortion at the age of 34 because I saw it as less intrusive and somehow a more natural process. I aborted after the [RU 486] tablet, so there was no need for me to go to the clinic for the [prostaglandin] pessary. It's never easy to make a decision to have an abortion, and I can't say that the RU 486 abortion was a pleasant procedure. But I was only a week overdue, so the abortion wasn't in any way painful— it was more like having a heavy period. I didn't need to take any pain medication. After the RU 486 abortion, I found it easier to return to my life quicker. I do a lot of horse riding, and after my surgical abortion, I didn't want to ride for 6–7 weeks, but with RU 486, I was able to get on a horse a day later. After my surgical abortion my belly felt tender for a couple of weeks, but after the RU 486 abortion I felt absolutely no ill effects at all. There was no difference for me emotionally. . . . After I took the RU 486 pill at the clinic, I sat there for 2 hours, during which time nothing really happened and I didn't feel anything. After I got home, I cried and felt sad. Although it wasn't the right time for me, the potential for a child was there, and that was why I felt sad . . . my tears and sadness came on completely spontaneously and lasted for about half an hour. When I had my surgical abortion, I felt the same sort of feeling when I came out of the anesthetic—a sense of loss.

When I went in to the clinic on the day that I was supposed to take the [prostaglandin] pessary, I told the nurse that I was pretty certain that I had aborted. The nurse asked, "Did you see the fetus?" I was stunned by the question because I had no idea that I was expected to see a fetus at the end of the first week of pregnancy. I saw tissue, but I didn't make a connection with a fetus. At 9 weeks, there would be a fetus, so I think I would be more squeamish about having an RU 486 abortion at that stage, because seeing an aborted fetus would make the abortion more real to me. It would look more like an unformed child as opposed to tissue. At that stage I think I'd opt for a surgical abortion.

The only disconcerting aspect of the whole process of the RU 486 abortion was that the doctor was uncertain from my description that I had in fact aborted after the first pill. I was unable to articulate it in a way that he could understand, but as it turned out, I was right. The idea that I had to go back two weeks later to check if I had aborted, and that I might have to undergo a surgical abortion, was disconcerting. The doctor didn't help in the process of determining whether I had aborted; he didn't give me any guidance. It was left up to me to figure out if I'd aborted. I would have liked a little more feedback. It was my call whether to take the [prostaglandin] pessary. I chose not to take it, because I felt certain that I had aborted. I asked the doctor whether he was going to examine me, but he declined, saying that there was nothing he could tell me because the pregnancy was so early.

During the RU 486 abortion, I felt like hibernating in a dark room by myself and nesting. Although I've heard that some women feel that an RU 486 abortion brings them closer to their partner, I didn't experience this reaction. While my lover was very supportive, he really didn't know how to respond sometimes. He wasn't sure whether I wanted to be left alone. I think it was difficult for both of us, because it's hard to know how to respond in such a situation. Having a supportive partner certainly makes having an abortion a lot easier.

If I became pregnant by mistake again, I would definitely chose an RU 486 abortion, because it's less intrusive, and you can get back to your life quicker. If my experience with RU 486 had been very painful, however, I think I'd be a coward the next time and opt for a surgical abortion.[7]

The nurse who asked "Mary" if she had seen the fetus was wrong to have asked that question, because at that stage of pregnancy there would not be a fetus, and the embryo would be so small as to be indistinguishable. Many women find medical abortion appealing because it is less intrusive. It is interesting to note that "Mary" underwent both a surgical and a medical abortion, and found no difference emotionally between them. Physically, there was a huge difference, possibly because her pregnancy was more advanced when she had the surgical abortion. Hormones are thrown into reverse regardless of the type of abortion, which may account for the similarity of emotional responses to the abortions. Fear of seeing an embryo or fetus is a strong factor in some women not choosing medical abortion. It is extremely important that medical staff communicate well with women undergoing a medical abortion, because bleeding alone at home, possibly in pain, and then expelling an embryo or fetus could be traumatic if the woman is not properly prepared.

A 26-year-old French Catholic woman confided that she chose RU 486 because she felt that it would be

less traumatic and more like a medical treatment. . . . I just had a baby girl 5 months ago. I thought that this second pregnancy was too close to the first, so for the well-being of my baby and our family I chose to have an abortion.[8]

Medical abortion is generally perceived as more natural and less painful.

Another French Catholic woman, a 22-year-old student, wrote that she chose RU 486 because "I was afraid of surgery and it could be done earlier, nobody touched me, there was no anesthesia and no dilation."[9] The negative aspect of the experience was that "between RU and the prostaglandin I had to wait alone. You never really know when you are going to expel."[9]

When women were asked by me whether they would prefer a surgical or a medical abortion (provided both were safe), most chose an early medical abortion. In France, 80% of eligible women (less than 49 days of amenorrhea) now choose medical abortion using RU 486. One Australian woman exclaimed:

> If I had a choice between a medical or a surgical abortion, I'd definitely take the pill! The whole process of going into a hospital and all the procedure that one has to go through for a surgical abortion, lying there on the bed, going into surgery, having the suction done—it's traumatic and horrible. I remember thinking before my abortion, "Oh God, don't let me die because I'm doing this." I was scared that I was about to have an abortion and that I wouldn't come out of it. After the abortion, they couldn't bring me out of the anesthesia—I had never had any history of problems with anesthesia—I just didn't seem to want to come back to consciousness, perhaps because I didn't want to have the abortion. I wanted my boyfriend's baby, but he said that he wouldn't stay with me if I didn't have the abortion. I thought that having the abortion would help keep us together. I think the guilt we both felt about the abortion contributed to our eventual divorce three years after we married.[10]

Ambivalence about an abortion can cause serious problems, both physical and emotional. Often, that ambivalence stems from problems in a relationship rather than from concern about the abortion itself. Having an abortion to keep a relationship together usually signals the end of the relationship.

Not everyone has a positive experience with RU 486. According to a British woman who had two RU 486 abortions in February and May, 1992,

The first time didn't seem to affect me at all . . . I was unaf-
fected physically by it. . . . The second time was awful. I
would not want my worst enemy to go through what I had
to go through. There was an extreme amount of bleeding
from the time I took the tablets to when I had the pessary. . . .
I was wiped out for three or four weeks. . . . But I didn't regret having that method again for the second time, because
I just felt so in control. That was very important for me . . . I
actually wanted to feel the pain . . . [and] experience my body
rejecting the fetus. . . . I think it's had quite a strengthening
affect on me mentally. The big drawback was having to be
in a ward with women who were desperate for children, who
had had numerous miscarriages, who were having infertility treatment. . . .[11]

This woman wanted to be in control of her abortion and "learn"
from the pain and reality of witnessing the fetus being expelled,
as if that would act as a deterrent to her becoming pregnant again.
Even if she was meticulous in her future use of contraception,
whatever she learned from the pain would not help her prevent a
future pregnancy with 100% centainty unless she gave up sexual
intercourse. Pain should never be welcomed as a punishment for
an abortion.

Another British woman recalled the following experience:

I chose medical abortion because I was frightened of invasive surgery. I was fearful of infection if I did have surgery,
and the chances, although they are very small, of not being
able to have children in the future. . . . I felt I would be far
more in control . . . [and] it seemed a more natural way for
my body to stop being pregnant—more like a miscarriage. . . . I felt I would recover faster. . . . I'd decided on an
abortion and I wanted to get it done as soon as possible. . . .
I was about six weeks pregnant. . . . Any longer would have
made the decision to terminate that much more difficult. It
was also important that my partner could be with me over
the weekend that I took the pills and I went into hospital.

That was important for both of us. . . . The weekend was fine. Having taken the tablets, I felt quite liberated. I felt free of my pregnancy even though I hadn't actually got rid of it at that point . . . The nurses were lovely . . . I felt some grumblings of pain and tried to ignore it. It got worse and worse and I took some tablets, but for some reason I had a very severe reaction and felt like I was going into labor . . . I had a very difficult time. In the end, because I was writhing around so much they took me down to surgery and I had a surgical abortion . . . I recovered very quickly. . . . I still have the idea that medical abortion is good, and if it happened again I'd still think it was a preferable method, but I'd have to be certain I wasn't going to get as much pain.[12]

Unfortunately, there is no guarantee about the degree of pain that will occur after any kind of abortion, surgical or medical.

Although RU 486 is not available in the United States, Dr. David Grimes, chief of the Department of Obstetrics and Gynecology at San Francisco General Hospital, noted in our telephone interview that

Among the few hundred women in Los Angeles who had experience with RU 486, the large majority were quite enthusiastic about having access to the drug. We know that most of the women who participated in the study of RU 486 had undergone one or more prior suction curettage abortions and most didn't like the experience. Most thought that the RU 486 abortion was preferable, but this was a self-selected population, so they can't be considered a random sampling of the population. You can't generalize at all from this data.[13]

Dr. Grimes may be correct from a scientific point of view when he says that we shouldn't generalize from samples of women who chose to participate in a scientific trial, but the fact that they want to participate at all seems significant to me.

I have not heard reports of any difficulty recruiting women for medical abortion trials anywhere in the world. The World

Health Organization is conducting trials of RU 486 all over the world at present and has no difficulty finding women willing to undergo medical abortion. Surely that says that women everywhere are interested in the possibility of having medical abortion available to them. Lawrence Lader noted in his book *RU 486* that the Chinese have synthesized their own "RU 486" and in the first trials on 2000 women, 80% preferred medical abortion to suction aspiration, largely because they felt less pain, recovered faster, and there was less psychological pressure.[14]

In England and Sweden, women have been using RU 486 to terminate pregnancy since late 1991. In the ensuing years, there have been well over 20,000 medical abortions in the two countries combined. To date, both have mainly used the vaginal prostaglandin gemeprost, but they have also begun using oral prostaglandin. Unlike France, where RU 486 is used until 49 days of amenorrhea, women in England and Sweden are able to obtain medical abortion using RU 486 until 63 days of amenorrhea. (Amenorrhea literally means an abnormal absence of menstruation, but the 49–63 days are actually counted from the beginning of the last menstrual period.)

Dr. Elizabeth Aubeny at the Broussais Hospital in Paris cautions:

> In France, women can have an abortion with RU 486 only until 49 days of amenorrhea. At this stage of the pregnancy, the embryo does not look like a fetus—it looks more like a tiny egg. . . . During the 14 days between 49 and 63 days, the embryo changes greatly. By 63 days it looks more like a fetus. That is one reason why we only use RU 486 up until 49 days in France—because women don't want to see the fetus. The other reason is that between 49 and 63 days of amenorrhea, the rate of success with RU 486 decreases a lot. RU 486 used before 49 days of amenorrhea with an oral prostaglandin is less painful than when it is taken with a vaginal prostaglandin. In France, 20% of women report no pain at all after using RU 486 in conjunction with an oral prostaglandin; 20% have pain that needs medication; 60%

have pain similar to that experienced during menstruation that lasts up to 1 hour. . . .[15]

As a lay person, I find it difficult to understand why the world medical community doesn't pay more attention to the French experience with RU 486, which has been well monitored and reported extensively in the medical literature. After researching this chapter, I most definitely would not recommend that women use RU 486 after 49 days of amenorrhea, even if it is available up to 63 days of amenorrhea. The French data are simply too powerful to ignore. Most trials around the world permit women to participate up to 63 days of amenorrhea, for reasons beyond me.

When I asked Dr. Aubeny whether she felt there was a moral difference between medical and surgical abortion, she replied:

> I do not believe that there is a moral difference between surgical and medical abortion. For women, it is the same, it is an abortion. . . . When we started using RU 486, people said that women will think that the abortion is nothing—that it is not an abortion. But that is not true. When women use RU 486, they are very involved in the abortion. They know exactly what happens and they are more in control. When a woman has a surgical abortion under general anesthesia, she doesn't know anything about what's going on during the procedure.[15]

Dr. Aubeny, Dr. Grimes, and the many other physicians interviewed by me may be right when they say that there is no moral difference between surgical and medical abortion, but I believe that some people do perceive medical abortion, particularly very early in the pregnancy, as more like a "natural" miscarriage. Although they may be more aware of the medical abortion procedure at the time, I have the impression that some women, in perceiving medical abortion as being more natural, may feel relieved of the full burden of responsibility for the abortion. Objectively of course, they are responsible, but psychologically, "just taking a pill" can make a significant difference to the woman, and her partner if he is involved.

In the first two weeks after conception, one could argue very strongly that use of RU 486 is less morally concerning. Surgical abortion is not an option at that stage, but RU 486 can be used as an emergency contraceptive after fertilization has occurred but before pregnancy is established. U.S. obstetrician and gynecologist Dr. David A. Grimes explains:

> Once fertilization takes place, most doctors don't consider pregnancy has been established until about two weeks later, when the fertilized egg has traveled through the Fallopian tubes to the uterus and implanted itself.[13]

If you're devoutly against abortion and see it as murder from conception on, then that first two weeks won't make a difference to your moral views. But to women who are uncertain about the point at which they might begin to feel a moral conflict, if at all, those first two weeks could make a big difference. Blocking a fertilized egg from becoming established in the uterus could be viewed as morally very different than halting an already established pregnancy, because it may be perceived as more like contraception than abortion. Preventing conception is morally acceptable to many people who oppose abortion, so that distinction could be profound.

In the United States and other countries, such as Poland, where there is passionate political opposition to abortion, this strong pressure has thus far discouraged Roussel-Uclaf, the French manufacturer of RU 486, from making the drug commercially available. After the initial U.S. trials of RU 486 from 1984 to 1990 in Los Angeles (at County–USC Medical Center's Women's Hospital) caused such a furor, Roussel-Unclaf was unwilling to provide RU 486 for further trials, because it did not see a "safe" market for the drug in the United States and didn't want to run the risk of their other products being boycotted.

Since pro-choice Bill Clinton defeated strongly anti-abortion President George Bush in the 1992 presidential election, Roussel-Uclaf had a change of heart, because it saw a healthier political climate emerging regarding abortion. In one of those brilliant lateral mind leaps that men make when trying to solve seemingly insoluble problems, the company donated the formula for RU 486 to the New York-based nonprofit, nongovernmental research organization, The Population Council. As I write, up to 2000 women are participating in The Population Council-sponsored trials that are under way around the United States, though ironically RU 486 for the trials had to be obtained outside the country because as yet no U.S. pharmaceutical company has agreed to manufacture the drug. Data from these trials will be submitted to the U.S. Food and Drug Administration (FDA) in a bid to get the drug approved for use here. It is hoped that these studies will reinforce French data regarding the safety, effectiveness, and acceptability of RU 486. The current U.S. trials are also investigating whether RU 486 should be available for termination of pregnancy up to 63 days of amenorrhea in the United States (like England and Sweden) rather than 49 days, as is the case in France.

The World Health Organization (WHO) also has ongoing RU 486 trials around the world, including in the United States. They are investigating the use of RU 486 as an emergency contraceptive (without a prostaglandin) and as an abortifacient. The WHO has supported or organized about 60 studies on mifepristone since 1983, in over 20 different countries. Dr. Helena von Hertzen and Dr. Paul Van Look, WHO researchers, believe that RU 486 has potential as an anti-implantation agent, a once-a-week contraceptive, and possibly even as a daily "minipill," as well as for ovulation inhibition and menses (menstrual) induction. Results of WHO trials to date have shown that as an emergency contraceptive, RU 486 is more effective and causes less nausea, vomiting, and other side effects than the Yuzpe regimen, which is the most commonly used morning-after pill at present.[16]

There are many other ways in which RU 486 can be medically useful, including as an aid during difficult births, because it makes the uterus contract and hastens the opening of the cervix. Researchers have shown that it can be helpful in treating Cushing's syndrome (a disorder of the adrenal cortex that causes obesity, hypertension, diabetes mellitus, and other associated conditions), endometriosis, ulcers, brain tumors, breast cancer, ovarian cancer, and adrenal cancer. Dr. Etienne-Emile Baulieu explained in our telephone interview in September, 1994, that he and fellow researchers believe they may have found

> a possible cure for a brain tumor using RU 486, which has been lifesaving in a number of cancer cases. In adrenal cancer, there is often no other possibility of surgical removal of the cancer because of the high level of cortisone secreted in the glands. RU 486 can calm cortisone activity and make surgery possible. The first case in which RU 486 was used to help a cancer patient occurred in about 1984. It was a great joy for me to visit the patient in hospital and see the result of that lifesaving activity. Other brain tumors which contain progesterone receptors are either stabilized or regressed by RU 486. We are trying to use RU 486 in the treatment of breast cancer, but it is not easy.[3]

In early 1994, Marie Stopes International in London began providing RU 486 to American and other nonresident women for a fee of $500. Until then, only British residents had been permitted to use RU 486. The change in the law required that the pregnancy be less than 9 weeks and that the woman remain in the country for a follow-up exam 1 week after the abortion. This in effect would make the abortion much more costly than $500 and therefore too expensive for most people.

Many American women have investigated the possibility of undergoing an RU 486 abortion in London, though few can afford it. English abortion counselor Andrea Butcher noted in our telephone interview in July, 1994, that

> We've seen less than ten American women at Marie Stopes International so far. Even that number is amazing, given that these women traveled from all over the U.S. to have an RU 486 abortion here. They had to stay in the U.K. for 3 weeks, so it made the abortion very costly. Only a tiny minority of women can afford to make such a trip. We have many more women phoning from America to inquire about RU 486, but

when they learn the practicalities, they realize that it's not really an option for them. They then seek a surgical abortion in the U.S. Almost all the women who have come to Marie Stopes in London for an RU 486 abortion cited a very bad experience with surgical abortion as their reason for wanting an RU 486 abortion. The bad experience might have meant a bad reaction to the anesthetic or problems with a doctor, or complications after the abortion such as infection.[17]

There is absolutely no guarantee that a medical abortion will be a better experience than a surgical abortion, although for many women that is the case.

During my research, counselors in England and France have observed that many women, including Americans, seem to have misconceptions about what a medical abortion entails. Counselor Andrea Butcher explains:

Some people perceive RU 486 to be akin to the morning-after pill—very simple and straightforward, not really like having an abortion. They think that they'll be taking a pill that will bring on their period. We have to make it very clear that RU 486 is a medical abortion as opposed to a surgical abortion, but it *is* an abortion. There seems to be a sense that an RU 486 abortion is more "natural" and like a miscarriage rather than an abortion. For some women that seems to be a bonus. There is so much confusion about RU 486. Women phone us and ask if we can send them the pills. They don't seem to understand that they're having an abortion and need to see a doctor. Women often express surprise when we tell them that in some senses, an RU 486 abortion is a more complicated procedure, because you have to make more visits to the clinic than you do with a surgical abortion.[17]

A French nurse whom I interviewed by telephone emphasized that

RU 486 is *not* an easy method of abortion. People keep saying that it is easier than surgical abortion, but it's not true.
Women who have an RU 486 abortion reflect upon the abortion much more than women who have a surgical abortion.
They think more about what they are doing because they are
more involved with the abortion process and are in control
of taking the pill—they realize that they are aborting the
fetus. When a woman has a surgical abortion, someone is
taking care of her and doing something to her. The experience with RU 486 is completely different.[18]

In addition to misunderstandings about the actual procedure
and its emotional effects, there are some very unhealthy reasons
for wanting an abortion, medical or surgical, being confessed by
women who feel ambivalent about abortion. Abortion counselor
Andrea Butcher explains:

Occasionally, a woman will say that she wants an RU 486
abortion to punish herself for having become pregnant, even
if it was a failure of contraception. She feels guilty and wants
to punish herself with what she believes will be hours of
strong period pains and consciousness of the procedure. She
believes that she will be aware of the miscarriage and body
changes and that remembering the procedure will force her
not to let it happen again. That is not a good reason for having an RU 486 abortion. I have also heard women say that
they want to have a local anesthetic prior to a surgical abortion for the same reason—to remain conscious through the
procedure so that it won't happen again. Consciousness is
seen as a form of punishment.[17]

Women who feel this way should seek counseling prior to having
an abortion.

The most extraordinary aspect of women traveling to England
for an RU 486 abortion in 1994 was that the trip was unnecessary,
because early medical abortion using methotrexate was available
in the United States. Why was methotrexate's potential as an abortifacient such a well-kept secret? Dr. Richard Hausknecht was on

the faculty of Mt. Sinai Medical School and a senior physician attending at Mt. Sinai Hospital in New York when I interviewed him several times by telephone in 1994 and 1995. He broke rank and "let the cat out of the bag" in 1994, causing a furor that rankled academic physicians who viewed his use of methotrexate as an abortifacient in private practice as irresponsible, because they felt that the drug was still experimental.

Dr. Hausknecht passionately defended his position when we spoke:

When I asked Dr. David Grimes in May, 1994, why everybody was keeping so quiet about methotrexate ... and why it wasn't at least being talked about behind closed doors at medical meetings, he replied that they hadn't done enough cases yet to be satisfied that it was safe. Dr. Mitchell Creinin is an obstetrician and gynecologist at Magee Women's Hospital in Pittsburgh, Pennsylvania. He and I thought of using methotrexate simultaneously, but he was the first one to publish. In October, 1993, he published the results of the first ten cases. When I asked Dr. Creinin for his protocol [procedure], he wouldn't give it to me, so I drew up my own. There's a lot of that sort of protectiveness in the medical world. One of the real reasons I'm doing abortions using methotrexate and the prostaglandin misoprostol is related to a major problem that we're having in this country. Abortion clinics are being bombed and burned. Doctors are being shot. This is a means of taking first trimester abortion away from women. I'm tired of sitting around and waiting for RU 486—I didn't get into using methotrexate for medical abortions as an academic project. I wanted to make this drug available, at least in the United States, on a universal basis. I said, okay, I'm going to do 100 cases in 6 weeks, and then we'll see. And that is basically what I did. Now I have more cases than everybody else in the country, and it's sheer happenstance that a woman from the *Chicago Tribune* asked for an interview and I was willing to be interviewed by her. If it hadn't been for that, all the ensuing publicity wouldn't have happened.[19]

Dr. Hausknecht's motives for performing medical abortions using methotrexate are noble and humanitarian.

Despite some academic researchers' concerns about his work being done in an "uncontrolled" setting, Dr. Hausknecht's protocol is currently being used in a trial entitled "The Ethicacy and Safety of Methotrexate and Misoprostol Therapy for Early Abortion" that is under way at five different medical institutions in the United States. The trial will continue until 1500 women have undergone medical abortions using this drug combination.

When I spoke with Dr. Mitchell Creinin about methotrexate in October, 1994, he remarked that "some people are doing the wrong thing with an experimental drug." I asked Dr. Richard Hausknecht for his response to the idea that methotrexate was an experimental drug. He replied, "When does a drug stop being experimental? My sense of timing is different from that of Dr. Creinin."[19] Dr. Hausknecht went on to point out that some researchers are more conservative than others, but in his view, methotrexate had proven itself to be safe and effective in the treatment of both ectopic and intrauterine pregnancies. He no longer considers the drug "experimental" in that sense, but acknowledges that further research into methotrexate is appropriate.

Dr. Hausknecht began using methotrexate in his private practice in July, 1994. He has performed well in excess of the 100 cases he originally set out to perform and has been deluged with calls from doctors around the United States asking for his protocol. If he had chosen to let his practice go in the direction it was pushed by all of the publicity in 1994, he could have concentrated solely on performing medical abortions because the demand became great.

The reasons given by women for desiring a medical abortion using methotrexate are much the same as those given for RU 486: a bad experience with surgical abortion, fear of the risks of surgical abortion, fear of pain they believe a surgical abortion will cause, less invasive, and seemingly more natural.

According to statistics published by the Alan Guttmacher Institute in 1992, there are 2380 abortion providers in the United

States, but 84% of counties offer no abortion services. Medical abortion could solve that problem, provided doctors are trained appropriately in suction curettage as a backup in the event that the medical abortion fails. Planned Parenthood of New York City (PPofNYC) has developed a special training program for physicians seeking to learn abortion techniques. This program was developed by PPofNYC's President and CEO, Alexander Sanger, to fill the need for abortion providers after training in abortion techniques was dropped from the curriculum in many U.S. medical schools. (Although, on February 14, 1995, the Accreditation Council for Graduate Medical Education mandated that abortion training be included in all OB/GYN residency programs, PPofNYC's program will continue as long as necessary.) Dr. Hausknecht offered this cautionary tip to prospective medical abortion providers during our interview: "My advice to doctors contemplating medical abortion is, if you don't have the backup for a suction completion, don't use methotrexate or RU 486."[19]

In 1990, Dr. Bernard Nathanson of Cornell University Medical College warned that RU 486 was an "experimental" drug, just as methotrexate is now being labeled "experimental" by some physicians:

> This drug [RU 486] has not been sufficiently tested and will not be for another 20 years. . . . We've had some fairly horrendous experience with drugs that have been represented as perfectly safe, but 20 or 30 years later, we discover they're lethal . . .[20]

Dr. Nathanson is against abortion, so his way of interpreting "the facts" is influenced by his personal views. Dr. David Grimes, former USC School of Medicine professor, recalls that

> There were some deaths from early birth control pills. The complications were so rare they couldn't be found in pre-marketing studies. You can never evaluate a drug in a vacuum. But on balance, contraceptives saved many women's lives: childbearing can be dangerous. In terms of public

health, the birth control pill has been one of the resounding success stories. . . . We know a lot about RU 486. It's a circular argument to say we don't know anything about this drug, so let's not study it.[21]

Any drug can produce an adverse reaction in a susceptible individual, no matter how many people have successfully taken it without a negative reaction. As long as women are fully informed about the known risks and possible side effects of a drug, the decision to undergo what may be deemed by conservative physicians to be an "experimental" treatment should be up to each individual woman.

Dr. Etienne-Emile Baulieu has encountered a good deal of opposition to RU 486 over the years, much of it based on beliefs rather than any objective fact. These days he refuses to debate people who suggest that the RU 486/prostaglandin regimen is a "chemical cocktail," just as Dr. Richard Hausknecht has refused to enter into such debates in the various media that have bombarded him with requests since his work with methotrexate became public in September, 1994. It is futile to try to convince those who believe that abortion is absolutely wrong in all circumstances that medical abortion is a welcome advancement in women's health care.

Sinister criticism that comes disguised as concern for women, however, does need to be addressed. That is sometimes difficult, as Dr. Baulieu discovered while visiting Australia. He explains:

> In Australia, there is a woman, Dr. Lynette Dumble [a senior research fellow in the surgery department at the Royal Melbourne Hospital] whom I call an "integrist leftist" . . . her speciality as a physician does not relate to hormones, gynecology, or abortion. She is an old-fashioned feminist, who is against everything if it is masculine, scientific, or related to a chemical device. She belongs to a miniscule group of three women (the other two reside in Boston) who have written a book on RU 486 which is an uninteresting collection of stupidities. When Dr. Dumble speaks of RU 486/prostaglandin

as a "drug cocktail," it is ridiculous. She is fantasizing when she suggests that RU 486 may affect the uterine lining in such a way that it increases women's risk of developing pelvic inflammatory disease which can in turn lead to infertility and ectopic pregnancy. There is no scientific evidence to support these fantasies. Unfortunately, these days you can say anything you want and there will always be some media willing to transfer your ideas, however stupid they may be. People like Dr. Dumble are more interested in becoming "famous" than in reality. She has in fact done nothing of note in this field of medicine and seems to me to be seeking a cause onto which she can graft herself to make a name.[3]

When media repeat idiotic ideas often enough, they gain credibility, unfortunately. I asked Dr. Baulieu about Dr. Dumble's ideas because her articles regularly appear in Australian newspapers, and I didn't have the knowledge to refute what she was saying.

Dr. John Willke, president of the National Right to Life Committee in the United States, believes that "RU 486 will kill thousands of women in Third World countries from bleeding. . . ."[22] His concern stemmed from reading a 1990 *New England Journal of Medicine* report that some women who had bled after a failed RU 486 abortion required a D&C, and one even needed a blood transfusion. Dr. David Grimes countered this concern by noting that

> This drug, if anything, would reduce the number of women who die from complications of illegal abortion dramatically. To say that thousands of women in Third World countries will die from bleeding assumes there would be no backup if the pill failed. Five thousand people per year die from botched abortions in Bangladesh alone. Given the alternative of having a stick stuck in your uterus, I think RU 486 is preferable.[23]

All of the abortion providers interviewed in this book have welcomed medical abortion as a great advance for women's health care. In the United States, the methotrexate and misoprostol needed for an abortion cost about $6 at most. Office visits, sonograms, and other tests would be additional, but it is likely that medical abortion would cost less or at least no more than surgical abortion. It is unknown what the cost of RU 486 would be in the United States, but in England the government has stipulated that clinics cannot charge more for a medical abortion than for a surgical abortion. (Dr. Hausknecht presently charges $500 per medical abortion in New York, but notes that most of this expense results from office visits, lab work, and sonograms.)

Brilliant maverick physicians are often laughed at initially, only to be vindicated when the new treatment has proven itself to the satisfaction of the medical establishment. Provided that women are properly informed of the possible risks associated with a drug trial or newly available treatment, politics and the conservatism of medical science should not prevent them from having the opportunity to choose that option. American women should not have to travel to Britain to obtain RU 486, and it is high time that they knew about methotrexate.

The development of abortifacients such as RU 486 and methotrexate could potentially be the most significant advance in women's health care since the development of the pill. Every woman has a right to be informed about these options so that she can make an educated choice between surgical and medical abortion.

9

What Happens when You're Pregnant and Can't Make the Decision for Yourself Regarding Abortion?

When I began researching abortion in 1984, a friend in London presented me with a newspaper clipping that related the story of a hospitalized, comatose woman who, during or after transfer from one hospital to another, had been raped, and as a result became pregnant. A decision had to be made: should she be permitted to carry her pregnancy to term, possibly threatening her life, or should she undergo an abortion?

The article was short and did not reveal the outcome of the case, but the impact of that scenario struck me as being very profound. Sadly, since then I have learned of other cases of comatose pregnant women and the serious choices that have been made for them by family members trying to do whatever would save their lives.

I presented the above extreme case of the raped comatose woman to the various clergymen whom I interviewed, as well as to philosophers, doctors and other professionals. The clergymen were virtually unanimous in their belief that the woman should *not* be given an abortion, unless her life was in immediate danger. The fact that she was raped while comatose did not seem to be significant to them.

The doctors felt that the woman should undergo an abortion, because of the risks associated with pregnancy. For the doctors, as for the clergymen, the fact that she had been raped did not seem to be a morally significant factor in their decision.

The philosophers, who viewed morality in a more theoretical and pure sense, held that the woman should have an abortion if her life were to be threatened by the pregnancy. They also reasoned that because she had been raped, she would probably not want to bear the child of a rapist. Regardless of whether she had the baby or an abortion, the woman would be subjected to a degree of physical trauma. She had no control over either decision, thus making it an almost amoral situation. One simply had to do what was regarded as best for her physical health. Most importantly, the philosophers suggested that an attempt be made to learn the woman's views on abortion. If it could be determined that she believed abortion to be morally wrong, then that would argue against performing the abortion. Of course, it could be difficult to obtain information regarding the woman's position on abortion unless she had written her thoughts down, but if family members concurred that the woman believed abortion to be morally wrong, then she should be permitted to carry the baby to term and give birth by cesarean section, even if that meant risking her life.

On December 13, 1988, Nancy Klein went into a coma as a result of injuries suffered in a car accident in a snowstorm on Long Island, New York. She was pregnant with her second child at the time of the accident. On the advice of doctors, her husband, Martin, and her parents decided that Nancy should undergo an abortion, as this would greatly enhance her chances of emerging from the coma and recovering from her severe head injuries. They believed that Nancy would have agreed with their decision. If she remained pregnant, doctors would be unable to use specialized diagnostic testing and provide her with medications and other forms of treatment that they felt would assist her recovery.

In January, 1989, Martin Klein applied for legal guardianship of his wife, so that he could authorize the abortion. The judge ruled in his favor, but the ruling was challenged by John Broderick, an attorney who has represented the militant anti-abortion group Operation Rescue, and John Short, founder of a Long Island group called Coalition for Life. Broderick and Short applied for legal guardianship of the fetus and Mrs. Klein, respectively. Each of the three times that the case went to various New York courts, Broderick and Short lost, but they kept appealing, forcing Martin Klein to fight them all the way to the U.S. Supreme Court.

On February 10, 1989, U.S. Supreme Court Justice Thurgood Marshall rejected Broderick and Short's stay request, lodged in desperation after New York's Supreme Court Appellate Division (Second Judicial Department) ruled against them on February 9, 1989, stating in the Opinion and Order that "ultimately, the record confirms that these absolute strangers to the Klein family, whatever their motivation, have no place in the midst of this family tragedy."

Nancy Klein had the abortion on February 11, 1989, at North Shore University Hospital on Long Island, where she had been hospitalized since the ordeal began. She was about 17–18 weeks pregnant at the time of the abortion. A few weeks after the abortion, Nancy emerged from the coma and began the long process of recovery. She has had to relearn the simple tasks most of us take for granted and had no recollection of the accident when she regained consciousness. She continues to undergo extensive therapy.

In a similar incident, Barbara Blodgett became comatose after being thrown from her vehicle after it was struck by a drunk driver on June 30, 1988. She was 3 months pregnant at the time. Although her family was advised that the pregnancy could threaten Barbara's chances of survival, her husband, David and her parents refused permission for an abortion because of their religious beliefs.

Slowly, Barbara began to show small signs of sensibility as the weeks went by, such as wincing when a nurse who was combing her hair tugged at a knot. At 37 weeks, after amniocentesis revealed that the baby's lungs were mature, Dr. Benedetti, her treating physician, induced labor. Barbara's condition improved considerably within a few days of the birth, and has continued to improve since then, though her prognosis remains uncertain.

Experts have speculated but do not agree on why her condition improved so radically after the birth. Dr. William Blackerby, a Nashville head injury specialist, has suggested that the massive hormonal shifts triggered by the birth may be the explanation. Dr. Loren Winterscheid, the medical director at University Hospital in Seattle where Barbara gave birth, doubts that there is any connection between the birth and her improvement. He believes that there is no way of knowing when or how much a patient in a coma like Barbara Blodgett's is going to recover.

Barbara Blodgett's family gambled with her life when they made the decision to permit her pregnancy to continue. She is one of only six known cases of a comatose woman giving birth to a healthy baby.

I present Barbara Blodgett's case, in contrast to Nancy Klein's, because her survival represents hope to those families whose religious beliefs might prevent them from accepting abortion under any circumstances, even if the woman is comatose and her life may be threatened by the pregnancy. If Barbara Blodgett had undergone an abortion, she might have begun the process of recovery sooner, or she might not have recovered at all. There is simply no way of knowing.

I believe that everyone should make a "living will" or designate in writing a "health care proxy." It is especially important that pregnant women declare in writing whether they would wish to undergo an abortion in the event of serious injury that leaves them unconscious or unable to make the decision for themselves. I have presented the contrasting cases of Nancy Klein and Barbara Blodgett because they highlight ethical issues not present when a woman is consciously contemplating an abortion.

* * * * *

Who makes the decision about the fate of a pregnancy for mentally retarded, mentally ill, imprisoned, and severely physically disabled women? The answer to that question varies to some degree from state to state.

California has unique laws covering the rights of disabled people. If a woman is in a coma in California, the decision regarding her pregnancy would be made by a judge. In California, once a person turns 18, there is provision for a conservatorship, but there is no guardianship for an adult in California as there is in other states, such as New York. In California, guardianship is only for minors.

There are two types of conservatorships, probate and LPS. A probate conservatorship is the old type; for instance, if someone is in a coma and needs an abortion or any kind of invasive surgery, then the case will go to the probate court. The judge will grant or not grant permission for the procedure, depending on the circumstances. An LPS (Lanternan, Petris, and Short) conservatorship applies only to the mentally disabled and takes care of people having to be committed to a hospital, enforced medication, and locked facilities. In New York, there is no LPS conservatorship, only probate. When it comes to the LPS conservatorship, which we have in California, the petition is handled by the district attorney's office, and the public defender's office is the one that defends the conservatee, so there is some safeguard. All the while that the conservatorship is in place (it has to be renewed every year but might continue for years), the conservatee always has access to a public defender. Under the probate system of conservatorship, there is no such safeguard, which is a real problem. Then the probate conservatorship just stays in place until someone goes back to court to undo it. Usually, the disabled person doesn't have money to hire an attorney and can't go back to court. Under the LPS system, they have the public defender to go to court for them. That's an overview of the system here in California. No other state has the LPS system, to the best of my knowledge.

A conservatorship court in California has to say that some powers can be taken away from a citizen before a conservatorship can be established. The guidelines are numerous. Under the LPS system, the person is unable to provide food, shelter, and clothing for themselves and because of a mental disability is defined as *gravely disabled*. The family is always consulted. Under LPS, there's an automatic 30-day investigation that's done by the public guardian's office in the appropriate county.

A woman in prison is under the criminal system. Probate cases are civil, not criminal. In California, when someone has committed a crime, they are imprisoned under criminal law, but there is a transfer code that would enable them to be transferred to a locked mental health facility.

Under a conservatorship, if a woman becomes pregnant, she has a say in the decision on whether to have an abortion or continue the pregnancy to term. The public defender will represent her interests. In most cases, if the person is coherent, the judge will let her do whatever she wants. *If the woman is not coherent enough, there would be no abortion, because there won't be anyone asking for it. The woman would automatically be allowed to carry the pregnancy to term.* The presumption in California is that the pregnancy will continue. The fact that the woman may have a condition, mental or physical, that could be inherited doesn't mean that the woman would automatically be given an abortion. If the mother's life is in danger or the fetus is in danger because the mother's doing things to herself that might harm the fetus, the case might well go to the judge and he most probably would grant permission for an abortion. The idea that because someone is under a conservatorship, therefore they cannot bear children, is not the position in California. The only time that discussion of abortion arises is when continuing the pregnancy might be injurious to the woman, such as when a woman is in a coma. If the woman is HIV positive, she would still be left to continue the pregnancy to term unless she requested an abortion. The possibility of illness, mental or physical, being transmitted to the fetus does not automatically warrant an abortion in California.

The baby would be put up for adoption, but the immediate family would have priority. First of all, the father would have to be considered, because you can't adopt without the father's signature in California. To some extent it depends on how the pregnancy came about. If there was a father involved, the father would have the first option to take the child. If the father was gone, did not want or did not know about the baby, first her parents and then other relatives would have a right to adopt the child. Any family member willing to adopt the child would have priority over strangers, providing that they would not hurt the child. Dependency courts always look for a blood relative to adopt the child. If no blood relative is willing and able to raise the child, strangers would then be given the option to adopt.

Judges around the country vary dramatically in how they rule on such situations. In the southern states, they almost never rule for abortion. In California, which is probably the most flexible state in the country, judges rule on a case-by-case basis and try not to have a bias one way or the other. The decision whether to abort or continue the pregnancy is definitely up to the mother in California, but sometimes it is difficult to figure out what a very disabled person wants. The feelings of people under conservatorships who know whether or not they want to be pregnant are taken into consideration by the judge.

If a woman wants to have the baby but not adopt it out, the Dependency Court would want to know who would be responsible for the child and who would help the mother before letting her keep the baby. For example, if she has a mother who would share custody with her, that might be one solution.

Very often people who are disabled or developmentally disabled will not necessarily have a developmentally disabled child. If amniocentesis reveals that the fetus will be developmentally disabled, that may sway the way a judge rules. If the judge thinks the woman should have an abortion because a prenatal diagnostic test reveals an abnormality, but the woman doesn't want the abortion, he may rule against her. Such a decision would not be coming from a philosophical bias, but rather from the details of her case. In certain circumstances, a judge might order a woman to undergo prenatal diagnostic testing, such as when a severe fetal abnormality is suspected.

If a pregnant woman is imprisoned, she will be permitted to have the baby if she wants. The father would have a right to raise the child. The only time that is not the case is when the mother doesn't know who the father is or she doesn't know the where-abouts of the father. She can make a unilateral decision regarding whether or not to have an abortion, but once the pregnancy has been brought to term, the father has a right to raise the child if she cannot care for it.

If I wrote the law, a pregnant woman under a conservator-ship would automatically be given an abortion, unless she re-quested otherwise. The presumption that continuing the pregnancy is the natural course for events to take is born of a logic I fail to understand. There is no such thing as a natural law that all pregnancies must be carried to term, especially if the mother is mentally incompetent to decide otherwise. I find the California State law on this issue baffling.

Does society have a right to tell a woman who will be unable to care for her child that she has no right to give birth? Should women raising children on welfare be permitted to have more chil-dren who will also be raised on welfare, or should they be forced to use contraception, and that failing, abort future pregnancies until they can provide for their children? Should women convicted of child abuse be permitted to have more children?

The answer to all of these questions is surprisingly simple in my view. Those who have legal guardianship and/or will have to provide for the child have the right to decide, be it the family or community. It should not always be a question of what is in the "best interest" of the woman if she is incapable of providing or caring for a child. It's a question of what the community is will-ing to do to help.

Sterilization or contraceptive implants should be mandatory for women convicted of child abuse. That failing, abortion should be mandatory. Convicted abusive mothers forfeit their right to bear children.

Welfare has become a way of life for many women, and their children. If a woman is on welfare with a child, it should be manda-tory that she use a contraceptive implant such as Norplant and that failing, that she have an abortion if she becomes pregnant and wishes to remain on welfare. The community should pay for the contraceptives and abortion. We simply cannot allow people to think that it's acceptable to have children without contributing to the financial kitty that has to pay for raising them. That's communal suicide. The law of the land should be, if you want to bring a child into the world, you have to make a reasonable effort to provide care. If the community can afford to help and chooses to do so, that's a gift. Welfare should be a safety net in the event something goes wrong, not a way of life for raising families.

A community that will have to provide financially for children whose mothers cannot has the right to order that the women have an abortion. It also has the right to mandate contraceptive use, provided that it does not harm the woman's health. There are times when the "best interests" of the community should be paramount, not those of the individual.

10

Facts to Consider if You're HIV Positive and Pregnant

Acquired immune deficiency syndrome (AIDS) causes a breakdown in the immune system. As a result, individuals infected with the AIDS virus develop infections or cancers, and it is these secondary infections that kill them. The AIDS virus is found in blood, semen, vaginal secretions, and breast milk. It is also found in saliva, but there are no known cases of transmission of the virus through saliva alone, largely, doctors believe, because the concentration of the virus in saliva is not high enough for it to be transmitted.

According to the U.S. Centers for Disease Control and Prevention in Atlanta, *all* babies born to women who have tested HIV positive before giving birth are born HIV antibody positive, because the mother's antibodies cross the placenta. Only those children in whom the virus itself crossed the placenta are HIV-infected. Around 75–80% convert to being negative during the first 1 1/2 to 2 years of life, as they lose the mother's antibodies. The remaining 20–25% who acquired the virus are expected to develop HIV disease. For mothers who take AZT during pregnancy, the risk of transmission may be as low as 8%. Pregnancy exacerbates a number of chronic diseases, but to date, there is no evidence suggesting that it exacerbates HIV. The average life expectancy of an HIV-infected child is about 8–9 years, but many live into adolescence.

*   *   *   *   *

On November 7, 1991, Laker's basketball player Earvin "Magic" Johnson announced at a press conference that he was HIV positive, meaning that he was carrying the AIDS virus, but had not developed the disease. It was as if a bomb had fallen on the American people. Suddenly, AIDS was no longer a disease restricted to homosexuals, intravenous drug users, and hemophiliacs. Heterosexuals were also at risk.

Of course, heterosexuals had always been at risk, but most were unwilling to acknowledge that risk. Women and men around the world have not been diligent enough in practicing safer sex and refraining from sexual promiscuity. Cookie Johnson, Magic's wife, and her baby were lucky that the HIV virus was not passed on to them. What I found extraordinary regarding Magic Johnson's announcement was the certainty with which most journalists, news anchors, and doctors pronounced that Cookie Johnson and baby were not at risk of contracting the disease. That was not true, but wishful thinking seemed to take precedence over truth after Magic's announcement, with only one or two doctors acknowledging that Cookie and baby were at risk. Cookie was reportedly 2 months pregnant when Magic made his announcement. Even if she had not had sexual relations with her husband since conceiving 2 months earlier, she could not be certain that she would not become HIV positive for at least another 4 months. Because she probably had sexual relations after conception, it would be more like 6 months before doctors could safely say that Cookie was probably out of danger, provided that she and Magic had not in the meantime engaged in unsafe sexual relations.

On average, it takes between 2 and 12 weeks for the body to develop antibodies after exposure to the AIDS virus, but it can take up to 6 months. In the interim, the infected person will test negative. Cookie Johnson tested negative for the virus by the time she gave birth, and her baby was born HIV negative. Although semen contains white blood cells, sperm do not, so AIDS can't be transmitted to the baby if only the father is HIV positive. Even when the woman tests HIV positive before giving birth, only about 20–25% of children born to infected women are infected. Oddly enough, the chance of the AIDS virus being transmitted to the fetus increases with second and third pregnancies after a woman has tested HIV positive. The most likely explanation for this increase is that the woman has progressed in her disease process with the passing of time, thus increasing her viral burden, which would in turn increase the rate of transmission.

As AIDS is terminal, an HIV-positive pregnant woman may not live to raise her child. There are three important questions that must be answered before making a decision to carry the pregnancy to term if you're an HIV-positive woman:

1. Who will care for my child when I'm dying and after my death?
2. Am I willing to risk giving birth to a child who may suffer a terrible, painful death if AIDS develops?
3. Can I afford to have this child, knowing that he or she may become seriously ill with a terminal disease like AIDS?

Making a decision in this situation is heartbreaking and excruciatingly difficult. If you do continue the pregnancy and the virus is transmitted to your baby, you may not die first. Inspirational Pediatric AIDS Foundation cofounder Elizabeth Glaser suffered unimaginable grief watching her 7-year-old daughter Ariel die of AIDS in 1988, and lived in fear (until her death on December 3, 1994) that her HIV-positive 10-year-old son Jake would also develop the disease. Elizabeth Glaser was infected with the AIDS virus in 1981, from a blood transfusion she received immediately after the emergency delivery of Ariel at Cedars–Sinai Medical Center in Los Angeles. Unaware of the infection, she breast-fed Ariel, transmitting the virus to her through breast milk. Elizabeth gave birth to her son Jake in 1984, still unaware that she was carrying the virus. It was not until 1986 that Elizabeth was diagnosed HIV positive. By that time her daughter Ariel had already developed the disease. After Ariel's death, Elizabeth devoted the rest of her life to trying to save her son's life, by raising funds and support for AIDS research. She became a high-profile public speaker on AIDS and gave a very moving speech at the 1992 Democratic Convention that brought her cause to the attention of millions. Perhaps the message for all women who may have been exposed to the virus is *be tested for HIV before getting pregnant*, or if your pregnancy is unplanned, have the test as soon as you discover that you are pregnant. Let Elizabeth Glaser's tragic experience as an HIV-positive mother be a lesson for us all.

Mary Lucy is a well-known AIDS activist living in California. I interviewed her on February 28, 1992. Mary's story will help you understand some of the problems HIV-positive pregnant women may encounter.

When I learned that I was pregnant in 1989, my first thought was that I had to have an abortion. I went for a pregnancy test at a clinic where they suggested alternatives such as adoption. It turned out to be one of those clinics that is against abortion, so they kept telling me that abortion wasn't the right thing to do. I was vulnerable, pregnant, and a drug addict, so I was very confused. My life was a disaster. When you're vulnerable, you'll take any information that offers comfort. The counselor at the clinic was clever and she got to me, so I didn't have the abortion. Instead, she hooked me up with an adoption agency, but I didn't feel comfortable with the whole process involved, even though I also knew that I didn't want to raise the child. I didn't want to go through a state adoption agency, so I decided I was going to adopt the baby out privately, to people I could get to know and who would accept my staying in touch with my child. By this time I was about 4 months pregnant.

As soon as I discovered that I was pregnant and that I was going to have the baby, I stopped using heroin and began taking methadone, which I was advised would not harm the fetus. But I had this feeling that I had been exposed to the AIDS virus, because I'd been using drugs intravenously and didn't practice safe sex. I had an AIDS test, but the clinic didn't call to tell me that I was HIV positive until 2 months later, by which time I was almost at the end of my sixth month of pregnancy. [Clinics and hospitals generally do not give this information over the phone.]

When I tested positive to the AIDS virus, my immediate response was again that I wanted to have an abortion, but the doctors told me it was too late.

Before I tested for the AIDS virus, I had picked out a couple to adopt my baby. They lived in Upper Walnut Creek. We corresponded for a couple of months. I felt that out of responsibility to myself and the couple, I had to test for the AIDS virus, as I was in the high-risk category. When I tested positive, I called them and asked them to come and visit me, because I had something important to discuss with them. I told them that I was HIV positive, and that they needed to make a decision about whether or not they were willing to go ahead with the adoption. The lady thought about it for a couple of weeks and made a lot of calls in order to collect information. She decided not to adopt my baby, but she did put me in touch with a woman whom she believed might want to adopt my child.

The "Sister" who adopted my baby lives with friends in a very spiritual, religious, latent Roman Catholic community, but they believe in abortion and are very supportive of people with AIDS. They believe in living life to the fullest. She came to meet me and offered unconditional love to my child, saying that she really wanted to adopt it, no matter what the consequences. Her attitude moved me deeply and gave me confidence that she would love my child. She said after we'd talked for a couple of hours during our first meeting that every day with my child, even if she was HIV positive, would be a holiday. She said that if my baby turned out to be HIV negative, then she would start saving for college. Those thoughts touched a soft spot in me, and I knew that she was going to raise my baby. So I went to live with her and the other members of her community. They taught me how to live with this virus and reassured me that everything was going to be okay. They also got me much-needed medical attention.

The community has adopted two children who turned out to be HIV negative, and they have two foster children who have full-blown AIDS. Two other children have already died of AIDS, and they have just now received another baby. Caring for the children of parents who have the AIDS virus or AIDS is their whole life. These are the people who began the foster parent program for Romanian babies with AIDS, establishing homes for them in Romania when the government refused to let them be adopted out to other countries. They train volunteer foster parents here in America and then send them over to Romania for 6 months to a year. They are very caring people.

When my daughter was born, she was formally adopted by the Sister (she's not a nun) and her friends. It was a private adoption—the State had nothing to do with it, except for coming to inspect their home to ensure that the conditions were suitable. I visit her as much as I want, but she does not know me as her mother. She's only 2 years old, so to her I'm just a lady who comes to play with her once in a while. The Sister is her mother, but my daughter will learn when she gets older that I was, or am, her birth mother. We've prepared scrap books and tapes for her so that she'll have some idea of who her birth mother was. . . . My daughter's immune system switched to negative when she was 7 months old.

Even if I had not tested positive for the AIDS virus, I would still have gone ahead with the adoption, because I felt that my baby deserved more than I could offer as a parent. But if I hadn't gone to that clinic where they convinced me that abortion was wrong and that I should have the baby and give it up for adoption, I would have had an abortion. I wanted an abortion when I went to that clinic, not a pep talk.

I took AZT during my last 3 months of pregnancy and became very ill. I lost 50 pounds and continued to lose weight after I gave birth. Eventually I could barely walk. I was in agony, and all my joints ached. I thought all these symptoms were a result of the AIDS virus, but they weren't. They were the result of the medication, AZT.

My T cells were very low after I gave birth and I had abscesses on my kidneys. I was a complete mess. I stopped taking AZT about a year after I gave birth and began vitamin and diet therapy, taking B12, garlic, alfalfa, lots of vitamin C as well as vitamins A and E. When I gave up taking AZT, my health began to improve and I gained weight. Miraculously, the high dose of AZT didn't affect my baby. It nearly killed me, but had no effect on her. She weighed 8 pounds and 8 ounces when she was born. She was a big, fat, healthy child, and I was emaciated, nearly dead. I felt like a vector or an oven in which my baby had been baked. Now my doctor says that whatever I'm doing I should keep doing it, because I feel great and I've regained my health. It's been 2 years since I gave up AZT, and I'm doing better than ever.

When a pregnant woman tests positive to the AIDS virus, she's caught between a rock and a hot spot. There are a lot of women who are infected who want to have children, but they fear for their own health and for the health of the child. And yet part of the woman wants to have the baby so that she can experience, even if just for a couple of years, what it feels like to be a mother.

I believe that children have a right to life, but I don't think that fetuses are children, so they don't have a right to life in that sense. I was sterilized the day after I gave birth. If I hadn't been sterilized and had become pregnant again, I would have had an abortion.[11]

Mary Lucy's experience with AZT was very bad, but for other HIV-infected people, AZT has prolonged their lives, sometimes by years. Doctors are learning more about AIDS and AZT every day.

AZT is now widely used to help prevent the development of AIDS in babies whose mothers are HIV positive. The drug is administered to the mother during pregnancy, usually in the second and third trimester, as well as to the infant after birth.

As this book goes to press in 1995, there is much controversy in the United States over attempts in various states to legislate mandatory HIV testing for all pregnant women and/or all newborns. The argument in favor of mandatory testing is that infants and women in need of treatment would be identified and provided with appropriate medical care. While that is a noble goal, mandatory testing will not necessarily ensure quality care for mother and baby. The latter is impossible without the mother's cooperation. Mandating that all pregnant women be tested for HIV will antagonize and frighten many women into not accepting any kind of medical care, which in the long run, will endanger both mother and baby. Women should routinely be offered counseling and encouragement to take advantage of the opportunity to be screened for HIV, at no cost to them, during early pregnancy, along with other prenatal testing. All Americans should have access to affordable health care, but it is especially imperative that pregnant HIV-positive women receive appropriate care.

Women want to be good mothers. If HIV testing is presented as one aspect of good mothering, most women will consent voluntarily, provided that confidentiality about the results of the testing and treatment are assured. "Susanna" is an HIV-infected woman who feels lucky that her pregnancy was confirmed at a county-funded clinic in California. She reflected on her feelings about being offered the chance to take a free AIDS test in a *Los Angeles Times* article on February 7, 1995:

> It's my first baby. My only one, I guess . . . I don't want to take any risks. . . . So when the clinic said I could get an AIDS test right along with all the other tests you take when you're having a baby, I took it. Why wouldn't I? . . . I have a chance to save my baby, I think, since I know he might get AIDS if I don't take the AZT.[2]

After testing positive for the HIV virus, Susanna agreed to take AZT five times daily from her 13th week of pregnancy through delivery. The cost of the treatment exceeds $3000, but is paid for by a federal program for women with no health insurance.

Fear of spousal abuse is one reason some women refuse to undergo HIV testing during pregnancy. Another is fear of loss of employment and abandonment by spouse, family, friends, and church if a positive HIV test result is revealed. Although some cities report that only half the high-risk women are willing to be tested for HIV, in California about 70% of women offered free tests at county clinics accept. According to John Schunhoff, director of the Los Angeles County AIDS program, mandatory testing for HIV will do more harm than good.

> We don't want to drive women away from health care. We want them to participate in it. . . . If the offer of the test is properly presented, and if we can keep track of the women who test positive and get them referred for treatment, this is a much better solution. I think most women want to know the truth so that they know their options as soon as possible.[2]

I urge all pregnant women to be tested for HIV voluntarily, because it is in the best interest of you and your potential baby to know as early as possible in pregnancy whether you are HIV positive. Only then can you make an informed choice on whether to continue the pregnancy to term with appropriate medical care, or seek an abortion.

It certainly should not be mandatory for HIV-positive women to take AZT during pregnancy, or for AZT to be mandatorily administered to HIV-positive newborns. Although that is fast becoming routine practice—because it lowers the risk of the infant remaining HIV positive once it loses the mother's antibodies—it should not be mandatory, because the long-term effect on infants is unknown, and there is no guarantee that the treatment will help. Parents have a right to choose whether they wish to take the risks associated with administration of AZT during pregnancy and to the newborn, however minimal they may be.

Around 7000 HIV-infected women become pregnant annually in the United States, according to the Centers for Disease Control. That is a surprisingly high figure, given the risks involved for the woman, her baby, and her partner. I had falsely presumed that HIV-positive women would not want to become pregnant, for fear of transmitting the virus to their baby and uncertainty regarding their ability to parent.

The head of the Los Angeles Black AIDS Consortium Commission, Dr. Wilbert Jordan of King-Drew Medical Center, says that the ethical dilemma in his practice

> comes in the form of all the infected women who want to get pregnant. . . . I have a woman right now. She came in with her boyfriend. She is HIV positive but healthy. I can't play God. She looks good. And with AZT, there is a good chance the baby can be born negative. . . . This burning desire to leave a legacy when you're faced with death yourself is not something affecting only African-American women. Like many . . . who are trying to leave a mark here before they die, they feel the best thing they can leave is a baby.[3]

I was stunned when I first read Dr. Jordan's remarks, because I simply couldn't believe that women would knowingly risk causing a child to suffer a terminal illness and probable loss of a parent in childhood. On reflection, I realized that the overwhelming desire for life in the face of death makes desperate people willing to gamble with life. I'm not sure they're right to take that risk when an innocent child will have to bear the consequences of the gamble, but neither can I judge them wrong. I only know that I wouldn't take that risk.

It's important that we all understand that so-called "facts" about AIDS can change from one day to the next. Intense research is underway on all aspects of HIV disease and its transmission. For agencies and organizations that provide reliable, updated information and assistance, refer to the "Help" Directory at the back of this book. The "facts" in this chapter are current, to the best of my knowledge.

11

Rape—The Paradox of a Violently Conceived Pregnancy

Webster's New World Dictionary defines rape as "the crime of having sexual intercourse with a woman or girl forcibly and without her consent; any sexual assault; plundering or violent destruction of a city, as in war; formerly, to seize and carry away by force; statutory rape—intercourse with a girl below the age of consent; any outrageous assault or flagrant violation."[1]

Pregnancy is the ultimate creation. Rape is an act of destruction. Therein lies the paradox.

It is important to understand the cultural context of a violently conceived pregnancy in order to appreciate the desperate need of most raped women to abort the pregnancy. It can literally be a matter of life and death for the woman. Consider the case of "Melisa," a Bosnian Muslim.

They tore all my clothes off of me until I was naked, and then two of them held me down and two of them raped me. They forced me to do it with my mouth. I was awfully scared, and they kicked me around and beat me. I don't remember exactly how many there were, 'cause I fainted." Before long she noticed that she was pregnant. At first she tried to abort herself with injections of hot water. She thought she had succeeded, because she was bleeding heavily . . . [but] she was still pregnant. She asked for an abortion at the first opportunity, in the Kiseljak hospital, but doctors denied her request. She did not arrive in Zagreb until December 1992, and then it was too late for an abortion . . . she referred to her child only as "the thing". . . . "Where I come from, everybody, my husband, my daughter, the whole town, everybody would think of the kid as filth." Her husband, who had stayed in Gorazde, knew nothing about the rape. "He'd never take me back again if he knew what happened". . . . In Spring 1993 she gave birth to a dead child in Zagreb. She left the hospital without telling anyone where she was going.[2]

"Melisa" was raped by Serbian troops in 1992, during the civil war in Bosnia–Herzegovina. Because many rapes and subsequent pregnancies go unreported, accurate statistics are virtually impossible to compile. A UN commission investigated rapes in former Yugoslavia in January of 1993; 119 cases of pregnancy resulting from rape were reported by major women's clinics in Zagreb (Croatia), Sarajevo, Tuzla (Bosnia–Herzegovina), and Belgrade (Serbia). The majority of women, 104, chose to have an abortion, and 9 more wanted an abortion but their pregnancies were too far advanced. The fate of the other 6 pregnancies is uncertain. As one doctor put it, "How can you expect any woman who's had to flee, who's lost everything, to bring a baby into the world?"[3]

Rape has been a heartbreaking subject to research. No woman should ever be forced to carry a pregnancy to term, especially if she conceived as a result of rape.

Genocidal rape is a form of gender persecution that aims to destroy a national, ethnic, racial, or religious group. Women and girls are the primary victims, but not the only intended ones. Their families and community are also meant to suffer, by being involuntary witnesses to the crime and suffering fear, shame, and humiliation. Many victims are maimed, tortured, and killed after being raped repeatedly by a gang of men. Genocidal rape occurs during both official and unofficial wars, but it can also occur during civil strife. It has been used by dictators to terrorize the local population into complicity.

Croatian psychiatrist Vera Folnegovic-Smalc has observed that:

> Suicidal thoughts are evident above all in women who have become pregnant as a result of rape. After an induced abortion the symptoms change, and depression is replaced by aggression and the wish for revenge. . . . In the beginning, rape victims came to us only if they needed a psychiatric certificate about their mental health to apply for a termination of pregnancy, after a suicide attempt, or if they were afflicted by other psychological disorders. I have known some women who tried to hide their rapes even then. . . .[4]

The abortion law of 1978 in former Yugoslavia permits termination of pregnancy without the need to give a reason during the first trimester. After that time, a psychiatric certificate supporting the need for termination can help convince a hospital ethics committee that the woman has a good reason to abort the pregnancy. During the war, however, some doctors were willing to bend the rules and perform an abortion after the first trimester without psychiatric support, on compassionate grounds.

The horrific rapes that occurred in 1992 during the Bosnian Serb conquest of Bosnia in former Yugoslavia aimed at exterminating the Muslim and Croatian women, and terrifying and shaming their families into leaving the country. But it wasn't only male Bosnian Serbs who raped. Croatian and Muslim men also raped (mainly Serbian women), just as some men—regardless of nationality, ethnicity, or religion—have done in wartime throughout history.

Concentration camps and special "rape camps" were set up by the Serbs, for the sole purpose of torturing women and making them bear Serbian children. By some absurd logic, even though genetically the baby would carry the "Muslim" genes of the mother, the Serbs felt that forcing Muslim women to bear their children would serve as revenge against the Muslims. Once pregnant, if the women didn't commit suicide and managed to survive the multiple abuses such as beatings and cigarette burn wounds on their bodies, they were usually set free. One woman named Senada recalls:

"They let us go because we were pregnant . . . they thought it was too late for us to do anything about it." . . . Senada decided to kill the child as soon as it was born. "I knew it wasn't my kid. I knew what I went through. It wasn't a child born of love or from a responsible marriage. If anyone had tried to show it to me after it was born, I'd have strangled them and the baby too. . . . If I'd ever had any chance to kill the kid inside me, I'd have done it." . . . The baby is now in England: a British journalist smuggled it out of Sarajevo. "This kid has nothing to do with me. He can do whatever he wants to with it, it makes no difference to me," says Senada.[5]

Men commit mass rape for various reasons: to humiliate and abuse their victims or "enemy" so that the rapists will be seen as the dominant power; to "ethnically cleanse" the community by either killing, expelling, or impregnating the women, thus making them unfit for marriage; to shame the women and their families into emigrating or committing suicide; to destabilize society; for revenge; to prove themselves as "men" and "bond" with male peers; because they are ordered to do so by commanding officers; out of fear for their own safety (rarely); possibly for sexual gratification.

In 1960, Congolese soldiers and civilian men celebrated their independence from Belgium by raping Belgian women, including nuns, as well as Portuguese, Greek, and American women. Because Belgian colonialists had raped black women for over 100 years, the Congolese men had supposedly raped for revenge, although they do have a history of raping their own race as well. Many Congolese soldiers viewed women as "property" and once independence was established, all "property" belonging to Belgians and other foreigners was theirs to take. Dr. Deniese Malderez recalls:

"I do not know how many rapes there were. We announced we had penicillin available as protection against venereal disease. Over 350 women were injected at this station. Approximately 50 women said they feared conception and asked for hormonal treatment. This we did not give because they were flying direct to Brussels. I believe many who were raped did not come to our station. . . . I went to four nuns who had been beaten and admitted they had been raped but would not come for treatment. The priests were shocked. You know Belgium is a Catholic country and abortion is illegal, but several priests said curettage must be performed. . . .[6]

Priests and nuns who have witnessed the brutalities of war, rape and forcible impregnation frequently have more practical views on abortion than their more sheltered brethren.

In 1971, Bengal (East Pakistan) declared its independence from Pakistan, with the support of India. West Pakistan dispatched troops to East Pakistan to try to crush the rebellion. Nine months of terror followed. During that time, an estimated 3 million people died, 10 million fled to India, and between 200,000–400,000 women were raped. (There are three sets of "official" figures.) About 80% of the women were Bengali Muslims, used to living in "purdah," i.e., strict, veiled isolation apart from men. Hindu and Christian women were also raped. Initially, it was West Pakistani Muslims from the Punjab who attacked them; their physique was different—they were taller, of lighter skin and different bone structure. "This racial difference would provide added anguish to those Bengali women who found themselves pregnant. . . ."[7] Gradually, as law and order disintegrated, Muslim Biharis known as "razakars" collaborated with the Pakistani Army and willingly joined in the raping. Even some Mukti Bahini "freedom fighters" of Bangladesh eventually began raping their own kind.

An estimated 25,000 women who had been raped became pregnant during that 9-month period of horror in Bangladesh.

Few cared to bear their babies. Those close to birth expressed little interest in the fate of the child. In addition to an understandable horror of rearing a child of forcible rape, it was freely acknowledged in Bangladesh that the bastard children with their fair Punjabi features would never be accepted into Bengali culture—and neither would their mothers.[8]

There was also the problem that Muslim Bengali men would not take back wives who had been touched by other men, despite a public campaign to try to convince these men that their women were national heroines.

For those with money, safe abortions were available in Calcutta, but many women were too ashamed and poverty-stricken to seek help. Suicide, infanticide, rat poison, and drowning were sadly their only recourse.

> Dr. Geoffrey Davis of the London-based International Abortion Research and Training Center . . . estimated that five thousand women had managed to abort themselves by various indigenous methods, with attendant medical complications.[8]

Mother Teresa offered free assistance to women wanting to adopt babies out overseas at a Catholic convent in Dacca; however, very few came to the shelter. Raped women risked becoming outcasts if they had a "bastard" baby outside of marriage or prior to wedlock, so secrecy and abortion were of paramount importance. When Planned Parenthood set up clinics in Dacca and 17 outlying areas in conjunction with the Bangladesh Central Organization for Women's Rehabilitation, women who learned of the clinics and could gain access chose to have abortions. The Dacca clinic did over 100 abortions in the first month after it opened. One Bengali doctor, Helena Pasha, admitted that before the war she had been totally against abortion, but after the war she made herself available to assist at the clinics, with little financial remuneration.

The most depressing aspect of studying the history of rape is that the above described examples are not unique. The incidence of rape per capita in Bangladesh was no greater than that of the horrendous one-month "Rape of Nanking" occupation by the Japanese in 1937, the rapes in Belgium and France as the German Army marched through during the first 3 months of World War I, and the rapes of women in Soviet Russia in World War II. At the Nuremberg war-crimes tribunal in 1946, captured German documents were used as evidence that rape was routinely used as a weapon of terror by the Nazis. Whenever men rape, women fear pregnancy, and abortion becomes a means of emotional and physical survival.

One young Vietnamese boat refugee interviewed by me recalled that when he escaped from Vietnam with his family at the age of 10, the two-day boat journey to Thailand was a nightmare. They were attacked by pirates and all of the women on the boat, with the exception of his mother, were raped. She was spared because her gestures had led the pirates to believe that she had just given birth. For the pirates, superstition held that intercourse with a woman who had just given birth would bring bad luck.

In Croatian psychiatrist Vera Folnegovic-Smalc's experience, the ability to cope with rape depends on a number of factors,

> including the victim's personality structure, her previous sexual experience, her sociocultural and religious character, the sort of rape, the victim's emotional relationship with her rapist, the consequences of the rape (e.g., pregnancy), the attitude of her family and those around her, and the therapy used.[9]

Posttraumatic stress disorder is the psychiatric diagnosis that most often applies to victims who suffer severe psychological damage as a result of rape and the additional trauma caused by the circumstances in which the rape occurred, such as war. Vera Folnegovic-Smalc explains:

> The most frequent symptoms occurring in our patients are anxiety, inner agitation, sleep disorders, nightmares, apathy, loss of self-confidence, and depression. . . . In all patients who have been primary or secondary victims of sexual abuse, we observe an aversion to sexuality. Some patients say, "For me there's no such thing as sex anymore; that's all in my past." Only one patient was prepared to resume sexual relations again after rape, and that was with her husband, who

knew nothing about the rape. She said, weeping, that they had stopped short of sexual intercourse at her request because she was afraid she would reveal everything to her husband, "and that could have meant the end of our life together." (In some cases husbands have gone so far as to kill their wives after hearing about the rape; in others, raped wives have committed suicide.).[9]

According to the 1990 National Women's Study in the United States, 31% of rape victims in the study developed posttraumatic distress disorder after being raped, even though only 4% sustained serious injury. At least 49%, however, feared that they would be killed or injured while being raped.[10] The incidence of posttraumatic stress disorder among women who have been raped in war is unknown, but it must surely be greater than the figures documented in the United States.

Most of us living in the United States are fortunate not to have faced the horrors of civil war. But rape does occur here, and whenever a women is raped, she may be haunted by the fear of pregnancy (61% of rape victims surveyed from 1987 to 1992 said that they feared pregnancy would result from the rape; see below).

According to the National Victim Center's 1992 publication entitled "Rape In America: A Report To The Nation," there are an estimated 683,000 forcible rapes of adult women every year in the United States. That translates to 78 rapes every hour. If statistics for adolescent and child rapes are included, the estimate at least doubles.

An estimated 12.1 million American women have been raped at least once, and 4.7 million of those more than once. A staggering 61.6% of rape victims in the United States were under 17 at the time of the rape, 29.3% of whom were under 11. Figures from the 1990 National Women's Study were based on 714 cases; 11% of victims were raped by their father or stepfather, 16% by relatives, and 29% by friends and neighbors. Among older victims, 22.2% were aged 18–24, 7.1% 25–29, and 6.1% over 29. Ten percent of victims were raped by a boyfriend or ex-boyfriend, and 9% by a husband or ex-husband. Unfortunately, most rapes (84%) are not reported to the police, because victims fear that their family and friends will find out and blame them for the rape.[10] There is a 5 to 30% chance that pregnancy will result from a single sexual assault during which sexual intercourse occurs, according to a report by C. Tietze that appeared in the journal *Fertility and Sterility* in 1960.

Because many rapes go unreported, it is not possible to establish accurate figures for rapes and subsequent pregnancies. In 1990, the year for which the National Women's Study produced the above estimates of the incidence of rape in the United States, an FBI Uniform Crime Report estimated the number of rapes reported to police to be 102,560, while the U.S. Department of Justice Bureau of Justice Statistics estimated the number of reported and unreported rapes of females over the age of 12 to be 130,000. The National Women's Study estimates did not include rape victims under the age of 18, so the number of rapes is in reality much higher than the estimates. A young Latino friend provides a typical example of why rape goes unreported. She was gang raped at gunpoint by three men in South Central Los Angeles, but refused to report the rape to police because the rapists threatened to kill her family if she did so (the rapists knew her home address from her driver's license). Given the history of gang violence in Los Angeles, she had no reason to disbelieve their threats.

Some women are so traumatized by rape and the fear of pregnancy that they experience a phantom pregnancy.

> Emma, a 17 year-old virgin at the time she was raped, had a "hysterical" pregnancy, complete with weight gain and nausea following her attack. She didn't get her period for 3 months. . . . Finally, she confided in her dorm director, who took a sample of Emma's urine for pregnancy testing. The results came back negative. The next day, Emma got her period.[11]

If women and girls were better educated to recognize the signs of ovulation, some of their fear of pregnancy might be alleviated, because they would have a better idea whether conception was likely at that time in their menstrual cycle.

When the rape counselor went to visit Loretta, all she could talk about was her fear that she was pregnant. She had taken Ovral in the emergency department and had had a period since the assault two weeks earlier, so it was highly improbable that she could be pregnant. She was from a strict religious background and sex outside of marriage was prohibited. While she had been a virgin prior to the rape, she was feeling considerable guilt because she had previously felt sexually attracted to men. She felt the rape was punishment for this unacceptable lust, and becoming pregnant would be the ultimate punishment.[12]

The physical trauma of rape passes, but the emotional effects can leave a permanent scar on the victim's psyche.

"Acquaintance" or "date" rape is the most prevalent form of rape in the United States, according to the National Victim Center's 1992 report. Included in the NVC's report were the results of the 1990 National Women's Study of 714 rape cases: 22% were committed by strangers and 78% by someone known to the victim.[10] Both "stranger" and "acquaintance" rape can be categorized as individual or gang rape, according to the number of males involved. Generally, the greater the number of males participating, the more severe are the trauma and range of symptoms that the victim experiences. The greater the number of times penetration occurs during gang rape, the greater is the chance of pregnancy if the victim has passed puberty and is premenopausal.

Force or the threat of force are estimated to be used against 60% of incest victims, according to The Children's Division of the American Humane Association, which published the findings of a 1969 study of 250 female victims of rape under the age of 16. The study found that 75% of the offenders were relatives, friends, or acquaintances of the victims. Rape-related pregnancy occurred in 29 girls. I have been unable to ascertain how many of these girls were victims of actual incest or acquaintance rape, or how many had an abortion, but I would hope that none of them were forced to carry the pregnancy to term. Statistics relating to pregnancy as a result of rape and incest are meaningless to a rape victim, because the threat of pregnancy is real regardless of the odds. Any girl who is raped and has passed puberty can become pregnant.

What happens to a child born of rape? Maybe he or she will be fortunate enough to be accepted by the mother, or adopted by relatives or strangers who know nothing of the violent conception. Sometimes, though, things don't work out well. An American woman recalls:

> About 3 years after my divorce, I was raped by a man whom I thought was a close, platonic friend . . . it was a shattering experience which destroyed the last vestiges of my ability to trust for many years. Nine months later, I gave birth to my son, Joseph, whom I never wanted, and whom I was never able to love. For health reasons, abortion was not an option. My only alternative was adoption, which I took in a sense by giving the baby to his father, saying that he would have to raise the child and that I would have nothing to do with his upbringing. Joseph's father agreed.
>
> When my son was a confused young man, his father requested that I agree to meet him. Joseph knew the reason why I rejected him but he wanted to meet me nevertheless. Perhaps he wanted my love—if he did, then I let him down. He said that he understood, and I guess that he did. I really didn't have any feelings about how he felt and experienced no maternal feelings for him. That may sound callous, but I was simply never able to feel anything for him.
>
> Rape is a terrible violation not only of the body, but also of the soul—having a child for me is an expression of love for the father of the child. You can't love a man who rapes you, and I certainly couldn't love my son, rape's child. In a sense, he too was a victim of rape. . . . Rape is cruel and violent, and a child conceived in that manner is a constant reminder of the horror of its conception.
>
> In 1987, my son died of a drug overdose, after battling drug addiction for many years. I felt no loss when he died. The thought of a person dying before they have managed to

truly live is always sad, and in that sense I was moved by his death, but I felt no personal sorrow.

There's no excuse to rape a woman—there are too many women who give away sex or from whom you can buy it. My son's father was secretly in love with me I later discovered, but that didn't give him the right to rape me. . . .[13]

It is impossible to know whether the child would have done better in life had his mother felt some love for him. A child born of rape is a constant reminder of the horror of the conception. Rejection of the fruit of violence is an instinctive female response.

Religion should provide comfort and help heal people in distress, but unfortunately it often compounds a woman's sense of guilt and confusion after rape. Loretta Lewis, a black female from an upper middle-class family, was 15 when she was raped by three white men. Her devout mother would not allow Loretta to have an abortion, because she believed that the baby had a "right to life." Loretta's parents adopted the baby and raised him as their own child. Loretta recalled:

I hated that child. To me he represented rape, pain, anger, and frustration. I didn't look at him until he was a toddler. I was in the same house and I wouldn't touch him. I wouldn't pick him up. I wouldn't do anything. He represented the worst experience I have ever been through in my life. . . . Then one day Mitchell, my son, toddled up to me and said, "You don't love me. You don't play with me," and started crying. That turned me around. . . . I started liking him as a little boy, and as he grew up, I really began to love him. He's here, we cannot put him back. If I had my choice, he would never have been on this earth. But he had nothing to do with it. He was an innocent bystander.[14]

To force a girl or woman who has been raped to bear the child is cruel and can have deadly consequences. It was pure luck that Loretta failed in her attempt to commit suicide after she was raped and developed seizures. She should have been permitted to have an abortion. Even though she eventually came to love her child, she will never be a mother to him.

Lee Ezell, author of *The Missing Piece*, offers a different perspective. She was raped and had a baby girl whom she gave up for adoption, because abortion was not accessible to her at that time. Her daughter turned out to be the only child she would ever have, and became "the missing piece" in her life. The following extract from her book was published in the *Los Angeles Times* on February 26, 1992:

> ... You can't imagine the impact when, a few years ago, I picked up the phone and a voice announced, "Hello, you've never met me, but I am your daughter. I've been searching for you to let you know you are a grandmother." Our remarkable reunion ... has been so fulfilling. My daughter's husband shook my hand and tearfully remarked, "Thanks for not aborting Julie; I don't know what my life would be like without her and our children." My daughter, Julie, born of sexual assault, did not inherit any 'evil genes.' As she puts it: "It doesn't matter how I began, but what I'll become." I'm so glad that ... I did not give this innocent child the death penalty for the crime of her father.[15]

Time heals many wounds. Lee Ezell's ability to embrace her daughter with love is touching, but had she been forced to raise her daughter, things might have turned out very differently. She was ready to be found when her daughter traced her, because she had never had any other children. Giving a child up for adoption is a very serious decision. Read Chapter 13 in this book before you make that choice or recommend it to anyone else.

If you've become pregnant as a result of being raped, you should seek professional counseling to help you through the trauma. Psychiatrist Vera Folnegovic-Smalc notes:

> There are various forms of therapeutic treatment for rape victims with psychological disorders; ultimately they depend on the intensity and type of symptoms, the victim's personality structure, her attitude toward treatment, and the train-

ing of the therapist. If the victim is positively disposed toward therapy, she usually receives individual psychotherapy in combination with chemical therapy. Anxiolytics, antidepressants, or both, are usually prescribed, and in the case of a psychosis neuroleptics are given as well. Family therapy can be undertaken only in exceptional cases, because the victims have usually been separated from their families or else want to hide the rape from them. They usually also receive gynecological treatment. . . . rape is one of the gravest abuses, with consequences that can last a lifetime. For that reason it is necessary to offer victims every opportunity to prevent or treat psychological symptoms ... [treatment should be covered by] health and welfare insurance ... it is important to support victims and their families emotionally, and in this respect religious and political communities can do their share. . . . the victim's wish for anonymity must be respected, and if no psychosis is present, the victim should have a role in deciding what type of treatment she receives.[9]

The National Victim Center in Virginia can help rape victims find sympathetic counseling and medical care located near them (see the "Help" Directory at the back of this book). Local telephone directories in the United States and other countries usually offer rape crisis counseling referrals in the list of emergency numbers at the front of the phone book.

It is very important that women who have been raped receive love and support from their family, friends, and community. Dr. Vera Folnegovic-Smalc offers hope:

If women experience strong emotional support from family and friends or even from new acquaintances in the refugee camps, their psychological disorders abate more quickly than those of women who keep the rape a secret or speak of it only to a therapist. We have discovered that women can discuss the actual act of sexual abuse and their subsequent psychological problems more fully in telephone conversations than face to face, and they also report their suicidal wishes more frequently by phone than when they come in for counseling. We believe this is because a telephone precludes the danger of being forcibly committed.[9]

As a community, we need to stop blaming women for rape and try to focus on helping them heal. We need to learn more about why men rape and seek ways to prevent it. Rape cripples a woman's ability to trust, sometimes for life.

Perhaps the ultimate irony is that of a woman with a history of infertility and trying to conceive, who then is raped and becomes pregnant within that menstrual cycle. A 26-year-old married Asian woman who found herself in that position underwent CVS and DNA testing in an attempt to determine whose sperm—her husband's or the rapist's—had impregnated her. The test results suggested at least a 98.6% chance that her husband was the biological father of her fetus. She decided to continue the pregnancy and gave birth to a healthy son.[16]

If you've been impregnated by a rapist, seek counseling. If you believe that abortion is morally wrong, don't have one. Having the baby and giving it up for adoption may be the best solution to your dilemma, even though that may also produce conflicts. Most of all, don't let anyone pressure you into making a decision you will later regret. Do what YOU believe is right.

12

Fetal Abnormality—Special Concerns

When I was pregnant with my son, I was referred for a variety of prenatal diagnostic tests. I chose to undergo chorionic villi sampling (CVS) at 9–12 weeks gestation rather than amniocentesis at 15–16 or 18–20 weeks, because I felt that it would be better to know of any fetal abnormality earlier rather than later in the pregnancy. (CVS sampling is a procedure in which a small amount of tissue—chorionic villi—is removed from the developing placenta. Chorionic villi tissue carries the same genetic information as the fetus and can be analyzed for many genetic disorders.)

In addition to CVS, I had a follow-up blood screening test between weeks 15 and 20 (MSAFP test) that reveals whether a woman is in a high-risk category for fetal abnormalities that cannot be detected earlier using CVS, such as neural tube defects (e.g., spina bifida, anencephaly) or ventral wall defects (omphalocele or gastroschisis).

During the counseling session prior to the CVS, the counselor suggested that my husband and I consider whether we would want to continue the pregnancy if the results revealed a fetal abnormality. She noted that the degree of abnormality would not necessarily be clear from the test results. After she had explained all of the details and risks associated with the procedure and the implications of positive test results, she remarked that if we were against abortion under any circumstances, we should forgo the risk of CVS.

My husband and I believe that you shouldn't knowingly bring a disabled child into the world, for the sake of both the child and the family, so we went ahead with the test. Fortunately, the results were normal, but if they had shown any kind of abnormality, I would have had an abortion. Believing as I do does not mean that disabled people aren't valued as human beings. Once a person is born—able-bodied or disabled—he or she deserves the chance to develop his or her full potential.

There are varying degrees of disability, and many disabled people are thinking, caring, productive, and loving members of their family and community. A disability doesn't make a person worthless, but it can cause a great deal of financial, emotional, and physical hardship for the disabled person and the caregivers. Dealing with the problems involved can bring people closer or tear them apart. Some grow through the experience, while others flounder in frustration and despair.

When I began researching this chapter, I wrongly believed that a disability automatically causes suffering, and that knowingly bringing a disabled child into the world was wrong because it inflicted suffering that could be avoided. I still believe that to be true, but I have learned that not all disabled people suffer. Suffering is a relative and very subjective term.

Glenn Little, president of the Disabled Persons Association in Victoria, Australia, taught me that lesson. He has cerebral palsy (caused by strangulation by the umbilical cord during birth) and was strapped into his wheelchair during our conversation because he has virtually no control over the movement of his body. Although his disability was caused during birth, his experience of being disabled offers great insight and a positive way of looking at disabilities. His arms flailed violently throughout our conversation, and his head made involuntary movements that sometimes made it difficult to understand him. But Glenn articulated his thoughts with crystal clarity and earned my respect as he answered my questions with generosity, compassion, humor, and intelligence.

Cerebral palsy is a disability which can happen in three major ways, one of which can be detected now during pregnancy. . . . If I had been given the choice about whether I wanted to live with my brain damage or be allowed to die, I would have chosen to live. I believe that I am serving a worthwhile purpose in my own way.

I would have liked to have been able to walk, particularly during the teenage years. I don't equate the frustration of being disabled with suffering. I think it's very bad to put it in that context. The individual can allow himself to suffer and wallow in self-pity, but that is the only way in which I would equate suffering with people with disabilities. . . . I'd like to be able to climb up and down cliffs and go swimming and pursue other similar activities, but my not being able to do so is not suffering. That's just frustration, a "Damn it, I can't do that," type of feeling. So we find other things that we can do and other outlets. I lead a very busy life. I'm on half a dozen committees outside the Association. I work a fifty-hour week keeping the Association going. We're having funding problems at the moment. So I don't have very much time to think about me or where I'm going. I enjoy music, getting lost in a good movie, and all manner of other activities.

I honestly don't think I've heard any disabled person say that they would prefer not to have been born. That's after twenty odd years of mixing in and out of the disabled community. If another disabled person and I decided to have a child and we were told that the child would be born disabled, we would go ahead and have the child. . . . I think that if you find out during pregnancy that the baby is likely to have a disability you will find nine times out of ten that they won't know the severity . . . the child might well grow up into someone like me or any of the other people you have met here at the Association today. Should we have been aborted? It's not just a question of what people need in the way of assistance— it's also a question of what they can give.

I am not a disabled person; first and foremost I am a person. I may be a person with a physical disability, but my identity is that of a person.[1]

Glenn Little was lucky to have been born into a loving family who were able to provide for him, with the help of the community and friends. Obstetrician Dr. Lawrence W. Scott has had the sad experience of working with children who were not as lucky. If you make the decision to carry the pregnancy to term and then cannot cope with the disabled child, foster care or adoption may be alternatives, but the child may also wind up in an institution.

During our interview, Dr. Scott reflected:

I believe that quality of life is just as important as life itself, but I don't know who has a right to say how much quality. I have seen many situations when children have been born with such grotesque abnormalities and medical problems that they're psychologically overbearing for the family. I recall delivering one baby that was so grotesque that everybody was totally happy when this child died shortly after it was born. It had a gross open defect on its head, a distorted eye, and a tumor on its spine which would have caused paralysis from the neck down. I have seen babies like this out at the State Hospital when I worked there between my first and second year as a doctor. That's a hospital for mentally retarded children in Pomona, California. I was doing some research there for a pediatrician during my summer break. I tested every child in that hospital. Many of them were so bad off that they had to be hauled around on carts—they were pathetic.

It's difficult to decide what to do when an abnormality is detected in pregnancy, because it's a gray area. Even a hydrocephalic baby may survive and grow up to be a normal, mentally sane person. It depends on the degree of hydrocephalus (increased fluid in the cerebral spinal spaces of the brain that causes marked enlargement of the head). They have ways of inserting drains now to decrease some of the fluid, so that the child may have a slightly larger than average head, but may function very well. But sometimes there is so much fluid that you know the cortex of the brain has been depressed to the point that it's just a shell and the child will be mentally retarded.

Most disabilities come in degrees, which is why it's so difficult to decide what's best. I don't think it's up to me as a doctor to decide if a fetus with a disability should be aborted. It's up to the parents to decide. But I do think that parents need to be better informed about what it means to have a disabled child, be it Down's syndrome or any other kind of abnormality. Only the parents and family can decide if they'll be able to cope.[2]

It is very difficult for any of us to know if we'd be up to the emotional and physical challenges of caring for a disabled child. Financially, the strain can be catastrophic, despite a variety of community and welfare support services and private insurance coverage. For those who can afford to hire a private nurse, as one Los Angeles family did when their third child of six was unexpectedly born with cerebral palsy, the cost can run from $25,000 upwards per year, depending on the qualifications of the nurse or aide. According to Dr. John Williams, medical director of the Prenatal Diagnostic Center in Los Angeles,

In 1993, the average cost of raising a Down's syndrome child from birth to age 18 was approximately $450,000. . . . That figure includes food, clothing, and medical care. Other disabilities can cost much more than that.[3]

I was surprised to learn while researching this chapter that most people don't consider the cost of raising a disabled child when making a decision regarding whether or not to continue a pregnancy after a fetal abnormality has been detected. According to genetic counselor "Elyse" at the Prenatal Diagnostic Center in Los Angeles,

Decisions are made on the basis of religious and family beliefs. Very few people could afford to take care of a disabled child on their own. Usually it's private insurance and community resources that pay for a disabled child, as well as the family. . . . Most people who chose to continue a pregnancy to term despite a fetal abnormality keep the baby. . . . A high percentage of patients terminate pregnancies where a fetal abnormality that isn't compatible with life has been detected. Anencephalies is an example (a condition in which the brain does not form properly).[4]

In my view, asking the community to fund personal religious beliefs is a questionable way to approach parenthood. If you knowingly bring a disabled child into the world, you should be able and willing to pay for all costs associated with caring for that child. Welfare and supplementary services should serve as an emergency safety net rather than a presumed way of life. A surprise disability that emerges after birth is clearly a different matter.

Dr. John Williams has well over 10 years' experience in genetic counseling and is a specialist in maternal–fetal medicine, clinical genetics, and clinical cytogenetics. He has observed that

Some couples will take a disabled baby and care for it as best as possible at home. Many find out after a few years that a Down's syndrome child becomes very hard to manage. They're very good babies and tend not to cry a lot or get into trouble. But as they get older, they are often difficult to control and hard to discipline because they don't really understand some of the aspects of why you're disciplining them and that they've done something wrong. So then the child will often be placed in foster care or an institution that will be paid for by tax dollars. There are families who do care for Down's syndrome children throughout their life span. Sometimes these children have serious heart defects and if they aren't repaired in the early years, they're not very repairable later. They become chronically debilitated by their heart condition and die as teenagers or young adults. Private insurance companies will pay for the medical care in most situations, but they don't necessarily pay for custodial care and special programs that handicapped children need. There are state-funded agencies that do provide funding for that,

but again, it's the taxpayers who are paying for it. Spina bifida is also usually covered by medical insurance, provided
that it's not an excluded condition. Some state-funded re-
gional centers in California will only cover disorders associated with mental retardation, including spina bifida,
chromosomatic abnormalities like Down's syndrome, and
other structural abnormalities associated with mental retardation.

Sometimes children with disabilities suffer physically.
If a Down's syndrome child has a defective heart, it may be
short of breath all the time and may not feel well . . . but in
the absence of a physical defect that would cause pain and
discomfort, who can really say if Down's syndrome children
are suffering because they're mentally retarded?

Spina bifida children often have problems with paralysis and increased risk of bladder infections and other problems that can accompany paralysis.

Tay–Sachs children generally don't survive beyond
three to five years after they're born. They are probably unaware of what's going on, because they're so debilitated, but
we don't know what they're actually perceiving. The family
certainly suffers watching the child deteriorate. Debilitating,
progressive, fatal diseases like Tay–Sachs are devastating for
the family because they watch an apparently normal, healthy
baby be well until about 6 months of age and then begin to
lose what developmental milestones that he or she has
gained and progressively become demented, blind, and con-
vulsive. The last few months and sometimes years of life are
agony to the family. There are other disorders similar to
Tay–Sachs that have a similar course. Some couples choose
to abort the pregnancy and others don't. It really depends
upon the family situation and if they've been through a serious illness with a prior child or a sibling. The only reasons
in favor of continuing a pregnancy when you know that the
fetus has tested positive for fetal abnormalities are religious
and moral.[3]

Unfortunately, many of the diagnostic tests that reveal fetal abnormalities such as CVS and amniocentesis are not routinely performed, except on women over age 35 or those in a high-risk category. CVS on average in the United States costs $1500, so the cost is prohibitive. But some women who could be tested are scared off by the perception of the risks of the procedure itself. Inaccurate media hype can easily scare people away from prenatal diagnostic testing, as Dr. John Williams learned in 1992 following TV reports that CVS was suspected of causing fetal abnormalities. Dr. Williams explains:

> It has been clearly shown through various scientific data that there is not conclusive evidence of an association between CVS and limb abnormalities. However, you cannot erase the fear from people's minds once they see an alarmist news media report.[3]

Inaccurate, sensationalist media reporting is greatly disturbing, because the media has such tremendous power over the way people think. Among the thousands of articles collected during 11 years of research on abortion-related issues, I cannot recall a single article that didn't have at least one mistake in it. Don't be scared off CVS because of alarmist news reports. What is important is finding a highly experienced physician such as Dr. Williams to do the procedure.

Women need to understand their diagnostic testing options and take advantage of them whenever possible and appropriate during pregnancy. Dr. John Williams explains:

> Chromosome abnormalities, inherited metabolic disorders such as Tay–Sachs Disease, and an ever-increasing number of single gene disorders can be diagnosed by analyzing the molecular structure of DNA. Cystic fibrosis, muscular dystrophy, hemophilia, and sickle-cell anemia can all be diagnosed by molecular genetic techniques using cells obtained by chorionic villi sampling (CVS) and amniocentesis, or later on in pregnancy by fetal blood sampling. There are disorders

that cannot be diagnosed by any biochemical or chromosome tests, but are associated with a physical abnormality, such as a structural defect like spina bifida or heart and limb defects. Visualizing the fetus with ultrasound (sonogram) is another way of making these diagnoses. A chromosome abnormality can be detected in the first trimester, between 10–12 weeks with CVS or between 13–20 weeks by amniocentesis. Most of the structural abnormalities can be detected between 16 and 22–24 weeks with ultrasound. Ultrasound is noninvasive, so it's a painless way of looking for structural abnormalities. CVS and amniocentesis involve invading the uterus, through the cervix for CVS or through the abdomen with a needle for amniocentesis or transabdominal CVS.

There are procedure-related risks such as having a complication like bleeding or infection or the ones that people fear the most, a miscarriage or some sort of injury to the fetus that could result in a defect. That's the theoretical explanation for the significantly increased rate of limb abnormalities that have been described by two of the roughly 150 centers worldwide doing CVS. The majority of the other centers have not been able to demonstrate an increased rate of limb abnormality. The theory is that you could do something to disrupt the development of an organ or a structure such as a limb. Although this fear is linked with CVS, there have been similar reports linked with amniocentesis. These problems are probably not caused by the amniocentesis any more than they are by the CVS. They are probably developmental abnormalities that are already present at the time of the CVS or amniocentesis, and in some cases are just not seen on the ultrasound because structures such as fingers and toes are so small that it's very difficult to visualize and count them to ensure that they're entirely intact in every fetus.

There's no test that is infallible. There are very low false-positive rates and even lower false-negative rates, but false-positive and false-negative results do occur. It is possible due to rare instances of low-level mosaicism (more than one cell line) to miss the abnormal cell line and we tell the patient that the fetus has normal chromosomes. It is possible that maternal cell contamination could cause us to tell the mother that she is carrying a normal girl when in fact she is carrying a boy with Down's syndrome, because the Down's syndrome cells didn't grow. These kinds of false results are very rare. The chances of a false negative are probably somewhere in the vicinity of 1 in 4–5,000 cases. A false positive with amniocentesis is less than one percent, and with CVS, it's about one percent. Ultrasound can also have false-positive and false-negative results because of artifact or an inexperienced ultrasonographer seeing something that's not there or, more commonly, failing to see something that is there.

Even if you think that you might not terminate the pregnancy, there still can be some benefit to having the information that prenatal diagnostic testing can provide. For most people, the rationale is that if you're not going to terminate the pregnancy, then why go to the expense of having the test. But sometimes couples change their mind. Having an abnormal child is often an abstract concept. When faced with the harsh reality of having an abnormal fetus, many couples who otherwise would never have terminated the pregnancy will change their mind and terminate the pregnancy. There are also medical advantages to having information regarding an abnormal fetus ahead of giving birth, as it can affect such decisions as whether or not to have an emergency cesarean section.[3]

In an ideal world, all pregnant women would be able to undergo prenatal diagnostic testing. Although the tests are not 100% accurate, I agree with Dr. John Williams when he says that "it is better to detect the abnormalities that are detected than none at all."[3] The other problem with diagnostic testing is that even if an abnormality is detected, the degree of disability will not necessarily be clear from the test.

For couples in a high-risk category of pregnancy (such as

women over 35), who have spent years trying to conceive, the thought of risking miscarriage through prenatal diagnostic testing is sometimes too unbearable for them. One woman, a smoker in her 40s when she had her first child, said she would prefer to have a disabled child than risk having a miscarriage. Her child was born apparently normal, but has since developed learning difficulties and a mental slowness. His problems would not have been detectable by diagnostic testing. Another woman, a geneticist in her mid-40s, who had spent 15 years and over $100,000 trying to conceive, at first declined CVS and amniocentesis, for fear of having a miscarriage. In the end, she decided to risk having amniocentesis, because she felt that she had to know if there were any fetal abnormalities. She was uncertain whether she would have had an abortion had abnormalities been detected; her decision would have depended on the type of abnormality.

Some couples gamble and continue a pregnancy despite test results showing a fetal abnormality, hoping that the results are wrong. Rarely do they get lucky. I wouldn't take that risk.

13

Adoption as an Alternative to Abortion

Adoption is repeatedly suggested as an alternative to abortion by those who are against abortion, but the truth is that most women would not consider it. What the advocates of adoption as an alternative to abortion fail to realize is that a born baby is NOT the same as an embryo or fetus *in utero*. A willingness to have an abortion does not mean that a woman would be willing to give up a baby. A 22-year-old French Catholic woman who had undergone an RU 486 abortion confided that she did not consider adoption as an alternative because "I would not be able to give my baby to someone else."[1] Abandoning a baby to fate is out of the question for most women.

Sharon Kaplan Roszia is an expert in adoption issues, especially "open" adoption. She is the director of the Kinship Alliance (headquartered in Orange County, California), an organization that believes in creating large clans or kinship systems for adoptee children, including previous foster families and other caring relatives. She observes:

> Women who struggle with adoption often verbalize their conflict by saying that "adoption seems unnatural." Many young women are brought in by their parents or boyfriends or even their husbands, who want them to consider adoption. To the young women involved, adoption is abhorrent. They think, "How could anybody do this to a child?" ... I

am very appreciative of people who approach adoption with great caution, because there is a lot of pain connected with the choice of adoption, as there is with other choices that require loss. . . . The bumper stickers that say "ADOPT, DON'T ABORT" offend me, because two very major impacting decisions are combined as if one cancels the other. Adoption does not cancel out abortion, and it should not be viewed as an alternative to abortion. There are gains and losses in both choices that have to be measured separately. Once the decision whether or not to abort occurs, if the pregnancy is going to be carried through to term, the next set of decisions has to be made regarding whether to parent or not parent on a daily basis.[2]

Most women perceive giving a baby up for adoption as far more traumatic than having an abortion.

When I had an unplanned pregnancy in Australia around late 1944, we considered having an abortion or having a baby as possibilities, but at no stage did we consider adoption a viable alternative, not even to the horror of an illegal abortion. It was outside the range of possibilities. I have always believed that once you have a child, you do the very best you can for it, and handing it over to strangers is not included in that. I would have grieved and suffered immensely if somebody had been in a position to force me to do that.

Those thoughts of my mother on adoption as an alternative to abortion echo my own feelings. My innate prejudice against adoption has made me work especially hard to try to be fair in writing this chapter. There are some women, and children, for whom adoption was a necessary choice, and it has worked out well.

Peggy Soule is executive director of Children Awaiting Parents, Inc. During a telephone interview with me, she related:

My dilemma has been that I support a woman's right to choose to have an abortion, and yet I have six adopted children. If their mothers had been able to get abortions in the early 70s, I wouldn't have my wonderful family. I would support and help my children if they wanted to search for their families. . . . Any birth mother considering adoption has many choices of prospective parents—single, two parent or gay—she has control. Even babies born HIV positive or with disabilities can usually find an adoptive home—some couples actually specify that they want to adopt a child with special needs. There are wonderful groups to work with. Open adoption is now more common. Adoptions don't have to be closed and secretive.[3]

Peggy Soule's son Mark has never had any desire to search for his birth parents, and yet some of his adopted siblings are curious to find their birth parents. He explained his feelings to me in a telephone interview:

My parents are my parents and the fact that I'm adopted is secondary to me. I've always been happy in my home. I believe that children should be told that they're adopted when they're young. Adoption really can work, as long as we remember that adoption is finding homes for kids, not finding babies for parents.

Some women who chose adoption or were forced by circumstances to accept it, deeply regret parting with the baby and have been scarred for life.

When you write your book, please, please tell women that adoption is a terrible choice to make. I had three illegal abortions in America. The physical pain and danger associated with the abortions were nothing compared with the agony and lifelong regret I have experienced as a result of adopting out my baby. I have never been able to stop wondering if she's alright. I have never regretted my abortions, but I will regret adopting out my baby for eternity.

That impassioned plea by a saleswoman employed at Sisterhood bookstore in Los Angeles was delivered as I left the shop. She took me aside on the pavement outside and implored me to include her thoughts on adoption in this book on abortion. I have done so because I believe that both the woman and her child were victims of a cruel system of closed adoption that is rarely appropriate.

Many women who feel ambivalent about their pregnancies bond intensely with the baby during birth, making adoption unfeasible.

> The process of the nine months was quite extraordinary. The effort I put into trying to have an abortion on the one hand and yet trying to love this unborn child I was carrying was remarkable. I was trying to muster up some love for this creature whom I saw as coming to destroy my life. During labor, I said to my husband that I felt as if someone had given me some strange drug. The moment that little skinny, scrawny, hairy creature emerged, I thought, "What a poor little thing she is." My fantasies and fears had envisioned this full-blown entity that was going to come and ruin my life. My husband held her in one hand and then put her on my breast. She immediately stopped crying and latched on. I felt "my creature"—she was mine. She instantly became everything. My husband felt the same way. I bless the day that she was born. No, I have never for a single moment regretted the birth of my daughter.[4]

Intense love for a newborn baby doesn't necessarily alter the woman's situation that made her contemplate an abortion, but it does mean that she will have to decide how best to express her maternal affection and protectiveness of her child. She may keep the child and run the risk of both of them starving if there is financial hardship, or she may decide to give the baby up for adoption and possibly regret it for the rest of her life, even though her maternal instinct at the time tells her that adoption would be best for the baby. Fortunately, open adoption has become more acceptable over the last 20 years, at least in the United States. It offers a woman an almost miraculous chance to find a compromise between keeping her baby and giving it up completely, by allowing her to share her child's life to an extent that is feasible and agreeable to all parties concerned. It is, however, still a painful choice.

Sharon Kaplan Roszia, coauthor of *The Open Adoption Experience*, has worked for 32 years as a social worker in the field of adoption and has been a foster mother and an adoptive mother to children of different races. She is acutely aware of the conflicts associated with adoption and the reasons why women choose that option.

Adoption is very painful, which doesn't mean that it doesn't have positive aspects. . . . Before placing a baby for adoption, a woman must have spread before her clear and honest choices, and she must be empowered to keep that child first and foremost. I really believe that adoption always has to be a second choice. I work very hard with women to make sure that they have examined every single way to parent that child, or to parent that child within family support, before they create an adoption. Ultimately, after women have taken that path, some tell me that they want their child to have something more than they feel that they can give at this point in time. It's really a time-based issue. If it was happening a year or two later, things might be different, but they know that children can't wait. So often, women say, "I've explored everything. I want my child to have what I can't give it." Typically they're talking about a two-parent home, financial stability, and an "at home" mother. More and more women have said to me in the last couple of years that they could parent this child and put it in daycare all day, or take it off to college and put it in a college nursery all day long, but they really want someone at home, hands on, devoted to their child, which is not something that they feel they can offer. That becomes an issue with placing of a child with a single parent, because what these women want is a "complete life-style" for their child, including a father figure. I do run into women who are comfortable with single parent or gay and lesbian placement, but the majority of women say that they want their child to have what they can't presently provide.

The reason connected with that is the feeling of not being ready to make that day-to-day parenting commitment.

Very often, if I ask whether the woman has considered terminating the pregnancy, they look at me in absolute horror. But when I ask them why they're against abortion, they can't tell me why. It's just a feeling. . . . For some women, it's too late to have an abortion, for others abortion is not within their religion, and some believe that some good can come out of their pregnancy for another family, so there's an altruistic tone to their reasoning. Those are the things I hear most often.

I fostered and adopted a large number of children of all different races, but our children came home as toddlers and teenagers, not as babies. So my experience of adoption from an adoptive parent perspective is with some extraordinary needs children with attachment difficulties and all kinds of "acting out in the community" types of difficulties. The children whom I fostered stayed with me into adulthood, no matter whether they came home as toddlers or teenagers. Some of the children have done well and some have not done well at all, but we're still in touch with them all.[2]

There is no guarantee that any parent, birth or adoptive, will be able to fulfill all of the needs of a child, no matter how much goodwill and desire there is to meet those needs on the part of the parent. The notion that a two-parent family will by definition be better able to meet the needs of a child than a single parent is simply not true, although it may be the case for some children.

Adoption may cause great trauma for children and their adoptive families, because at some point most adopted children want to know who their birth parents were and why they were adopted out. Many problems and much suffering may be caused to all concerned by this process of inquiry on the part of an adopted child in search of roots and identity. A 40-year-old American man poignantly confided:

I love my parents very much, but I have always felt like an outsider, as if I didn't belong to the family because my personality and physique are so different to those of my parents and the rest of my family. It did not surprise me when I was told as a teenager that I was adopted. I have been searching for my birth parents for some time, but now that I may have the opportunity to meet my birth mother in the near future, I'm scared—I'm afraid she will not like me and that she will reject me again, or worse still, that I will not like her.[5]

Sharon Kaplan Roszia explains:

I think the costs [of adoption] are very high for children. I'm not a "Rah-rah, let's vote for adoption" fan. The cost of adoption for children is connection with their family of origin and a chance to grow up like every other child with their own family. It's difficult to be raised in a clan that's not your own. The way I address that is by advocating open adoption. I won't participate in adoptions where we can't preserve some family linkage for children. I absolutely cannot tolerate totally disconnecting children from their family. I don't think that it's necessary for a child to lose a family in order to gain a family. If people who come to see me are really having a difficult time and can't see themselves adequately parenting but on the other hand the thought of never knowing where their child is and never contributing to their child's life in any way beyond birth is abhorrent, then we examine what an open adoption relationship could do. That sometimes creates an option for them that wasn't there before.[2]

It is the concept of open adoption that changed my totally negative view of adoption.

Amanda Crawford is both an adoptee through the closed adoption system and an open adoptive mother. She is the director of a newly forming organization called the OPTIONS Alliance, which will specialize in placing children for open adoption whose parents are dying of AIDS. In one of those rare coincidences engineered by fate, I first spoke with Amanda the day after she had just been reunited with her birth mother, at the age of 36. During the interview, she was passionate and full of the thrill of a happy reunion with her biological mother. Her story and thoughts on adoption capture the essence of the adoption conflict from the perspective of a child and parent.

I was adopted at 6 weeks old by a Chinese family. . . . When I was around 9 years old, I found out that I was adopted when a 10-year-old friend of the family became mad at me and said angrily "You don't know anything and you're adopted anyway!" When I asked my mother whether I was adopted she told me the story about a young Korean couple that had given me up for adoption.

I was very angry at everybody when I learned that I was adopted. I used it against my adoptive parents big time, saying things like, "You won't let me have this and you don't really love me because I'm adopted." In retrospect, I couldn't have been more wrong. I was incredibly angry with my birth mother and I kept asking myself how she could abandon me. Was I really that ugly? What did she do, just leave me by the trash? I kept imagining bizarre pictures about what had made her abandon me. With maturity, I gradually grew out of that anger, especially as I learned how to be compassionate. I realize now that maybe my birth mother didn't have a choice . . . it wasn't fair of me to judge my birth mother for her decision to give me up for adoption.

It is really overwhelming to meet my birth mother. . . . When I first called her on September 15, 1994, she thought that I was a prank caller. She had been convinced that I was dead . . . 11 days after I called she flew to California to meet me, once she realized that I wasn't a prank caller. During the initial phone conversation, she asked me my name a couple of times and seemed in shock when I answered Amanda, but that I was called "Mandy" as a child. She then asked if it would be alright if she called me "Mandy." It touched my heart because it was almost as if she wanted to go back to the years when I was little. Her attitude, overall, has helped me to overcome a lot of insecurity.

A lot of women don't remember giving birth to the child they gave up for adoption. Women seem to do one of two things: they either blank out memory of that period or they recall every detail vividly. My mother, who is here with me now, is trying to reconstruct the story of what happened to me. She does recall that she did not see me after I was born and didn't really know if I was a boy or girl. She did say that if she had had the opportunity to hold me and see me, she is pretty certain she would not have gone through with the adoption, no matter what my birth father would have said. She believes that she would have found a way to keep me.

As an adoptee, you often go through your entire life not looking like a soul. Because of this, there are three areas that are very distinct black holes in the life of a child who is adopted. Do I look like somebody? Who do I look like? That's the most overwhelming one. Why did you let me go? Do you hate my guts? What is my medical history? For me, it turned out that my mother had married my father approximately 18 months after I was born, which is very rare. Usually when adoptees go searching for their birth parents, they find one or other parent, not both. I look very much like my sister.

The day after I first spoke with my birth mother, she says that she just kept saying sorry all day long. I think that she was trying to deal with all the emotions that learning I was alive brought up in her. She seemed to be in shock. I kept waiting for my birth mother to say, "What are you, one of those ever-bouncing clowns?" (The ones with weights in the bottom that keep bouncing back upright. You can't push them over.) I thought she would say something like, "I got rid of you the one time and now you're bouncing back up into my life." That's every kid's nightmare. When you're adopted, growing up there is that wish for the fairy-tale ending when you find out that your birth mother and birth father are a prince and princess and they couldn't keep you because Rumpelstiltskin was going to come and take you. . . . This is the kind of stuff you make up when you're trying to get a sense of who you are. I was so thrilled that my birth mom turned out to be a fairy princess. I was so scared that she'd hang up on me when I first called. She said, "How could I hang up on you?" Even so, I fretted after we made contact and I still fret a little that she might hate me. I wasn't raised under her roof so I'm not anything like her or the kids. We have a facial resemblance, but otherwise I'm nothing like her or the family. We have very different personalities and attitudes to life. I told my birth mother today that I keep thinking that she's going to hate me, and she replied, "How can I hate you? I don't even know you." I said, "It's real easy. You say you hate me and don't call me again." It's scary stuff. A lot of emotion.

My birth mother told me after we first spoke that she had always hoped that she would get one of those phone calls, just like the one she received when I called to say that I was her birth daughter. She says that 10 years ago she brought up the subject with my birth father, who is now deceased, about whether I might still be alive. He said, no, the baby is dead. But she says she still kept wondering and couldn't understand how I could be dead.

My birth mother has been very generous. She brought me a gift that her mother gave her 37 years ago when she first came to the United States. It's a 24-carat gold charm, a Korean good luck pouch on a chain. It belonged to her mother, so I feel very honored that she gave it to me. She bought my son toys and clothes and has been so warm and loving and generous and receptive and kind and everything that you would want a mother to be.

I am not able to conceive. The only way I could ever have had children was via surrogacy, which is extremely expensive, or by adoption. We were fortunate enough to be able to travel to Romania almost 4 years ago and adopt our son. He was 8 months old when we brought him home. My son was the youngest of five children in a Romanian family. That year, his mother gave up two children. She was almost going to give up three, but in the end, she would up relinquishing the two youngest boys. With the state of their economy, she couldn't afford to raise five children, so she had to let some go. To this day, I am still upset that my son was given back to his mother by the orphanage between the time that we first agreed to the adoption and the time when we came to pick him up. He stayed with her again for about 3 weeks, so that he would get preferential care and be well fed and nourished by the time we came to pick him up. The attorney had her under lock and key in a home, however, so that she wouldn't run away. When I came to pick up my son, I thought I'd be picking him up at the orphanage. But I actually had to take him from her arms and walk out the door. To this day, I can hear my son's howling and horrid screaming. She was also crying uncontrollably with this incredibly deep, wrenching, and intensely emotional wail. This is a picture I will live with forever. It was just terrible seeing the grief in her face and knowing my son's anguish. . . . After that I started to wonder if my own mother had felt that kind of grief, and in that moment I felt as though I had to let my birth mother know that I was okay.

The ultimate sacrifice is when a woman says that because she trusts you she will give you her baby. I feel honored that another woman entrusted her baby to me. The birth mother is the hero in adoption . . . She has to live for the rest of her life with that sacrifice. I feel privileged to have the responsibility of raising the life that my son's birth mother gave to me. I want my little boy to know that his birth mother made a huge sacrifice for him, that she suffers and probably wonders how he is and if he's well. I keep a one-sided contact with my son's mother, because they have a tendency in Romania to beg for money, and I didn't want him to think that he was "sold." I send her pictures and letters once every 6 months, to keep her updated on her son's development, but I don't include a return address. She can see the family resemblance, because he looks very much like her. I'm honored to be able to participate in my son's life and share bits of his birth mother's life with him. . . . My son tells everyone that he's adopted. He's forever saying, "I'm adopted. I'm from Romania. My birth mother's name is Maria." Now he's into, "My mommy has a birth mother. Her name is Chaiha Rhee." Adopting out a child lives with a woman forever.[6]

Those who are against abortion cite adoption as some kind of idyllic alternative, but it's not. Adoption is an incredibly painful and often tragic last resort.

Obstetrician and abortion provider Dr. Lawrence W. Scott has a unique perspective on abortion and adoption, because he has been involved with both as a professional and from personal experience.

Adoption always sets up someone, either the parent(s) or child, with the anxiety of curiosity. I went into private practice in 1966, when abortion was illegal. I became the doctor who delivered about 60 babies a month for Big Sister League in Los Angeles, 90% of whom were adopted out through the County Adoption Agency. As abortion became progressively easier to obtain, the number of mothers coming to Big Sister League dropped, and by 1972, there were very few. Still, I had established a name for myself as a doctor who was sympathetic to women who wanted to adopt out a baby. I tried to approach the situation with heart, and make it comfortable for the girl and her parents. Women who were too far along in their pregnancy to have an abortion were also sent to me for assistance with adoption.

Unfortunately, a woman who has a baby and elects to adopt it out as opposed to having an abortion has a picture to remember. Too frequently, she will be haunted by doubts about whether she did the right thing adopting her child out. I think it's better for the woman to terminate the pregnancy early, before there's anything she can relate to, and get on with her life. Another problem that arises when a woman adopts a baby out is explaining to a future potential spouse why the baby was adopted out. I've seen a few situations when that has created a lot of problems and disrespect for the mother on the part of the future husband. It shouldn't make a difference, but the truth is, a lot of men have trouble accepting a woman who has adopted out a baby. The third problem is that most adoptive parents do the right thing and at some point tell their child that it was adopted. That triggers curiosity and the child often sets out to find the natural parents, who may be embarrassed at being found. Most children who are adopted out go to couples who really want them, so they stand a better chance of getting love, affection, and a college education than the average child. But to this day, I have young ladies calling me who have learned from their birth certificate that I delivered them 20 years ago and now they want to know the name of their parents. I go through my files and if I have the information, I tell them.

I have my own personal experience with adoption. I got a white, Catholic girl pregnant, which was totally taboo at that time, because I am black. She had to hide the pregnancy from her father. We could have had an abortion, but she was Catholic and totally against abortion. She did not see the baby after it was born, but I did. Over the years, I always had an image of the baby in my mind and I wondered what happened to her.

Three years ago, my daughter came back into my life. She's now almost 30. My daughter's happy to be back in my life now, and my curiosity has been satisfied. But the reunion has not been without problems. The adoptive parents of my daughter were white bigots, and my daughter was never told that she was half black. As she looks white, she never realized her heritage until she met me. Fortunately, my daughter was not upset when she found out—she actually found it amusing. She was taken home by many white couples as a child and then when they found out that she was half black, she was returned to the foster home. This went on until she was about 8 or 9 years old. She became confused about why so many people rejected her. Learning that she was half black at least helped her make sense of the rejection.

When my daughter was adopted out, the adoption laws were very strict. She couldn't find us and we couldn't find her. Anyone who broke that chain was in serious trouble. I wanted to adopt her when she was born, but her mother refused to allow me to adopt her. She wanted her raised by a Catholic family. I wanted her to go to a loving black couple if I wasn't going to be allowed to adopt her, but the problem was, my daughter looked white! So no black couple would adopt her. She wound up being adopted by the foster home parents where she had been sent.

My daughter bugged the hell out of the social worker who followed her case and finally, about 4 years ago, at the age of 25, she was told that her mother was part Italian, part Irish and a nursing student, and her father had been a resident doctor at a local hospital. As the social worker held up the piece of paper to read, my daughter could see her parents' names backwards, even though they had been whited out. Then she called the licensing bureau and found out where I practiced. My daughter's a smart girl, very bright.

To this day, my daughter is very angry with her natural mother. She feels that she "gave me away, without even looking at me." When my daughter first called me, I was delighted. I sent her money to come and visit me as she lived in Sacramento and I lived in Los Angeles. We had a wonderful time together and since then we've seen a lot of each other. She now lives in San Diego, but we often talk and travel together. I called her natural mother who was married to a doctor whom she was in the process of divorcing. Ironically, this doctor had made most of his lucrative income doing abortions. I hadn't talked to her since our daughter was born. She said that she had three children whom she would have to tell, as they didn't know about her adopted daughter. Her husband knew. Her kids were thrilled—they thought it was super and liked the idea that they had another sister.

My daughter has never been able to accept that her mother didn't want her. I've tried to explain to her that it wasn't a personal thing against her—she didn't want any child—but still, my daughter finds it hard not to take her mother's decision personally. She knows that I wanted to adopt her as it was recorded on the official paperwork at the adoption agency.

When my daughter goes to visit her natural mother, she sees her half-sister who has been given everything. It's hard for her, because she was adopted out by what I would describe economically as an upper lower-class family with stereotypical ideas about church and family life. The people who adopted her had three natural children of their own to whom they gave everything, and they had three adopted children whom they treated like stepkids. So my daughter left home when she was 16 ... I think finding her natural parents was very important to her because she was looking for a bonding that she never got with her adoptive parents.

My daughter is ambivalent about abortion. She obviously believes in abortion as she's had one herself, but on the other hand, she's tickled to death that her mother didn't have an abortion, because otherwise she wouldn't be here. She doesn't believe in adoption.[7]

Every child's birthright is love. If a woman doesn't want to have an abortion or raise her child after it is born, it should be an absolute right for the father to raise the child, unless there is a good reason to deny him custody. Single parenthood isn't necessarily a good reason. A woman should not have the right to deny a father custody because his religious views differ from hers. If the father of the child has not abandoned the mother, the decision to place the child for adoption should be made by both parents, not unilaterally by the mother.

Professionals in adoption have emphasized repeatedly during my research that virtually all infants can be placed, and in their view, adoption is very often a really happy ending. While I acknowledge their expertize and don't doubt the truth of what they say, I still don't think adoption should be viewed as the solution to 50–60 million unwanted pregnancies per year. Even if women seeking an abortion were willing en masse to have their babies and place them for adoption, to suggest that there would be prospective families willing to adopt 50–60 million infants world-wide each year is fanciful. But supposing there were families willing to adopt all those babies, what would happen to the world population? It would increase at a catastrophic rate that could endanger mankind's survival, because the earth could not sustain that kind of population growth for very long. Adoption is not a feasible alternative to abortion for unwanted pregnancies on a mass scale, but it may be the right solution for individuals.

Social worker Sharon Kaplan Roszia recalls:

> I have often said to people who link adoption and abortion that "I'll get behind you if you'll put your money where your mouth is. If you're willing to start adopting some of these kids who are sitting in foster care who are very difficult children to parent, then I might be able to get behind what you're saying." I really want to see some action from the anti-abortion community that lines up their money, their homes and their parenting skills behind the large numbers of children who don't have a place in our society.[2]

The tragedy of children winding up in long-term foster care should serve as a warning to all prospective parents. The rewards of caring for a child are enormous, but so is the responsibility. If for any reason things don't work out as hoped and your child is placed in protective custody by the state, or you voluntarily surrender custody, your child will have to pay the price. It's so easy for most women and men to conceive, and yet so difficult to imagine the reality of parenthood.

While trying to find a positive way of looking at adoption, I remembered Aldous Huxley's last novel, *Island*, in which he related his vision of Utopia. Children could visit their second "family" without fear of upsetting their birth parents, because society believed that children should not be soley dependent on their parents for love and sustenance. In Huxley's Utopia, parents were not expected to be able to fulfill all of the needs of their children. Now that open adoption is acceptable, perhaps perceiving the adoption process as extending a child's family is a more positive way of looking at it, for all concerned.

14

The Incongruous History of Abortion Legality and Parental Consent Laws

Abortions have been performed around the world for thousands of years, regardless of legal status. The choice we have as a community is whether it will be a relatively safe, legal procedure or illegal and extremely dangerous. Historically, abortion legality has depended for the most part on the need for population control and to protect women from being killed by quack doctors or by their own hands, rather than on any great concern for the rights of the fetus.

A society that is desperately trying to control the rate of population growth will not only encourage abortion but it will, if necessary, make it compulsory. In China, there are severe financial penalties for couples who choose to have more than one child. There have also been cases of forced abortions in late stages of pregnancy. While this seems cruel and immoral to many of us living in the West, it is considered immoral in China not to put the needs of the community before the needs of the individual, as proclaimed in the following excerpt:

> None of you has any choice in this matter. You must realize that your pregnancy affects everyone in the commune, and indeed affects everyone in the country. The two of you who are eight or nine months pregnant will have a cesarean; the rest of you will have a shot which will cause you to abort.[1]

Social duty is a very important aspect of Chinese morality. The Chinese believe that for the community as a whole to survive at an acceptable standard of living, population growth must be controlled. Having two or more children is considered a betrayal of the community. To elicit cooperation of the Chinese, persuasion is employed to convince women and their families that they have made the choice and done so out of a sense of social duty, even when there is no choice.

> We aren't forcing you to abort. . . . The decision to undergo an abortion has to be made by you yourselves. But in making this decision, you have to consider not only yourselves but the country and the collective as well. Obviously the country needs to control its population for the sake of the Four Modernizations. The collective, as well, needs to limit its population. . . . There is already only one-sixth of an acre for each person in the village. . . . Having more children is only going to make it more difficult for all of us to make a living.[2]

There are couples in China who defy the law, at a very high financial price, just as there are those in countries where abortion is illegal who risk their lives and spend large sums of money on an abortion, no matter how much the community encourages childbirth with financial incentives and moral blackmail.

A society that needs or desires population growth will not encourage abortion. In 1920, the Soviet Union legalized abortion in an attempt to stop the fatalities resulting from illegal abortions. But in 1936, Stalin introduced a new law that was supposed to increase the birthrate. Despite abortion being prohibited, the birthrate stayed the same, but there was an increase in the number of deaths from illegal abortions . In 1955, abortion became legal again, but only for medical reasons. Then in 1968, abortion became legal virtually on demand for all women in the former Soviet Union.[3]

Abortion frequently causes clashes between local culture, religion, and law. India is perhaps the most striking example of this conflict. Like the Chinese, the Indian government realized as early as 1951 that overpopulation was a problem. An intensive program was introduced encouraging birth control and sterilization. The latter was made compulsory for parents of three or more children by Mrs. Ghandi's government, a fact that contributed to her political defeat. The program was modified dramatically as a result to allow more freedom of choice on the issue.

Despite very liberal laws permitting abortion, which took effect in 1972, in 1977 only 278,000 legal abortions were recorded, the highest figure for any year since India introduced the new law. In 1982, however, Professor S. M. Dasgupta told a conference on population control that "nearly 4 million illegal abortions were carried out each year."[4] A number of reasons were suggested to explain the high incidence of illegal abortion: the law needed to be simplified to state that abortion on request was legal; 80% of the population live in villages, without electricity and running water or the benefit of coverage by the health service; there was a shortage of doctors willing to perform abortions as well as of facilities; and people were ignorant about the Act that legalized abortion.

Perhaps the most important reason for the number of illegal abortions is the enormous social stigma attached to abortion in India. Both Hinduism and Islam are against abortion, Hinduism more so (Islam permits abortion to save the mother's life). There is still a strong emphasis that a woman be a virgin when she marries. It is common practice for a young girl who has been "deflowered" to have an abortion and then on her wedding night to insert soft-membraned eggs in her vagina so that she bleeds appropriately when making love with her husband for the first time. The shame and fear of punishment for premarital or extramarital sex is a significant cause of the very high rate of secret illegal abortions in a country where abortion is legal.

Another interesting aspect of Indian culture is seen in the following excerpt:

> Modern medicine enables couples to indulge the ancient Indian preference for baby boys. So-called sex determination clinics flourish and in a recent study of 8,000 abortions in

Bombay, a medical researcher reported that 7,999 were of female fetuses.[5]

One reason for the preference for males is the Indian custom of giving a dowry with the bride who then no longer belongs to her own family but is more or less the slave of her husband's family.

Landed Indians have long paid a dowry. Hindu law precludes a daughter from inheriting her family's land, so a dowry of gold and jewellery would represent her share of the family wealth. India banned the dowry as a social evil in 1961, but never enforced the law . . . so the dowry flourished and spread. . . . Now, instead of jewellery, something more visible is required by inlaws and "izzat"—family honour. A refrigerator or television set perhaps, that will proclaim a family's wealth and in that way improve its social standing. And because "izzat" is at stake, the dowry is as popular with the rich and educated as with the poor, only the size of the dowry balloons accordingly.[5]

In order to avoid the burden of the dowry, Indians resort to abortion and, more extremely, infanticide.

So onerous are dowry demands that female infanticide is resurging in parts of India. . . . The magazine India Today estimates that 6,000 baby girls have been poisoned in just one county in the state of Tamil Nadu in the past decade. Parents freely admitted killing to avoid the burden of a dowry 15 or 16 years later.[5]

In Ireland, one of the major obstacles to obtaining even an illegal abortion is finding a physician who will perform the operation, because the country is predominantly Catholic and abortion was constitutionally banned in an amendment passed in 1983, except to save the mother's life. Irish women nevertheless abort unwanted pregnancies, but, needless to say, they do so in secrecy.

In February, 1992, a 14-year-old Irish girl was forbidden by a judge to travel to England to have an abortion. The girl had conceived as a result of being raped by the father of a close friend, and clearly indicated that she would commit suicide if she did not receive permission to have an abortion in England. Her case came to the attention of the Irish government when her parents called Irish police to inquire what the effect of an abortion would be on prosecution of the rapist, and whether they should have tests conducted on the fetal tissue after the abortion in England, so that positive identification of the rapist could be made and the evidence used in criminal proceedings. The Irish policeman who spoke with her parents apparently felt this was a serious case that needed to be brought to the attention of the courts and government, not because the girl was raped, but because she was about to violate Irish law by travelling abroad to have an abortion in England.

Over 4000 Irish women make the journey to England each year to have abortions, but their efforts are discreet and the government and police do not interfere. If the Irish government were truly that concerned about protecting fetuses and enforcing the law, then all Irish women would be required to have pregnancy tests before vacationing abroad.

The Irish government and people are strongly influenced by the religious belief that abortion is a terrible sin and morally wrong, and the Irish judge's decision was consistent with that belief as manifest in Irish law; however, it was also an outrageously hypocritical decision, as the English statistics regarding the number of abortions performed annually on Irish women in England are well known to the Irish government and, I presume, to the judge who made the decision. That decision was supported by Irish Attorney General Harold Whelehan, who must also be aware that Irish women have abortions abroad. The family made an appeal to the Irish Supreme Court to overturn the ruling and won. The girl was granted the right to travel to England for an abortion. In March, 1995, Irish President Mary Robinson asked the Irish Supreme Court to decide on the constitutionality of a pending change in Irish law that would guarantee Irish women the right to information on foreign abortion clinics. The Supreme Court debate is in progress as this book goes to press.

It is ironic that some women in countries where abortion is legal and socially sanctioned seek "secret" abortions. In Russia, where women often have as many as 20 abortions, there are still women who would prefer to pay for a private abortion than have one that would become public knowledge. Says one Russian woman:

> It's taken for granted that if a woman is absent from work for three days she's having an abortion. If she isn't married, people start talking; if she is, maybe she doesn't want people to know. Hospital records are public, so women try to avoid going there. Often women come to hospitals after they've tried to induce abortions by taking medicine or by other means and haven't succeeded. By that time the fetus is far along and the hospital staff bawls them out. "Tell us what you took," they say, "otherwise we won't help you." Here, everyone is afraid of getting pregnant, terrified of having to have an abortion. It's difficult and painful; I should know, I had one at the hospital. Now they've started to give painkillers. But outside the cities they don't—only some kind of injection that doesn't work. We hoped that things would improve when the Pill appeared. I heard the Pill mentioned for the first time seven or eight years ago. Sometimes you can get them, sometimes you can't. Now I haven't seen them for four months. That's the way it is. Sometimes they disappear for months and then turn up again. But now women are afraid of them too. It's considered safer to have an abortion than to take the Pill.[6]

Another reason for secrecy about abortion in Eastern European countries is shame, but it is not shame born of moral concern for the fetus or embarrassment at a failure of contraception. A 29-year-old, single professional woman explains that abortion "is like saying 'I'm too poor to raise a child.' It's a kind of shame felt over the conditions we live in."[7]

After the execution of Nicolae Ceausescu, Romania's former leader, startling facts emerged regarding his schemes for building socialism and increasing the nation's population from 23 million to 30 million by the year 2000. Romania's policies on abortion and childbirth under Ceausescu serve as a warning to all of the possible consequences of combining religious and political fanaticism under the umbrella of the law.

In 1966, a decree was issued in Romania that generally outlawed sex education, birth control, and abortion. In this decree, Ceausescu proclaimed that "the fetus is the property of the entire society. . . . Anyone who avoids having children is a deserter who abandons the laws of national continuity."[8]

As a result of this decree, Romania's birthrate almost doubled. Poor nutrition and inadequate prenatal care caused serious health problems for pregnant women, and the infant mortality rate rose to 83 deaths in every 1000 births, a statistic that was much higher than for any Western European country. The social-health system was not designed to help women care for newborns, so any newborns weighing less than 1500 grams were usually classified as miscarriages and denied treatment, in effect a form of infanticide. Many babies were "adopted" by the state and died horrific deaths or survived only to contract AIDS and other diseases in Ceausescu's notorious orphanages.

It was extremely difficult for women to avoid pregnancy in Romania under Ceausescu's rule. Sex education was forbidden and books dealing with human sexuality and reproduction were classified as "state secrets," and could only be used as medical textbooks. Birth control was virtually nonexistent as contraception was illegal, and smuggled condoms and birth-control pills were extremely difficult to find, even on the black market. Illegal and extremely dangerous abortions in effect became the main means of birth control. It has been estimated that 60% of all pregnancies ended in miscarriage or abortion under Ceausescu's rule.

The methods of enforcing these prohibitive laws were extreme and inhumane. Women under the age of 45 were rounded up at their workplaces once every 1–3 months and taken to clinics where they were examined to see if they were pregnant. These examinations were often conducted with government agents present who were cynically labeled by Romanians as "menstrual police." A woman who had shown signs of pregnancy during a routine examination of this nature and then failed to produce a baby at the appropriate time would be summoned for questioning and punished if it were discovered that she had terminated the pregnancy. Even women who miscarried naturally were suspected of arranging an abortion.

Because of the severe punishments for performing or having an abortion and for miscarriages, some doctors resorted to forging statistics. "If a child died in our district, we lost 10–25% of our salary" says Dr. Geta Stanescu of Bucharest. "But it wasn't our fault: we had no medicine or milk, and the families were poor."[8]

Under certain circumstances, abortion was legal in Ceausescu's Romania. If a woman was over 40, had four children, or was in danger of losing her life, then abortion was permissible. It was also acceptable if you had high-ranking Communist Party connections. Illegal abortions were expensive (they could cost from 2 to 4 months' wages), and if the participants were caught, the consequences could be devastating. Nevertheless, the rate of illegal abortions was higher than in any Western European country in which abortion was legal.[9] And of course, many women died as a result of illegal abortions, because they were too afraid to seek medical attention at a hospital.

Perhaps the most bizarre aspect of Ceausescu's policy was a quiz conducted by the Communist youth group in 1986, in which they questioned Romanian citizens about their sex lives. The questionnaire contained items such as, "How often do you have sexual intercourse?" and "Why have you failed to conceive?" Women who were unable to conceive or did not have any children had to pay a "celibacy tax" which could amount to as much as 10% of their monthly salaries.

In 1990, Ceausescu's highly restrictive abortion laws were rescinded. It is worth noting that prior to Ceausescu, first-trimester abortion was permissible on request in Romania from 1957 to 1966. Romania is a startling example of how a legal prohibition against abortion for political purposes could harm babies, for while Ceausescu was against abortion, he was in no way in favor of life and did nothing in his orphanages or in his policies to help those children he had decreed legally had to be born. Perhaps the lesson is that if we are going to have children, we must be able and willing to provide for them. Governments should not be responsible for raising children, except in extreme and sad situations where there is no other alternative.

In Japan, at least 800,000 abortions are performed annually. Without abortion, legal or illegal, it is doubtful that Japan would have succeeded in transforming itself into one of the richest nations in the world. Japan not only had overpopulation but, more seriously, the overcrowding created massive environmental pollution that would have presented almost insurmountable problems had abortion not controlled the rate of population growth.

> During the period of Seclusion, abortion and infanticide were common in Japan. The Samurai did not congratulate a friend on the birth of a child until it was clear that it was going to be allowed to live. In 1754 one commentator wrote "up to fifty or sixty years ago a couple on the farm used to bring up five or six or even seven or eight children, (but) it has become the custom in recent years among farmers for each married couple to rear no more than one or two children." However, with contact with Western civilization, anti-abortion legislation was introduced in 1873. Infanticide came to be treated with the full rigour of the homicide laws, and by the first half of this century, Japanese public policy treated abortion and contraception in much the same way as the West.[10]

In 1948, Japan introduced a more liberal abortion law which was further liberalized in 1949. Currently, abortion is permitted in the case of genetic disease, rape, and

> when "there is danger that, if the pregnancy continues or childbirth ensues, the mother's health will be impaired for

physical or economic reasons." This clause is invoked in more than two-thirds of all cases.[11]

It in effect offers abortion on request.

Among Scandinavian countries, perhaps the most interesting in relation to abortion is Iceland, which has always been independent and farsighted in its social legislation. In 1934, the Icelandic parliament led the way in abortion reform among Northern European legislatures: Law No. 38 of January 28, 1935 was without precedent, dealing with the social as well as the medical indications for abortion.

> When estimating how far childbirth may be likely to damage the health of the pregnant woman . . . it may be taken into consideration whether the woman has already borne many children at short intervals and a short time has passed since her last confinement, also whether her domestic conditions are difficult, either on account of a large flock of children, poverty or serious ill-health of other members of the family.[12]

That law remains in effect today.

In African countries, with the exception of Ghana, Togo, Tunisia, Zambia, and Morocco, the laws on abortion are conservative. Tunisia was the first Muslim country to allow abortion on grounds other than medical necessity. In 1965, the law was modified

> so that any mother with five or more children, or any woman who became pregnant after an IUD insertion, might request an abortion. Health administrators were formally reminded of this change and asked to perform terminations free of charge three years later.[13]

Abortion is available on request only in Tunisia; in Zambia, socioeconomic as well as medical reasons are acceptable. Abortion is legal in cases of rape, incest, fetal defects or when the woman's health is in jeopardy in Algeria, Botswana, Burundi, Cameroon, Congo, Egypt, Ethiopia, Ghana, Guinea, Kenya, Lesotho, Liberia, Morocco, Namibia, Rwanda, Sierra Leone, South Africa, Tanzania,

Togo, Uganda, and Zimbabwe. All other African countries permit abortion only to save the life of the mother, except Sudan, where rape and incest are also grounds for legal abortion.

Turkey is the only middle eastern country that permits abortion on request. In Iran, Lebanon, Oman, Iraq, Syria, Yemen, and the United Arab Emirates, as in most Muslim countries, abortion is permitted only to save the mother's life. In Jordan, Kuwait, and Saudi Arabia, the law has been interpreted more leniently in recent years, permitting abortion in cases of rape, incest, fetal defects, and when the mother's health is in jeopardy. Jordan has even permitted a legal abortion in extreme circumstances, such as the need to preserve family honor and reputation. It must be said, however, that there is still a high incidence of illegal abortion in Islamic countries where there is great emphasis placed on the need for virgin brides and faithful wives. Women in these countries do resort to secret illegal abortions frequently because the penalty for lost family honor can be death for the woman.

Ironically, Israel's law on abortion was for a time identical to Jordan's, as both inherited the law while under the British mandate. In addition, both had punishments of up to 14 years imprisonment for abortion. In 1952, the District Court of Haifa in Israel declared abortion legal provided there was documented medical justification. In the 1960s, the government of Ben Gurion offered financial incentives to Jewish Israeli women not to have induced abortions, because of the need for population growth, but to little effect. It seems that the factors that actually determine a woman's desire for abortion are more personally socioeconomic and practical than patriotic or religious. The extreme religious right is particularly against abortion, not so much because of concern for fetal rights but because they consider it an act of suicide for a country such as Israel to permit abortion for its Jewish population: the Arabs will eventually outnumber the Jews and it will become virtually impossible to continue to live by the democratic code on which Israel was founded. The anti-abortion movement in Israel is motivated by very different concerns than the movement in the United States and other Western countries.

In Latin America, the picture is very different. The combination of religious (Roman Catholic) and political influences in military-dominated systems has led to abortion being generally outlawed with the exception of Cuba and Puerto Rico, where it is available on request. However, abortion does occur on a grand scale illegally, with an estimated 4 million abortions per year. Interestingly, in Latin America, proof of pregnancy must be provided in order to convict an abortionist whereas in British-influenced legislation it is the intention of the abortionist that makes him or her liable to prosecution. This in effect provides a loophole that allows Latin American doctors to perform abortions under the guise of regulating menstruation. Abortion is permitted only to save the life of the mother in Chile, Colombia, the Dominican Republic, Guatemala, Haiti, Honduras, Nicaragua, Panama, Paraguay, Uruguay, and Venezuela. Brazil and Mexico permit abortion in cases of rape or incest, in addition to saving the woman's life. All other Latin American and Caribbean countries permit abortion for fetal defects as well as the above-mentioned reasons, and if the woman's health is at risk.[14]

In Asia, abortion is permitted on request in China, Mongolia, Singapore, and Vietnam. Australia, India, Japan, North Korea, and Taiwan permit abortion for socioeconomic and medical reasons, making abortion freely available if not literally on request. In Hong Kong, South Korea, Malaysia, New Zealand, Pakistan, Papua New Guinea, and Thailand, fetal defects, rape, incest, and a risk for the woman's health are legally acceptable reasons for an abortion. Afghanistan, Bangladesh, Cambodia, Indonesia, Laos, Myanmar, Nepal, the Philippines, and Sri Lanka permit abortion only to save the woman's life.[14]

In Europe, abortion is available on request in Albania, Austria, Belgium, Bosnia-Herzegovina, Bulgaria, Croatia, the Czech Republic, Denmark, Estonia, France, Italy, Macedonia, the Netherlands, Norway, Romania, Slovakia, Sweden, Slovenia, and Yugoslavia. Finland, Britain, and Hungary permit abortion for socioeconomic and medical reasons, which makes it almost as freely available as if it were on request. The most conservative laws in Europe are in Ireland, with Poland, Portugal, Spain, and

Switzerland following close behind. Abortion in the latter countries is permitted only in cases of risk to the woman's health, fetal defects, rape, and incest.[14]

In Canada and the United States, abortion is available on request.

Some countries that permit abortion virtually on request limit that free choice to the first trimester and set limits on the availability of abortion in the second trimester. In France, abortion is provided on request in the first trimester, but is permissible only rarely in the second trimester and never in the third. The French chose 12 weeks as the cutoff point for abortion on request because at that point the embryo becomes a fetus and the placenta takes over from the ovaries in producing the hormones necessary for pregnancy, thus making the fetus hormonally autonomous from the mother. The other main factor that influenced the French law was safety for the woman: it is considered better for the woman's health if she has an early abortion.

In 1988, the Morgentaler Decision was passed in Canada. Dr. Henry Morgentaler explains:

> Due to me, there is no criminal law in Canada at all on abortion. The Supreme Court invalidated the previous abortion law. . . . Parliament has been unable to craft a new law, so we have been operating for six and a half years in Canada without a criminal law. . . . It's not necessary to have an abortion law . . . The Canadian Medical Association has set an upper limit of 20 weeks, but most doctors prefer to perform abortions in the first trimester, when there is less risk to the woman.[15]

Of the former Soviet bloc countries where communism legalized abortion, predominantly Catholic Poland is the only one that now has laws strictly prohibiting abortion except when the mother's life is threatened, in cases of rape or incest, and if the fetus has a severe and irreparable abnormality. In 1994, President Lech Walesa successfully vetoed an attempt to liberalize those laws. In March of 1994, it was reported that a 48-year-old gyne-

cologist hanged herself in Poland after she was charged with terminating a five-month pregnancy. The penalty would have been
a two-year prison term and loss of her medical license.[16] It is tragic
that "Zofia S." felt driven to commit suicide when her work became illegal and she was caught.

In 1990, after the reunification of East Germany, where abortion was legal on request, with West Germany, where abortion laws
were the most conservative in Western Europe, a battle raged over
abortion. The former Catholic-influenced West German abortion
laws permitted a doctor to decide if a woman could have an abortion. It was legal only in the most terrible medical, psychological,
or social circumstances. So extreme was the enforcement of this
law that women who sought abortions elsewhere risked criminal
prosecution, and there were even reports of German police ar-
resting women returning from Holland (where abortion laws are
liberal) and forcing them to undergo gynecological examinations
to see whether they had undergone an abortion.[17]

On June 25, 1992, the Bundestag (lower house of parliament that
makes laws) decided that "West" German women should be given
the same liberal abortion rights as "East" Germans. Abortion became
available virtually on request within 12 weeks from conception, provided that the woman received counseling at least three days prior
to the procedure, and on "eugenic"(the word used in my sources)
grounds up to 22 weeks after counseling. No time limit was set for
abortion on medical grounds, which would not require the compulsory counseling. The new law also stipulated that abortion would
be paid for by statutory health insurance and social assistance benefits. But the state of Bavaria and the majority of Christian Democrat
members of the Bundestag appealed to the Federal Constitutional
Court, asserting that abortion on request was unconstitutional, as
were the accompanying benefit payments. Therefore, the parts of the
law pertaining to these issues never came into effect.

The Federal Constitutional Court ruled on the suit on May 28,
1993. The Court held that abortion within 12 weeks from conception (and after counseling) was not unconstitutional, but that lawfulness (justification) was not established by the procedure, thus

making it unconstitutional for state health insurance to pay for abortion. A majority of five of eight judges argued that paying for abortion under those circumstances might well mean that the state would be participating in possibly unlawful behavior. Lawmakers have a unique ability to confuse even the most rational of thinkers. The German Federal Constitutional Court in effect made it illegal for the state to fund abortion because it might be unlawful while simultaneously saying that abortion should be available on request. That kind of "doublespeak" is absolutely exasperating. The Court also mandated that state health insurance would have to pay for abortions performed for "eugenic" or medical reasons, as well as in cases of rape and incest. In such cases, however, a second physician would be required to verify that one of the legal grounds needed for state funding was applicable.

The bizarre consequence of the new laws being passed was that funding assistance for abortion became difficult to obtain. State health insurance was then required to pay only for services not immediately related to the abortion. But, if the woman could not afford an abortion and her income was under the legal limit, then she could apply for state social assistance, which in effect said that one state department won't pay for abortion on request but another will. It is difficult to imagine how reasonable people could conceive such a garbled law.

Bills presented by the Free Democrats and a majority of Christian and Social Democrats, respectively, have a good chance of passing and would in effect bring abortion legislation in line with the more reasonable (and comprehensible!) 1992 Supreme Court decision. Both parties recommend that statutory health insurance pay abortion providers and attendant physicians' fees, although they differ in their recommendations on the level of income that would disqualify a woman from assistance. Although more acceptable, the conservative Christian Democratic proposal is still mind boggling—their law would make abortion illegal but unpunishable during the first 12 weeks of pregnancy. If abortion is illegal, then punishment should be implicit![18]

The sad consequence of Germany's yo-yoing abortion laws

since reunification has been a dramatic rise in the number of women in Eastern Germany seeking sterilization. Serious unemployment with no perception of hope for future improvement, lack of funds to pay for an abortion, employer prejudice against women seeking employment or promotion whom they think may become pregnant, the high price of contraception, the disappearance of abortion on request, and fear that they will be unable to provide for themselves and their children, are the prime motivating factors for women seeking sterilization, according to a report in the Australian newspaper *The Age* on January 19, 1995.[19] If abortion were available on request and subsidized by state health insurance in Germany, women would not have to choose irreversible sterilization as a method of contraception.

Incongruity is not the province of Germany alone. Abortion is the second most prevalent surgery in Australia, where approximately 80,000 women annually undergo the procedure. But abortion remains listed under the Crimes Act, and an illegal abortion can be punished with up to 15 years in jail for both the doctor and patient. Although abortion has been relatively easy to obtain since Australian Judge Menhennit's clever ruling in 1969 in the state of Victoria, keeping it under the criminal code leaves the door open to prosecution of women and abortion providers should a judge choose to play doctor.

Menhennit used necessity and proportion as key principles in his definition of the lawfulness of abortion. He said:

> For the use of an instrument to procure a miscarriage to be lawful, the accused must have honestly believed on reasonable grounds that the act done by him was (a) necessary to preserve the woman from serious danger to her life or physical or mental health (not being merely the normal dangers of pregnancy and childbirth) which the continuance of the pregnancy would entail; and (b) in the circumstances not out of proportion to the danger to be averted.[20]

In order to prove that an abortion provider had performed an unlawful abortion, a prosecutor would have to prove that the physician didn't really believe that the woman needed an abortion, virtually an impossibility unless the doctor "confessed" as much. Part (b) in effect meant that the woman would need to be in danger of significant proportion to warrant as strong a measure as abortion.

In 1994, Justice Newman of the New South Wales Supreme Court ruled against a woman seeking damages from doctors who failed five times to diagnose her pregnancy early enough for her to have an abortion, because he believed that termination at any time in her pregnancy would have been illegal in her case. In his view, her mental or physical health would not have been at risk if she were to have a baby. It is absolutely outrageous for a judge to presume to make that decision. The problem with the Menhennit ruling (which was adopted with various modifications in other states, more liberally in New South Wales) is that it leaves the door open to just that kind of judicial arrogance. As this book goes to press, the case is being heard in the New South Wales Court of Appeal.

Judge Mrs. Hadassah Ben-Ito (Judge of the District Court in Tel Aviv) had to hear a controversial abortion case while sitting as an Acting Justice in the Israeli Supreme Court. In 1986, during an address at a Round Table Discussion titled "The Ethical, Legal and Religious Aspects of the Modern Diagnostic and Therapeutic Approach to the Fetus," she observed that historically there never had been a consensus on abortion, and she felt that there never would be one. In her experience, "The real problem arises when there is a conflict between the mother and the unborn child."[21] She went on to note that in 1981, while sitting as an Acting Justice in the Israeli Supreme Court, she helped write a majority opinion in the only real abortion case that was ever heard in the Israeli Supreme Court. The case involved the father of a fetus who had influenced the judge in a District Court and obtained an injunction against the mother and hospital not to perform the abortion that the woman had requested.

> The poor woman was running around between courts. Finally, she came to the Supreme Court, very far advanced in her pregnancy already, asking us to rescind the decision

of the judge, and we had the difficult task to decide whether a judge can appoint a guardian for the fetus, especially a father, when there is a conflict of interest not only between the fetus and the mother but also between the father and the mother, to plead its right to be born. The outcome was that we did away with the decision of that judge and the woman did have her abortion. But that case taught me something that I want to share with you . . . this should not be a legal matter. This is no matter for the courts, and . . . no matter for the legislature. I do not think it is a matter of rights. I think it should be a matter of ethics. . . . Legislatures in modern countries are political bodies. Do we want a legislature to decide on moral issues and tell us what to do according to changing political conveniences? Would we agree that one legislature today should decide that abortion is allowed because life begins at birth and four years later if a Catholic party for instance gained power, change the law and say that abortion is not allowed because life begins at conception? Is that acceptable? . . . if we speak of rights and applications of laws, we must be practical. . . . People do whatever they feel they have to do and we cannot enforce laws which people will not accept . . . it is impossible to treat the fetus as a patient separate from the woman. . . .[21]

If we must have abortion laws, it is vital that they be clear, consistent and practical. The current laws in Germany and Australia are prime examples of how not to legislate, because women can so easily be abused by legal ambiguity.

In the United States, since the Supreme Court invoked the constitutional right to privacy as a basis for legalizing abortion in the 1973 case of Roe versus Wade, abortion has been an ongoing major political issue. Anti-abortion protesters fail to realize, or perhaps just don't care, that making abortion illegal again in the United States would cause the deaths of millions of pregnant women AND their embryos or fetuses. The most extraordinary aspect of the movement against legal abortion is the complete denial of this fact by those who are against abortion.

It is incomprehensible to me that people who are "pro-life" would lobby in favor of legislation that will unquestionably lead to a great many deaths. If you believe that abortion is murder and that life is sacred and must be protected at all costs, why should it be more desirable to have both mother and embryo or fetus die? Illegality does not stop women from having abortions; if we have learned anything from the history of abortion, it is that women will continue to seek to terminate unwanted pregnancies, despite the risk to their own lives.

While it is true that some women may be deterred from having an abortion if it is illegal, most women will proceed with an illegal abortion, or attempt to abort themselves. And while some women who can't obtain an abortion will later be grateful, the opposite may also be true. A Hungarian woman sadly confided:

> When I see Operation Rescue demonstrations on television, I often ask myself if the people demonstrating know what it means to be an unwanted child. My mother committed suicide when I was three and my father rejected me because I wasn't born a boy. I was a desperately lonely and unloved child. When my father remarried several years later I clung to little bits of affection occasionally tossed my way by my stepmother. Most of the time she rejected me too. There is no doubt in my mind that it would have been better for me not to have been born. My mother should have aborted me.[22]

Those who are adamantly opposed to abortion on principle don't seem to really care about children, just about an abstract principle of the right to life. What about the right to love, the right to food and shelter, the right to an education, the right not to be abused, and most of all, the right to hope? What's the point of caring for the fetus if we don't care for it once it's a born baby?

If we encourage women to bring unwanted children into the world, who will pay the price? Are U.S. taxpayers willing to foot the bill for an extra 1.5 million babies[23] and their mothers every year? Realistically, some of those women might find other means to provide for themselves and their child, but many won't. The United States is already overwhelmed with domestic problems and a severe shortage of funds and political will to provide basic food, shelter, education, and medical care for its population. Nurturing and protecting fetuses and then abandoning unwanted babies to fate is tantamount to infanticide.

It is social suicide to overpopulate. If we encourage the population in the United States and the world to increase at an even faster rate, we will be inviting self-destruction as a species. Abortion is an extremely important aspect of our program to limit population growth.

In August, 1991, I attended an exhibition entitled "Just Call Jane" by Kerr and Malley, at the Shea Bornstein Gallery in Santa Monica, California. With the kind permission of Suzy Kerr and Diane Malley, I am including some of the texts that accompanied their art exhibit of extraordinary "dying declarations" by women who were about to die after having an illegal abortion.

The years 1850 to 1880 saw abortion emerge as a mass political issue in America for the first time. In 1857, the newly formed American Medical Association, with the cooperation of the Church and State, initiated a successful campaign to make abortion illegal. By the end of the century, every state had restricted abortion.

The history of criminal abortion reveals the state's intrusive role in regulating women's reproductive behavior and demanding conformity to marriage and motherhood. Women who had illegal abortions and sought medical care after a botched abortion were denied help until they gave a "dying declaration" which was used as evidence by the state to prosecute abortionists.

"A dying declaration is a statement made by a victim of a homicide while about to die, and without any hope of recovery, concerning the facts and circumstances under which the fatal injury was inflicted and offered in evidence in the trial of the person charged with having caused the death of the declarant." (American Jurisprudence)

Dying Declarations were humiliating, official interrogations about sexual matters, conducted by doctors, prosecutors, police officers and special investigators from the coroner's office. Women were questioned repeatedly about their private lives, their sexuality and their abortions. Although most women who had abortions were married, the state's prosecutors focused on unwed women and the formula of the dying declaration assumed the dying woman was unmarried.

The state concentrated on collecting dying declarations as a method of prosecuting abortionists until the 1930's. By the 1940's, the system had changed and abortion control depended upon hospital therapeutic abortion committees, raids on abortionists' offices and testimony from women who had been abortionists' patients. The process remained punitive for women caught in it, and criminal trials continued to require public exposure of women's sexual histories and abortions.[24]

Dying Declaration: July 1896 . . .

"I, Cora Alice Grimes, of the village of Nebo, while of sound mind and knowing I am about to die, make this statement: I live with my mother, three miles east of Nebo. On the second day of July, 1896, James Dunn, a retail merchant in the village of Nebo, stopped at the gate which led from the public road to my home and gave me a packet of calomel. He directed me to take it in certain specified doses and assured me it would produce a miscarriage. I took two doses of the calomel on the same day. I believe the abortion occurred on the nineteenth day of July." (Cora Alice Grimes: Reports of Cases at Law and in the Chancery Supreme Court of Illinois Vol 172, February, April 1899.)[24]

Dying Declaration: August 29, 1899 . . .

"I, Maria Hecht, now lying dangerously ill at the St. Elizabeth's Hospital, and believing I am about to die, make this my ante-mortem statement: in January I became acquainted with John Schockweiler, who is employed in a freight house on the south side. I had sexual intercourse with him for about five or six times, and in the month of May I noticed that I was pregnant. On August 24, 1899, I went of my own free will to visit Dr. Louise Hagenow. She first laid me on a lounge and began to use an instrument on me, and during that time I suffered considerable pain. Then the doctor made me get up and walk around the room. The doctor then came in and began to use the instruments again. I felt as though I was being cut to pieces, and at about 5.30pm she took the child away from me. I suffered great pain, and the following day, Friday August 25, I left and took a car for 941 North Clark Street, a friend of mine named Spitzer, where I remained until Monday morning at ten o'clock, August 28, when I left and was brought to the St. Elizabeth's Hospital in a carriage. I now see the woman standing at my bedside who performed the abortion." (Maria Hecht: Reports of Cases at Law in Chancery Supreme Court of Illinois Vol 188, December 1900–February 1901.)[24]

Dying Declaration: February 12, 1907 . . .

"I, Nellie Walsh, of the city of Chicago, county of Cook and state of Illinois, while in sound mind and knowing I am about to die, make this statement: That on Wednesday, February 6, 1907, Dr. Adolph Buettner, Clyborn Avenue, near North Avenue, performed an abortion on me at my request, he making the statement that there would be no danger. The abortion was produced by the use of an instrument, a catheter, and the fingers of the right hand. On the 11th of February, 1907 I was taken to the National Emergency Hospital in very critical condition. An operation was performed on me at four o'clock on the same day which consisted in curetting the womb. On the next day I was informed by the nurse that I was in a very critical condition. Dr. Nelson informed me I had no hopes and I requested that a priest be sent for. The priest was called somewhere between nine and eleven o'clock and administered the last sacrament." (Nellie Walsh: Reports of Cases at Law and in Chancery Supreme Court of Illinois Vol. 233, February, April 1908.)[24]

Dying Declaration: March 18, 1928 . . .

"Understanding that I, Mrs. Lyman, am not going to get well, I make this my dying statement. Having no hope of recovery, I understand that I am not going to live. On the night of March 9, 1928, I called Dr. Murphy to my home. He made an external examination of me that night and considered it nothing more than an ordinary miscarriage. During the night I had chills, had run a temperature of 103, complained of being cold and there was a very foul odor. Dr. Murphy concluded the next morning that I had an illegal abortion, or an abortion of some type or form. He also said that he saw the fetus on the night of March 9; that it was lying in the bed. The doctor who operated on me was Dr. Herbert of Holyoke. He was paid $25.00 by my husband. All the statements I signed a day or two before this interview were true. I don't see why I can't get well, other people have been through the same thing." (Mrs. Lyman: Massachusetts Reports Vol. 264 Supreme Judicial Court of Mass., May 1928–October 1928.)[24]

Kerr and Malley revealed another facet of illegal abortion in their exhibition:

They called themselves "the service." In Chicago in the late 1960's and the early 1970's, if you needed an abortion, you called "Jane." Jane was an illegal, underground abortion collective run by women. From 1969 until 1973 Jane performed over 11,000 safe, affordable abortions.

Jane began as a counseling and referral service, of which there were thousands all over the country. Referrals to Jane might come from a free clinic, a friend or a doctor. Jane was listed in the phone book under "How." You called Jane and Jane would tell you how to get an abortion.

Originally, Jane referred women to a doctor who performed abortions for the service. He was, however, very secretive and expensive. When Jane discovered that the doctor was not licensed, they realized they needed more control and learned to perform abortions themselves. No woman was ever turned away and the average price paid for an abortion was $40.

When a woman called Jane she got a tape recording saying: "This is Jane from Women's Liberation. Please leave your name and number and someone will call you back." On the day of the abortion, women went to an apartment called "the front." From there they were taken to another apartment or house where the abortion was performed. Someone from "the service" remained with the women throughout the operation and for follow-up counseling.

By May 1972, 250 women each week depended on Jane for abortions. That month Jane was raided and seven women were arrested although charges were eventually dropped. Jane was back at work within two weeks operating more clandestinely than before. By the fall of 1972, 300 women each week counted on Jane for abortions. Jane operated until the first legal clinic opened in Chicago in the Spring of 1973.

If Roe v. Wade is overturned by the Supreme Court . . . women all over this country could once again find themselves in the position of just calling Jane.[24]

Illegal abortion doesn't always kill, but it does consistently inflict great suffering. This is most poignantly revealed in the following excerpt from an interview with an American woman, who to this day becomes angry and very distressed when recalling her three illegal abortions.

I was 15 years old when I had my first abortion. I became pregnant as a result of rape. I came from a very poor family—my father would have been furious if he'd discovered that I was pregnant. I had no mother to turn to for advice or support. I would have felt humiliated and he would have abused me terribly. I was conscious of the life growing in me and I felt that it was somehow wrong to have an abortion, but I truly believed that it was a choice between me or the fetus. We couldn't both live. There was simply no way that I could provide for a child and survive mentally, physically, or financially. Having a baby then would probably have killed us both. I went to a woman who inserted a catheter which caused me to abort. There was no anesthetic and it was traumatic beyond words—I don't know how I survived the torture of that abortion.

My second abortion occurred 3 years later, and was performed by the same woman. It was equally terrifying and painful.

My third abortion took place when I was 24 years old, during the 1960s. I was impregnated by a man who was an Olympic Gold Medal winner. I trusted him when he told me that he was sterile and that we didn't need to take contraceptive precautions. He lied. The third abortion should have been a less traumatic experience in principle, because it was performed by a doctor, and I was by then better educated and moved in a different cultural setting which was more sophisticated. But it turned out to be a horrible, degrading experience which was sheer agony. It was performed by a doctor who couldn't get my uterus open. He had a knife in my uterus for an hour while he tried. It is impossible to describe the pain of such a procedure—it's simply beyond words. So he called in a man to help him with the abortion. I'm not even sure if this man was a doctor, but I do know that he was frightened of being caught and punished for performing illegal abortions. They didn't want me to identify this other man, so I was tied up and blindfolded during the abortion, just to make sure that I couldn't identify the man who was torturing me. I was given no anesthetic, and they listened to a basketball game on the radio as they butchered me. That abortion scarred me for life, both mentally and physically. I felt totally betrayed by the doctor. . . . I have never had children.[25]

Recriminalizing abortion would be barbaric.

Worldwide, parental consent laws represent the ultimate legal incongruity. Why should minors need parental consent to have an abortion but not to have a baby? Childbirth is considered 100 times more dangerous and likely to result in the need for major abdominal surgery than legal abortion, and 11 times more likely to result in death.[26] Teenagers are more likely to develop eclampsia and preeclampsia during pregnancy than are older women, thus increasing their health risk. And for those minors who choose to give the baby up for adoption, only the insensitive or those blinded by anti-abortion dogma would suggest that it is less traumatic for a minor to give a child up for adoption than to have an abortion. Parental consent laws actually increase the health risks for teenage girls. Worst of all, why is it acceptable for a child to beget a child without parental consent, when in all probability, if the child isn't given up for adoption, it will be the grandparents who pay for the care of the child, certainly for a few years, and quite likely wind up raising the child as well. If the grandparents don't pay, taxpayers will. Perhaps minors should have to seek parental and taxpayer consent for having a baby rather than having an abortion.

The arguments in favor of parental consent laws are specious. Not one stands up under close scrutiny. The typical arguments cite health and emotional risks as being too great for a minor to bear the burden of responsibility. Even former U.S. Surgeon General C. Everett Koop, who is strongly anti-abortion, acknowledged that abortion causes only a "miniscule" negative mental impact on women from a public health standpoint.[27] Minors are no more likely to suffer infection, hemorrhage, perforation of the uterus, complications from anesthesia, subsequent endometriosis, injury to the cervix, or complications in future pregnancies than older women, and it has been shown conclusively in data from the U.S. Centers for Disease Control that abortion is in fact one of the safest surgical procedures, especially in the first 12 weeks of pregnancy, for all females, regardless of age. Some suggest that a minor is incapable of assessing the risks maturely. Frankly, that argument is bunk. Given the facts, minors are quite capable of making that assessment, though, like women of other ages, they may feel differently at a later stage in life. That doesn't mean that the minor's decision was wrong or based on immaturity. People do change, and that is the unknown factor when any female decides to have an abortion.

In the United States, parental consent laws force minors to face the risks of pregnancy and childbirth, and more sinisterly, to undergo more dangerous late abortions in the second trimester. The highest ratio of late abortions occurs among teenage minors, because they are the most likely to deny their pregnancy, largely out of fear of having to deal with the response of their parents.[28] In Minnesota, second-trimester abortions for minors increased by 18% when parental consent laws were introduced. In Missouri, they increased from 19% in 1985 to 23% in 1988, after parental consent laws were introduced in 1985.[26]

The inconsistency of medical laws relating to minors is extraordinary. A married or financially independent minor living away from home is considered capable of making medical decisions for herself, though there is absolutely no evidence suggesting that she is more emotionally and physically mature than a minor living at home. Similarly, a minor in the military is considered capable of making independent decisions, though why someone should be deemed a minor and yet mature enough to enter the military is beyond me. In 1967, the Supreme Court concluded that the Bill of Rights and the Fourteenth Amendment protect the rights of minors as well as adults. The Court later ruled that minors have a constitutional right to privacy that includes the right to contraceptives and to terminate an unwanted pregnancy.[29] However, the states have the right to create laws that contradict that Supreme Court ruling. If a minor is mature enough to seek contraceptives, she is certainly mature enough to make a decision regarding pregnancy and abortion. To confuse matters thoroughly, there is inconsistency regarding when a minor reaches the age of majority. In Mississippi the age of majority is 21, in Alabama, Nebraska, and Wyoming it is 19, and in all other states and the District of Columbia it is 18.

Twenty-five states presently mandate parental consent or notification in the United States.[28] Four states have laws permitting a minor to independently make the decision to terminate a pregnancy. The rest of the states have no applicable law. By contrast, 25 states have laws granting minors the right to make independent decisions regarding contraception; 28 permit them legally to make decisions regarding prenatal care (including diagnostic testing such as amniocenteseis and CVS) and delivery services, including cesarean section; 50 allow a minor to consent to treatment for sexually transmitted diseases and venereal disease without parental consent; 11 permit a minor to seek HIV testing and treatment independently; 47 consider a minor capable of deciding whether to seek treatment for drug and alcohol abuse; 21 view a minor capable of deciding whether he or she needs mental outpatient treatment; 19 consider minors capable of making decisions regarding inpatient health services; 21 permit a minor to make decisions regarding nonemergency medical care; 44 legally permit minors to drop out of school without parental consent; 10 permit minors to marry without notifying their parents; 47 have laws that permit minors to consent to adopting out their child; and 29 consider minors capable of deciding what kind of medical care their child should receive.[30] Those states that do not have legislation on these matters may prohibit minors from making these decisions or else they simply have no law at all. Denying minors the right to independently decide the fate of a pregnancy is inconsistent with all of the other important decisions they are legally permitted to make, most of all giving a child up for adoption.

Because of parental consent laws, some girls have had clandestine or illegal abortions and developed complications resulting in their death. Becky Bell is perhaps the most notorious example. She was the Indiana teenager who died as a result of an illegal abortion because she was too afraid to ask her parents for their consent so that she could obtain a safe, legal abortion. She was apparently convinced that telling her parents that she was pregnant would destroy them and invite some kind of terrible retribution on herself. Becky's parents were in favor of parental consent laws before her death, but now campaign actively against such laws. They believed their relationship with Becky was close and that she would have felt free to come to them during any crisis, especially an unplanned and unwanted pregnancy. They were wrong.

Abortion should be legal because it does *not* cause suffering and death of a viable human being capable of feeling. That is why every woman should have the right to privately choose to have an abortion, for any reason.

After more than a decade of research on abortion, I have learned that you can't argue with beliefs, because they spring from faith. You CAN protect the freedom of people to practice their beliefs without persecution. History repeats itself whenever abortion is criminalized, because the issues remain the same and people have not changed. When you think about whether abortion should be legal, remember the Dying Declarations in this chapter as well as the forgotten victims of illegal abortions—children who are left motherless, parents who lose a daughter, husbands who lose a wife, and all those who lose a loved one.

Epilogue

As I write, there is a case under appeal by both the prosecution and defense in Clearwater, Florida, where a fetus able to live outside the womb is considered a person. Kawana Michele Ashley, age 19, was charged on September 7, 1994, with third-degree murder and manslaughter after shooting herself in the womb. She was six months pregnant at the time. The bullet injured one of the fetus' wrists. An emergency cesarean section on March 27, 1994, delivered a female infant weighing a little over two pounds who died on April 11, 1994, after her underdeveloped vital organs failed.

According to a *Los Angeles Times* report on September 10, 1994, when questioned, Ms. Ashley said that she could not afford an abortion. She tried to obtain one at a St. Petersburg clinic while in her second trimester, that would have cost somewhere between $1300 to $1800.[1] Her health insurance, Medicaid, would not cover the abortion because of a Republican-influenced federal government mandate that stipulates that government funds cannot be used to pay for abortion, except in cases of rape, incest, or when the mother's life is threatened by the pregnancy. Ms. Ashley, an unemployed, single mother of a three year-old son, was living with her grandmother when she realized that she could not support another child. As her pregnancy progressed, she became increasingly fearful of the future and finally, in desperation, shot herself.

Third-degree murder is defined state by state; third-degree murder in Florida might be considered a misdemeanor in another state. *Black's Legal Dictionary* defines third-degree murder as the "killing of a human being without any design to effect death by a person who is engaged in the commission of a felony."[2] Seeking to cause an illegal third trimester abortion would be the only felony charge that could apply in Ashley's case, but that renders the definition of third-degree murder paradoxical in the extreme if not nonsensical. It is not a felony to try to commit suicide.

On January 23, 1995, Pinellas County Circuit Court Judge Brandt Downey heard the case and dismissed the third-degree murder charge but upheld the manslaughter charge. Ms. Ashley's defense team, attorneys Priscilla Smith and Catherine Albisa of The Center for Reproductive Law and Policy and public defender Bruce Johnson, have appealed the manslaughter charge, and the public prosecutor has appealed the dismissal of the third-degree murder charge.

Ms. Ashley's defense team argued that Florida's manslaughter and murder laws were not meant to apply to these circumstances, noting that the Florida legislature has not passed legislation to criminalize such behavior and indeed, "no court in the country has applied homicide statutes to actions by a pregnant woman which allegedly cause the death of her fetus."[3] Ms. Ashley could not be prosecuted for attempting to injure herself. Ms. Albisa noted that, "Whether she was trying to kill herself or dangerously self-abort, Kawana Ashley did not commit murder."[3] Florida courts have consistently refused to apply child abuse statutes to women's behavior that could threaten pregnancy or harm the fetus, most notably in the case of Johnson v. Florida, in which the state High Court refused to hold a woman guilty for taking controlled substances during pregnancy that caused a "drug delivery."[3]

Brenda Joyner is the director of the Feminist Women's Health Center in Tallahassee, one of the few clinics in Florida that provides free or low-cost abortions to poor women, and ironically, a clinic that might have helped Kawana Ashley. I concur with Ms. Joyner's response to Kawana Ashley's tragic solution to her unplanned pregnancy dilemma: "This woman was crying out for help and nobody heard her, as is so often the case with the poor . . . In this case, the women's movement has failed her, the Florida legislature has failed her, and the health care system has failed her."[1] The anti-abortion movement also failed her, by not reaching out financially to help pay for the baby they believe Ms. Ashley should have been forced to bear and by lobbying against federal funding of abortion.

Kawana Ashley should have been told that there are organizations that will help pay for an abortion and clinics that will provide them free of charge. She should have been counseled about open adoption or temporary foster care as possible solutions to her problems. She is not a danger to society and should not be punished with imprisonment. Rather, she should be educated and perhaps obligated to use contraception until such time as she can afford to have a second child if she becomes pregnant again. Laws are made to protect the community, but they are also meant to be just. Flexibility in interpretation of the law and sentencing are important elements of justice.

Kawana Ashley was guilty of ignorance and causing injury to the fetus, which in turn caused its death. She was so desperate to end her pregnancy that she was also willing to risk killing herself. There are times when leniency of sentence is appropriate even when a crime has been committed.

Should a person be convicted of murder if a fetus is killed during the course of an attack on a pregnant woman? This question has lead to the most extraordinary legal debate and legislation in California.

Robert Keeler had reportedly vowed to kill his ex-wife's unborn child. Around 1973, he attacked his 7-month-pregnant ex-wife, stomping repeatedly on her stomach during the attack. He fractured the head of the 5 lb. female fetus, killing her.

The California Supreme Court at that time ruled 5 to 2 that the killing of a viable, unborn child was not murder under state law because the fetus could not be considered a human being. As a direct result of that case, the Legislature changed the law, redefining "murder" as the unlawful killing of a "human being or a fetus." Appellate courts later held that the law could only be applied to a viable fetus, one capable of surviving outside the womb.

The key question remains unresolved—when is a fetus viable, and should viable mean with medical aid or without it? Judges have ruled both ways.

In 1993, the California Supreme Court reviewed the case of Maria Flores, who was shot in the chest by Robert Davis, causing her 22- to 25-week-old male fetus to be stillborn. Her attacker was initially sentenced to life without parole for murdering the fetus (the mother survived). This conviction sparked a widespread legal debate on the question of whether a person can be convicted of murder and face execution for killing a fetus so young that it could not survive on its own and could be legally aborted.

Some of the doctors who attended Maria Flores after she was shot felt that the fetus may have been viable despite its extreme prematurity, while others felt that it was not. The decision at the time was against performing a cesarean section because the chances of the fetus surviving were so minute. The most important aspect of the case from a legal standpoint was that the fetus could have been legally aborted at that time, raising the point that it is absurd to say that it's okay for a third party to kill the fetus within legally acceptable limits providing that the woman consents, but that if she and/or her fetus is attacked and the fetus is killed, then it becomes murder.

If the fetus *is* a viable human being, then killing it should be considered murder, manslaughter, or mercy killing in third trimester cases (depending on the circumstances), regardless of who does the killing. But if the fetus is not a viable human being (in the first two trimesters), as I have argued in this book, then it should not be possible to prosecute someone for murder for killing it, however horrific the crime. Instead, the killer should be prosecuted for inflicting grave bodily and psychological harm to the pregnant woman, and some special legal category should be created for the crime of injuring the fetus of a woman planning to carry her pregnancy to term. It might be argued that since the fetus may be viable in the third trimester, a special type of murder charge should be created for that particular crime, distinguishing it from lawful (and very rare) third trimester medical procedures that can cause fetal death. Redefining the word murder to include the fetus is not the solution to the legal and moral problem; it just creates confusion.

Twenty-one states in the United States presently consider the third-party killing of a fetus in a nonabortion context a criminal offense. Seven states carry penalties for killing an embryo, and Louisiana has reportedly even made it illegal to terminate an embryo in a petri dish. In Utah, the killer of an "unborn child" can be executed by firing squad or lethal injection.

On May 16, 1994, the California Supreme Court affirmed a Court of Appeal judgment that reversed the original Davis murder conviction. It was felt that it was unjust at that point in time to apply a new definition of murder as "the unlawful killing of a human being, or a fetus, with malice aforethought" that precluded fetal viability as a factor, and that the jury had been misled into believing that viability meant "possible survival" instead of the actual legal definition, which requires a better than even chance of survival outside the womb. Since the weight of the expert medical testimony was against the probability that the fetus was viable, the perception was that the jury would probably have concluded differently had it been properly instructed. The Court of Appeals affirmed the convictions for armed robbery and assault with a firearm.

*   *   *   *   *

If democratic, pro-choice President Clinton loses the next election, the United States could be thrust back into the dark ages of anti-abortion Republican Presidents Reagan and Bush. The November 1994 Republican electoral victories that created a historic Republican majority in Congress may well be a harbinger of ill-tidings for women.

It is preposterous that any president of the United States can appoint Supreme Court justices for life who lean toward his view on abortion or any other issue that may be complicated by subjective religious beliefs. Supreme Court justices are human beings with religious beliefs that affect their philosophy of life, justice, and law, just like the rest of us. While they may try to interpret the constitution objectively, their personal philosophies undoubtedly influence the way that they rule.

I believe that additional safeguards are needed to protect pluralism in the United States. Americans need to reevaluate the constitutional powers granted to the president of the United States. There are certain types of legislation that he should not have the power to veto, such as abortion and any other issues that require him to make a judgment that may be colored by his personal religious views (or more cynically, by political expediency). Supreme Court appointments should not be for life; justices should be appointed for limited terms of perhaps 10 years.

Hypocrisy reigns supreme among politicians and those who espouse militant religious views against abortion. Most of the abortion providers whom I interviewed around the world were exasperated by the fact that anti-abortion female activists and their daughters, or the wives and daughters of male abortion opponents, presented to them for abortions. Medical ethics prevent them from revealing the names of these hypocrits, who would undergo an abortion and then continue to publicly condemn the procedure. As Dr. Elizabeth Karlin, director of the Women's Medical Center of Madison, Wisconsin, so eloquently observed in her editorial, "An Abortionist's Credo" that appeared in *The New York Times Magazine* on March 19, 1995: "About 6 percent of my patients come from actively protesting, anti-abortion families, and 90 percent have said, 'I would never have an abortion.' "[4] Dr. Karlin shrewdly notes that when women who are publicly against abortion privately seek to terminate their own pregnancy, they see themselves and their personal pregnancy crisis as "different." Her candid response is: "I'm sorry, but I only know how to do one kind of abortion—the kind that results when your heart sinks when you discover you are pregnant and the despair won't go away. If that's not the kind you want, leave now."[4] Bravo, Dr. Karlin.

It is utterly exasperating to watch slimy Washington anti-abortion politics sully the outstanding reputation of distinguished physician Dr. Henry W. Foster Jr., whom President Clinton nominated for the position of Surgeon General in February, 1995. As this book goes to press, the result of the Senate confirmation hear-ings on Dr. Foster's nomination is pending. In a statement published in the *Los Angeles Times* on February 4, 1995, Dr. Foster noted that "My personal goal has always been to provide education, counseling, preventive health care and contraceptive access to patients needing such services . . . If abortion is provided, my wish is that it be safe, legal and rare."[5] It was noted in the same article that Dr. Foster emphasized that he had delivered more than 10,000 babies during his career, and performed probably less than a dozen abortions, all of which he stressed had been performed "primarily to save the lives of the women or because the women had been the victims of rape or incest."[5]

After his medical records were reviewed, it was revealed that Dr. Foster had performed closer to 39 abortions during his long years of service in the medical profession. What does it matter if he performed 5, 10, 20 or 1,000,000 abortions? If they were medically justified, legal, and requested by women, what difference does the number make? He wasn't being evasive when he said he believed that it was fewer than a dozen. I have worked around doctors since the age of fourteen, and I can say categorically that I have never met a doctor who could recall the exact number of patients he had seen or how many of each specific procedure he had done over 20 or 30 years work as a physician. To accuse Dr. Foster of deceit for not recollecting accurately the number of abortions he performed is ludicrous. He is not a criminal and should not be treated like one!

Should Dr. Foster have committed malpractice and let women whose lives were threatened by pregnancy die rather than perform an abortion? Should he have passed judgment on women who were victims of incest and rape and forced them to bear children that were forcibly conceived? What kind of ethics govern the Washington anti-abortion lobby that is hellbent on destroying a man who is a former dean and acting president of the black medical school, Meharry Medical College, and founded the highly successful "I Have a Future Program" in the Nashville housing projects. What's wrong with his support of condom distribution in schools, a practice that helps prevent teen abortions!

Dear Washington anti-abortion lobbyists—what would you do if the life of your wife, mother, daughter or sister were threatened by pregnancy, or if she became pregnant by a rapist? My guess is, if Dr. Foster were Surgeon General, you would welcome his counsel on abortion in such a crisis.

Dr. Max Sizeland is an abortion provider in Australia. He recalls that

> In the 1970's I felt it was my duty to determine who should have an abortion. One day I passed judgement that it was not in one woman's best interests to have an abortion and she threw herself off a building . . . I no longer sit as a judge; I just try to provide abortions for those who need them.[6]

Dear reader, beware of judging women who seek an abortion, or the providers who risk their lives to make abortion a safe procedure.

Ideally, abortion should not be the concern of courts and legislatures. But if I were asked to formulate an abortion law that would satisfy a broad spectrum of the international community (with the exception of the Vatican and militant anti-abortion fanatics), I would acknowledge the concerns of those who worry that the fetus may be viable and a human being earlier than 26 weeks and suggest a compromise that would make abortion legal on request during the first 12 weeks of pregnancy. Abortion would continue to be legal up to 20 weeks in cases of rape, incest, fetal defects, and when the mother's health is threatened. Thereafter, abortion would be illegal, but euthanasia would be acceptable if the fetus were severely defective (e.g., anencephalitic). If a woman's life were threatened by continuing her pregnancy after 20 weeks, she could undergo a cesarean section. Perhaps most important of all, I would make contraception universally available through an international fund and distribution network set up for the specific purpose of providing all human beings of procreative age with free contraception, on request.

Appendix

Excerpts From "Roe v. Wade"

The full text of the United States Supreme Court decision in the case of ROE et al. v. WADE appears in U.S. Reports, Volume 410, pages 113–178, which is available in law libraries and some general libraries. The version given here omits the voluminous footnotes.

A helpful analysis of Roe *et al*. v. Wade (Roe) can be found in Laurence H. Tribe's *Abortion: The Clash of Absolutes*, published by W.W. Norton & Company in 1990.

An important point to note in the Court's decision is that seven out of nine judges felt that the state has no compelling interest in the fetus until the third trimester. Under Roe, the state does have an interest in protecting the health of the woman in the second trimester, and therefore has the right to regulate the safety requirements for the procedure.

The media frequently mentions that Roe declared a woman's right to privacy as the justification for her to have the right to choose to have an abortion, but fails to mention that it is because the judges felt that the state has no compelling interest in the fetus until the third trimester that she has that right to privately decide. Why does the state have no compelling interest in the fetus in the first and second trimester—because abortion is not murder! If it were, the state would have a compelling interest in the fetus earlier in pregnancy.

Roe et al. v. Wade, District Attorney of Dallas County

Appeal from the United States District Court For The Northern District of Texas

No. 70-18. Argued December 13, 1971—Reargued October 11, 1972—
Decided January 22, 1973

Mr. Justice Blackmun delivered the opinion of the Court . . .

II

Jane Roe, a single woman who was residing in Dallas County, Texas, instituted this federal action in March 1970 against the District Attorney of the county. She sought a declaratory judgment that the Texas criminal abortion statutes were unconstitutional on their face, and an injunction restraining the defendant from enforcing the statutes.

Roe alleged that she was unmarried and pregnant; that she wished to terminate her pregnancy by an abortion "performed by a competent, licensed physician, under safe, clinical conditions"; that she was unable to get a "legal" abortion in Texas because her life did not appear to be threatened by the continuation of her pregnancy; and that she could not afford to travel to another jurisdiction in order to secure a legal abortion under safe conditions. She claimed that the Texas statutes were unconstitutionally vague and that they abridged her right of personal privacy, protected by the First, Fourth, Fifth, Ninth and Fourteenth amendments. By an amendment to her complaint Roe purported to sue "on behalf of herself and all other women" similarly situated.

VI

It perhaps is not generally appreciated that the restrictive criminal abortion laws in effect in a majority of States today are of relatively recent vintage . . . they derive from statutory changes effected, for the most part, in the latter half of the 19th century.

1. 'Ancient Attitudes.' These are not capable of precise determination. We are told that at the time of the Persian Empire abortifacients were known and that criminal abortions were severely punished. We are also told, however, that abortion was practiced in Greek times as well as in the Roman Era, and that "it was resorted to without scruple." The Ephesian, Soranos, often described as the greatest of the ancient gynecologists, appears to have been generally opposed to Rome's prevailing free-abortion practices. He found it necessary to think first of the life of

the mother, and he resorted to abortion when, upon this standard, he felt the procedure advisable. Greek and Roman law afforded little protection to the unborn. If abortion was prosecuted in some places, it seems to have been based on a concept of a violation of the father's right to his offspring. Ancient religion did not bar abortion.

2. 'The Hippocratic Oath.' What then of the famous Oath that has stood so long as the ethical guide of the medical profession and that bears the name of the great Greek (460(?)–377(?) B.C.), who has been described as the Father of Medicine, the "wisest and the greatest practitioner of his art," and the "most important and most complete medical personality of antiquity," who dominated the medical schools of his time, and who typified the sum of the medical knowledge of the past? The Oath varies somewhat according to the particular translation, but in any translation the content is clear: "I will give no deadly medicine to anyone if asked, nor suggest any such counsel; and in like manner I will not give to a woman a pessary to produce abortion," or "I will neither give a deadly drug to anybody if asked for it, nor will I make a suggestion to this effect. Similarly, I will not give to a woman an abortive remedy."

[The Oath] . . . represents the apex of the development of strict ethical concepts in medicine, and its influence endures to this day. Why did the authority of Hippocrates dissuade abortion practice in his time and that of Rome? The late Dr. Edelstein provides us with a theory: The Oath was not uncontested even in Hippocrates' day; only the Pythagorean school of philosophers frowned upon the related act of suicide. Most Greek thinkers, on the other hand, commended abortion, at least prior to viability. See Plato, Republic, V, 461; Aristotle, Politics, VII, 1335b 25. For the Pythagoreans, however, it was a matter of dogma. For them the embryo was animate from the moment of conception, and abortion meant destruction of a living being. The abortion clause in the Oath, therefore, "echoes Pythagorean doctrines," and "[i]n no other stratum of Greek opinion were such views held or proposed in the same spirit of uncompromising austerity."

Dr. Edelstein then concludes that the Oath originated in a group representing only a small segment of Greek opinion and that it certainly was not accepted by all ancient physicians. He points out that medical writings down to Galen (A.D. 130–200) "give evidence of the violation of almost every one of its injunctions." But with the end of antiquity a decided change took place. Resistance against suicide and against abortion became common. The Oath came to be popular. The emerging teachings of

Christianity were in agreement with the Pythagorean ethic. The Oath "became the nucleus of all medical ethics" and "was applauded as the embodiment of truth." Thus, suggests Dr. Edelstein, it is "a Pythagorean manifesto and not the expression of an absolute standard of medical conduct."

This, it seems to us, is a satisfactory and acceptable explanation of the Hippocratic Oath's apparent rigidity. It enables us to understand, in historical context, a long accepted and revered statement of medical ethics. . . .

VII

Three reasons have been advanced to explain historically the enactment of criminal abortion laws in the 19th century and to justify their continued existence.

It has been argued occasionally that these laws were the product of a Victorian social concern to discourage illicit sexual conduct . . . it appears that no court or commentator has taken the argument seriously . . . . A second reason is concerned with abortion as a medical procedure. When most criminal abortion laws were first enacted, the procedure was a hazardous one for the woman. This was particularly true prior to the development of antisepsis. Antiseptic techniques . . . based on discoveries by Lister, Pasteur, and others, [were] first announced in 1867, but were not generally accepted and employed until about the turn of the century. Abortion mortality was high. Even after 1900, and perhaps until as late as the development of antibiotics in the 1940's, standard modern techniques such as dilation and curettage were not nearly so safe as they are today. Thus, it has been argued that a State's real concern in enacting criminal abortion law was to protect the pregnant woman, that is, to restrain her from submitting to a procedure that placed her life in serious jeopardy.

Modern medical techniques have altered this situation . . . medical data [indicates] that abortion in early pregnancy, that is, prior to the end of the first trimester, although not without its risk, is now relatively safe. Mortality rates for women undergoing early abortions, where the procedure is legal, appear to be as low as or lower than the rates for normal childbirth. Consequently, any interest of the State in protecting the woman from an inherently hazardous procedure . . . has largely disappeared. . . .

The third reason is the State's interest . . . in protecting prenatal life. Some of the argument for this justification rests on the theory that a new human life is present from the moment of conception . . . . Parties challenging state abortion laws have sharply disputed in some courts the contention that a purpose of these laws, when enacted, was to protect prenatal life. Pointing to the absence of legislative history to support the contention, they claim that most state laws were designed soley to protect the woman. Because medical advances have lessened this concern, at least with respect to such abortions the laws can no longer be justified by any state interest. There is some scholarly support for this view of original purpose. The few state courts called upon to interpret their laws in the late 19th and early 20th centuries did focus on the State's interest in protecting the woman's health rather than in preserving the embryo and fetus . . .

VIII

[The] right of privacy, whether it be founded in the Fourteenth Amendment's concept of personal liberty and restrictions upon state action, as we feel it is, or, as the District Court determined, in the Ninth Amendment's reservation of rights to the people, is broad enough to encompass a woman's decision whether or not to terminate her pregnancy . . . some . . . argue that the woman's right is absolute and that she is entitled to terminate her pregnancy at whatever time, in whatever way, and for whatever reason she alone chooses. With this we do not agree . . . The Court's decisions recognizing a right to privacy also acknowledge that some state regulation in areas protected by that right is appropriate . . . a State may properly assert important interests in safe-guarding health, in maintaining medical standards, and in protecting potential life. At some point in pregnancy, these respective interests become sufficiently compelling to sustain regulation of the factors that govern the abortion decision. The privacy right involved, therefore, cannot be said to be absolute. In fact, it is not clear to us that the claim . . . that one has an unlimited right to do with one's body as one pleases bears a close relationship to the right of privacy previously articulated in the Court's decisions. The Court has refused to recognize an unlimited right of this kind in the past . . .

IX

Texas urges that, apart from the Fourteenth Amendment, life begins at conception and is present throughout pregnancy, and that, therefore, the State has a compelling interest in protecting that life from and after conception. We need not resolve the difficult question of when life begins. When those trained in the respective disciplines of medicine, philosophy, and theology are unable to arrive at any consensus, the judiciary at this point in the development of man's knowledge, is not in a position to speculate as to the answer.

XI

To summarize and to repeat:

1. A state criminal abortion statute of the current Texas type, that excepts from criminality only a life-saving procedure on behalf of the mother, without regard to pregnancy stage and without recognition of the other interests involved, is violative of the Due Process Clause of the Fourteenth Amendment.

(a) For the stage prior to approximately the end of the first trimester, the abortion decision and its effectuation must be left to the medical judgment of the pregnant woman's attending physician.

(b) For the stage subsequent to approximately the end of the first trimester, the State, in promoting its interest in the health of the mother may, if it chooses, regulate the abortion procedure in ways that are reasonably related to maternal health.

(c) For the stage subsequent to viability [which the Court accepted as 28 weeks gestation], the State in promoting its interest in the potentiality of human life may, if it chooses, regulate, and even proscribe, abortion except where it is necessary, in appropriate medical judgment, for the preservation of the life or health of the mother.

2. The State may define the term "physician," as it has been employed in the preceding paragraphs of this Part XI of this opinion, to mean only a physician currently licensed by the State, and may proscribe any abortion by a person who is not a physician as so defined. . . .

This holding, we feel, is consistent with the relative weights of the respective interests involved, with the lessons and examples of medical and legal history, with the lenity of the common law, and with the demands of the profound problems of the present day. The decision leaves the State free to place increasing restrictions on abortion as the period of pregnancy lengthens, so long as those restrictions are tailored to the recognized state interests. The decision vindicates the right of the physician to administer medical treatment according to his professional judgment up to the points where important state interests provide compelling justifications for intervention. Up to those points, the abortion decision in all its aspects is inherently, and primarily, a medical decision, and basic responsibility for it must rest with the physician. If an individual practitioner abuses the privilege of exercising proper medical judgment, the usual remedies, judicial and intra-professional, are available.

"Help" Directory

United States

Alan Guttmacher Institute
1120 Connecticut Ave. NW, Suite 460, Washington, D.C.
20036-3902
(202) 296-4012, FAX (202) 223-5756

Centers for Disease Control and Prevention
1600 Clifton Road NE, Atlanta, Georgia 30333
(404) 639-3311

Children Awaiting Parents, Inc.
700 Exchange St., Rochester, New York 14608
(716) 232-5110

National Adoption Center (800) TO ADOPT

National AIDS Hotline (800) 342-AIDS

National Victim Center, Victim Assistance (817) 877-8355 (hours
9–5 Central time) or Infolink (800) 394-225 (call for referral
to local victim assistance number) or check your local
telephone directory for a referral to a rape crisis center

Planned Parenthood Federation of America
810 7th Ave., New York, New York 10019
(212) 261-4662 or (800) 230-PLAN (7526) (the"800" number
refers you to the clinic nearest your location)

*Financial Assistance for an Abortion in the United States,
where the average cost of an abortion is around $300*

Center For Women Policy Studies
2000 P St. NW, Suite 508, Washington, D.C. 20036
(202) 872-1770
(Helps HIV-positive women fund an abortion)

Planned Parenthood—see above

Women's Reproductive Rights Assistance Project (WRRAP)
(213) 651-2930
(Funded and run by the National Council of Jewish Women, Los
Angeles)
Helps fund abortions nationally. Ask abortion provider to call;
grants are made directly to the provider.

Legal Assistance and Information

The Center for Reproductive Law and Policy
120 Wall Street
New York, NY 10005
Tel: (212) 514-5534
Fax. (212) 514-5538

Religious Information

Catholics for a Free Choice
1436 U St. NW, Suite 301, Washington, D.C. 20009
(202) 986-6093

Religious Coalition for Reproductive Choice
1025 Vermont Ave., NW, Suite 1130, Washington, D.C., 20005
(202) 628-7700

United Kingdom

Marie Stopes International
Marie Stopes House, 108, Whitfield St., London
W1P 6BE, England
011-44-171-383-0042

Notes

Preface

1. Bernard Williams, *Morality: An Introduction to Ethics* (London: Cambridge University Press, 1972), pp. 9–10.

Prologue

1. Steven W. Mosher, *Broken Earth: The Rural Chinese* (London: Robert Hale, 1984), p. 228.
2. Linda Bird Francke, *The Ambivalence of Abortion* (New York: Random House, 1978) p. 227.
3. Carola Hansson & Karin Liden, *Moscow Women* (London: Allison & Busby, 1984), p. 147.
4. Maria Rosa Cutrufelli, *Women of Africa: Roots of Oppression* (London: Zed Press, 1983), p. 140.

Introduction

1. Interview with Lawrence W. Scott, M.D., F.A.C.O.G., J.D., 1994.
2. Interview with an American woman, 1986.

Chapter 1

1. Telephone interview with Andrea Butcher, 1994.
2. Mira Dana, *Abortion And The Emotions Involved* (London: Women's Therapy Center, 1984), pp. 14–17.
3. Dana, *Abortion And The Emotions Involved*, p. 6.

4. Arianna Stassinopoulos, *Maria Callas* (New York: Simon & Schuster, 1981), pp. 277–278.
5. Interviews with Henry Morgentaler, M.D., 1986 and 1994.
6. Dana, *Abortion And The Emotions Involved*, p. 12.
7. Interview with Lawrence W. Scott, M.D., F.A.C.O.G., J.D., 1994.
8. Elizabeth Karlin, M.D., Sunday *New York Times Magazine* editorial, "An Abortionist's Credo," March 19, 1995, p. 32.

Chapter 2

1. Linda Bird Francke, *The Ambivalence of Abortion* (New York: Allen Lane, Penguin Books Ltd., 1978), p. 12.
2. Linda Gordon, *Woman's Body, Woman's Right: A Social History of Birth Control in America*, as quoted by Linda Bird Francke in *The Ambivalence of Abortion*, p. 12.
3. Malcolm Potts, Peter Diggory, & John Peel, *Abortion* (London: Cambridge University Press, 1977), p. 169.
4. Potts *et al.*, *Abortion*, pp. 259–260.
5. Maria Rosa Cutrufelli, *Women of Africa: Roots of Oppression* (London: Zed Press, 1983), p. 141.
6. Cutrufelli, *Women of Africa: Roots of Oppression*, p. 142.
7. Judith Djamour, *Malay Kinship and Marriage in Singapore* (London School of Economics: Monographs on Social Anthropology, No. 12, 1965), p. 88.
8. Potts *et al.*, *Abortion*, p. 261.
9. Potts *et al.*, *Abortion*, pp. 261–262.
10. Potts *et al.*, *Abortion*, pp. 262–263.
11. Potts *et al.*, *Abortion*, p. 263.
12. Potts *et al.*, *Abortion*, pp. 263–264.

Chapter 3

1. Interview with an American woman, 1986.
2. Interview with Frances Kissling, president, Catholics For A Free Choice, 1986. Updated 1994.
3. *Los Angeles Times*, January 3, 1995, p. A17, column 1.
4. *Boston Sunday Globe*, January 1, 1995, front page.
5. *The Outlook* (LA), January 2, 1995, front page.
6. *Los Angeles Times*, January 4, 1995, p. B4, continuation of article on p. B1.
7. *Los Angeles Times*, January 6, 1995, article by Susan Carpenter-McMillan.
8. *New York Times*, December 31, 1994, p. Y9, column 2.
9. *Time* magazine, January 9, 1995, p. 35, article by Michael D. Lemonick.
10. *Time* magazine, March 27, 1995, pp. 48–51 article by Douglas Frantz.

11. *New York Times*, January 5, 1995, p. A9.
12. Interview with Bertram Wainer, M.D., 1986.
13. Interviews with Henry Morgentaler, M.D., 1986 and 1994.
14. Interview with Bernard Nathanson, M.D., 1986.
15. Interview with Roy Rowland, M.D., Congressman, 1986.
16. Patricia Jaworski, *Abortion Rights and Fetal 'Personhood.'* Audio documentary edited by Edd Doer & James W. Prescott (Centerline Press, 1989 and 1990), Dr. Michael Bennett, p. 57; Dr. Patricia Goldman-Rakic, p. 58; Dr. Dominick Purpura, and Patricia Jaworski, pp. 60–61.
17. Malcolm Potts, Peter Diggory, & John Peel, *Abortion* (London: Cambridge University Press, 1977), p. 1.
18. William Brennan, *The Abortion Holocaust: Today's Final Solution* (St. Louis: Landmark Press, 1984).
19. Telephone interview with Etienne-Emile Baulieu, M.D., 1994.

Chapter 4

1. Dr. Anthony Kenny, *A Path From Rome* (London: Sidgwick & Jackson, 1985).
2. Interview with Father Michael Mannion, 1986.
3. Interview with Frances Kissling, 1986. Updated 1994.
4. *The Sunday Herald*, Melbourne, Australia, July 8, 1990, p. 207.
5. *Los Angeles Time*, October 27, 1991.
6. Interview with Rabbi Julia Neuberger, 1985.
7. Interview with the Venerable Sangharakshita, 1985.

Chapter 5

1. From Ernest Hemingway, *Hills Like White Elephants*, excerpt extracted from Scribner's *The Short Stories*, pp. 275–276. Excerpted with permission of Scribner's, a division of Simon & Schuster, Inc., from *Men Without Women* by Ernest Hemingway. Copyright 1927, Charles Scribner's & Sons. Copyright renewed 1955 by Ernest Hemingway.
2. Edward Kienholz, "The Illegal Operation," 1962. Photo reproduced by permission of E. Kienholz. From the collection of Monte & Betty Factor, Los Angeles.
3. Interview with Marc Marais, 1994.
4. Interview with an American actor/musician, 1994.
5. Painter living in (West) Germany. Response to author's questionnaire, 1984.
6. Interview with an American singer/songwriter, 1986.
7. A British-born poet living in Canada. Extract from letter to author, 1984.

Chapter 6

1. Linda Bird Francke, *The Ambivalence of Abortion* (New York: Allen Lane, Penguin Books Ltd., 1978), p. 148.
2. Interview with "Mariana," London, 1984.
3. Interview with "Fatima," Israel, 1984.

Chapter 7

1. Telephone interview with David Allan Grimes, M.D., 1994.
2. Telephone interview with Henry Morgentaler, M.D., 1994.
3. Telephone interview with Professor J. G. Schenker, 1986.
4. Interview with an Irish nurse living in London, 1985.
5. Telephone interview with Andrea Butcher, 1994.
6. *Los Angeles Times*, April 5, 1992.
7. Interview with Bernard Nathanson, M.D., 1986.
8. Interview with Roy Rowland, M.D., 1986.
9. Telephone interview with Bertram Wainer, M.D., 1986.
10. Interview with Lawrence W. Scott, M.D., F.A.C.O.G., J.D., 1994.
11. *Time* magazine, January 9, 1995, p. 34, article by Margot Hornblower.

Chapter 8

1. American Journal of Obstetrics and Gynecology 1952; 63:1298–1304, article by J. B. Thiersch
2. Mitchell D. Creinin, M.D. Journal of the American Medical Association (JAMA), October 19, 1994, Vol. 272, No. 15, p. 1194.
3. Telephone interview with Etienne-Emile Baulieu, M.D., 9/5/94.
4. David Paintin, FRCOG, Chairman, Birth Control Trust, "Running an Early Medical Abortion Service." Published by the Birth Control Trust, 1994.
5. Mitchell D. Creinin, *Contraception* (December, 1993), p. 520.
6. Article by Beth Ann Kirier, *Los Angeles Times*, April 22, 1990, View section, Part E, page 1, column 2.
7. Telephone interview with "Mary," 7/26/94.
8. Response to author's questionnaire by a 26-year-old French-Catholic woman, 1994.
9. Response to author's questionnaire by a 22-year-old student, 1994.
10. Telephone interview with an Australian woman, 1994.
11. "Woman A": *Running An Early Medical Abortion Service* (Birth Control Trust, 1994), p. 44.

12. "Woman C": *Running An Early Medical Abortion Service* (Birth Control Trust, 1994), p. 45.
13. Telephone interview with Dr. David Grimes, 7/29/94.
14. Lawrence Lader, *RU 486* (Reading, MA: Addison–Wesley Publishing Co., 1991), pp. 63–64.
15. Telephone interview with Dr. Elizabeth Aubeny, 9/1/94.
16. Helena von Hertzen, D.D.S., M.D., & Paul Van Look, F.A., M.D., Ph.D., M.F.F.P., *Antiprogestogens: From Abortion To Contraception.* Yearbook of the Flemish Society of Obstetrics and Gynecology, 1994.
17. Telephone interview with Andrea Butcher, 7/19/94.
18. Telephone interview with a French nurse, 9/2/94.
19. Telephone interview with Richard Hausknecht, M.D., 9/30/94.
20. Dr. Bernard Nathanson, as quoted in "RU 486: The Abortion Battle's New Frontier," *Los Angeles Times,* April 22, 1990, View section, Part E, p. 1, col. 2, p. 14, col. 1.
21. Dr. David Grimes, "RU 486: The Abortion Battle's New Frontier," *Los Angeles Times,* April 22, 1990, View section, p. 14, col. 1.
22. Dr. John Willke, as quoted in "RU 486: The Abortion Battle's New Frontier," *Los Angeles Times,* April 22, 1990, "View," Part E, p. 14, col. 1.
23. Grimes, *Los Angeles Times,* April 22, 1990, View, Part E, p. 14. col. 1.

Chapter 10

1. Interview with Mary Lucy 2/28/92.
2. *Los Angeles Times,* February 7, 1995, p. E5.
3. *Los Angeles times,* February 7, 1995, pp. E1 and E5.

Chapter 11

1. *Webster's New World Dictionary of the American Language* (New York: Simon & Schuster, 1980).
2. Alexandra Stiglmayer, "The Rapes in Bosnia," in *Mass Rape: The War Against Women in Bosnia–Herzegovina.* Edited by Alexandra Stiglmayer. Translations by Marion Faber. Forward by Roy Gutman. (Lincoln: University of Nebraska Press, 1994), pp. 136-137. Used by permission.
3. Stigmayer, in *Mass Rape: The War Against Women in Bosnia–Herzegovina,* p. 135.
4. Vera Folnegovic-Smalc, "Psychiatric Aspects of the Rapes in the War Against the Republics of Croatia & Bosnia–Herzegovina," in *Mass Rape: The War Against Women in Bosnia–Herzegovina,* pp. 176–177.
5. Stiglmayer, in *Mass Rape: The War Against Women in Bosnia–Herzegovina,* p. 133.

6. Susan Brownmiller, *Against Our Will: Men, Women, and Rape* (New York: Ballantine Books, 1993), pp. 136–137. Used by permission.

7. Brownmiller, *Against Our Will: Men, Women, and Rape*, pp. 80–81.

8. Brownmiller, *Against Our Will: Men, Women, and Rape*, p. 84.

9. Vera Folnegovic-Smalc, in *Mass Rape: The War Against Women in Bosnia–Herzegovina*, p. 177.

10. "Rape in America: A Report To The Nation." Published by the National Victim Center, April 23, 1992. Prepared by Crime Victims Research & Treatment Center.

11. Robin Warshaw, *I Never Called It Rape: The Ms. Report on Recognizing, Fighting, & Surviving Date and Acquaintance Rape* (Harper Perennial, A Division of Harper Collins Publishers, 1994), p. 72.

12. Linda E. Ledray, R.N., Ph.D., L.P., F.A.A.N., *Recovering From Rape* (New York: Henry Holt & Company, 1994), p. 58.

13. Interview with a black American woman, 1988.

14. Interview with "Loretta." Reprinted by kind permission of Catholics For A Free Choice.

15. Lee Ezell, *The Missing Piece*. Extract published in the *Los Angeles Times*, February 26, 1992.

16. Lee P. Shulman, David Muran, & Patricia M. Speek, "Counseling Sexual Assault Victims Who Become Pregnant After the Assault." *Journal of Interpersonal Violence*, Vol. 7, No. 2, June, 1992 (Sage Publications Inc., 1992), pp. 205–210.

Chapter 12

1. Interview with Glenn Little, 1986.

2. Interview with Lawrence W. Scott, M.D., F.A.C.O.G., J.D., 1994.

3. Telephone interview with John Williams III, M.D., 10/4/94.

4. Telephone interview with "Elyse" at the Prenatal Diagnostic Center in Los Angeles, 10/3/94.

Chapter 13

1. Response to author's questionnaire by a 22-year-old French-Catholic woman, 1994.

2. Telephone interview with Sharon Kaplan Roszia, director of the Kinship Alliance, 1994.

3. Telephone interview with Peggy Soule, executive director of Children Awaiting Parents, Inc., Rochester, New York, August, 1994.

4. Interview with an American woman, 1986.

5. Interview with an American man, 1991.

6. Telephone interview with Amanda Crawford, 9/27/94.

7. Interview with Lawrence W. Scott, M.D., F.A.C.O.G., J.D., 1994.

Chapter 14

1. Steven W. Mosher, *Broken Earth: The Rural Chinese* (London: Robert Hale, 1984), p. 226.
2. Mosher, *Broken Earth: The Rural Chinese*, pp. 227, 229, 230.
3. Carola Hansson & Karin Liden, *Moscow Women* (London: Allison & Busby, 1984), p. 114.
4. Colin Francome, *Abortion Freedom: A Worldwide Movement* (London: George Allen & Unwin Ltd., 1984), p. 156.
5. *Wall Street Journal*, August 21, 1986, front page, column 1.
6. Carola Hansson and Karin Liden, *Moscow Women*, p. 147.
7. Carol J. Williams, "An Abortion Debate Divorced From Morality," *Los Angeles Times*, July 31, 1990.
8. *Newsweek*, January 22, 1990, p. 35.
9. Stanley K. Henshaw, Deputy Director of Research, Alan Guttmacher Institute, *Induced Abortion: A World Review, 1990* (Family Planning Perspectives, Vol. 22, Number 2, March/April 1990).
10. Malcolm Potts, Peter Diggory, & John Peel, *Abortion* (London: Cambridge University Press, 1977), p. 412.
11. Potts *et al.*, *Abortion*, p. 413.
12. Potts *et al.*, *Abortion*, p. 383.
13. Potts *et al.*, *Abortion*, p. 436.
14. Sources: Population Action International (1993 data); "Induced Abortion: A World Review, 1990 Supplement, by Stanley Henshaw of the Alan Guttmacher Institute; and United Nations publication, "World Abortion Policies 1994."
15. Telephone interview with Henry Morgentaler, M.D., 1994.
16. *The Outlook*, March 26, 1994.
17. Tamara Jones, "Abortion is Legalized in Germany," *Los Angeles Times*, June 26, 1992.
18. Planned Parenthood in Europe, Volume 23, No. 1, pages 5–7. Article by Joachim von Baress, Deputy Director of Pro Familia, the International Planned Parenthood Federation member in Germany.
19. Johannes Frewel, *Eastern Germans Choose Jobs Before Babies*, *The Age*, January 19, 1995.
20. "Abortion, Child Destruction, and Murder." John R. Vallentine. Australian Medical Defense Union, March 28, 1987, p. 10.
21. Judge Mrs. Hadassah Ben-Ito, "The Ethical, Legal & Religious Aspects of the Modern Diagnostic and Therapeutic Approach to the Fetus." Roundtable discussion in Jerusalem, Israel. © 1986, Elsevier Science Publishers B.V. (Biomedical Division). J.G. Schenker and D. Weinstien, eds., pp. 15–16.
22. Telephone interview with a Hungarian woman, 1991.
23. That figure comes from the Alan Guttmacher Institute, Facts in Brief: "Abortion in the United States," 1994.
24. Exhibition by Suzy Kerr & Diane Malley, "Just Call Jane," 1991.

25. Telephone interview with an American woman, 1991.
26. Patricia Donovan, *Our Daughters' Decisions* (Alan Guttmacher Institute, 1992), p. 21.
27. Donovan, *Our Daughters' Decisions*, p. 21.
28. AGI, Facts in Brief, "Abortion in the United States," 1994.
29. Donovan, *Our Daughters' Decisions*, pp. 6–7.
30. Donovan, *Our Daughters' Decisions*, pp. 12–13.

Epilogue

1. *Los Angeles Times*, September 10, 1994.
2. Henry Campbell Black, M.A., *Black's Legal Dictionary* (St. Paul, Minnesota, West Publishing Co., 1968), pp. 1170–1171.
3. The Center for Reproductive Law and Policy, "Attorneys for Woman who Shot Herself in Stomach while Pregnant Seek Dismissal of Charges," press release dated November 23, 1994. "Florida Court to Consider Request for Dismissal of Homicide Charges against Pregnant Woman who Shot Herself," press release dated January 20, 1995.
4. Dr. Elizabeth Karlin, "An Abortionist's Credo," the Sunday *New York Times Magazine*, March 19, 1995, p. 32.
5. Marlene Cimons, "Surgeon General Choice Tells of Abortions." *Los Angeles Times*, February 4, 1995.
6. Dr. Max Sizeland, as quoted by Tania Ewing, "Case Adds Fuel to Abortion Debate: A Doctor Who Has Stuck to his Beliefs on Abortion." *The Age*, February 21, 1995, p. 2.

Index

Disclaimer

The interviews, stories, comments, and all information presented in *The Abortion Dilemma* are included solely to show the many complex personal, moral, religious, cultural, physical and emotional health, financial, and legal factors that contribute to the deep conflict that people have all over the world when wrestling with the decision to have, or not to have, an abortion. Consequently, all information contained herein *is not*, nor is it to be construed as, any endorsement or recommendation for any woman (or any person to counsel) having an abortion performed where it: (1) would be in violation of any valid, existing civil law; (2) place a woman seeking an abortion under any increased risk of incurring physical and/or mental harm; (3) would be against commonly accepted, professional medical practices; and (4) would not include the services of a legally licensed medical doctor, practitioner, or clinic, performed only at a place designated by the supervising professional. Specifically, but not limited to the above, any interviews, stories, comments, or information pertaining to "self-performed" abortions (or an abortion not performed by a legally licensed medical doctor, practitioner, or clinic, including any of factors (1) through (4) being present) are *not* presented as an endorsement of those described occurrences; to the contrary, such "self-performed" abortions aren't recommended.